MW01703294

NTC's Super-Mini Dictionary of EASILY CONFUSED WORDS

NTC's Super-Mini Dictionary of EASILY CONFUSED WORDS

With Complete Examples of Correct Usage

Deborah K. Williams

McGraw-Hill

Chicago New York San Francisco Lisbon London Madrid Mexico City Milan New Delhi San Juan Seoul Singapore Sydney Toronto

McGraw-Hill

A Division of The ***McGraw-Hill*** *Companies*

1 2 3 4 5 6 7 8 9 0 TCP/TCP 1 0 9 8 7 6 5 4 3 2

ISBN 0-07-139653-5

Printed and bound by TransContinental Printing

This book is printed on acid-free paper.

Contents

Introduction

English is generously endowed with several types of easily confused words. Some of these words are homophones (*homo* 'same,' *phone* 'sound')—words that are pronounced alike but are different in spelling, meaning, or both. Examples of common homophones include *sail* and *sale; their, there,* and *they're;* and *knight* and *night*. Other easily confused words are troublesome because of the grammatical rules that govern their use. Unless one knows the rules that dictate which word should be used in a particular context, it is easy to misuse such pairs as *can* and *may; among* and *between;* and *shall* and *will*. Finally, some words are easily confused simply because they are easy to mix up. Such word pairs as *infer* and *imply; disinterested* and *uninterested;* and *flounder* and *founder* are often used incorrectly because they are similar in meaning and form yet have subtle differences in definition.

This book is an easy-to-use reference guide that will help the user understand confusing words and their usage and to then choose the correct spelling or meaning of a word for any given situation. The dictionary consists of word groups arranged alphabetically by the first word of each set. All sets of words are alphabetized internally as well. For example, *aisle—I'll—isle* is the full entry preceding *all—awl*. Cross-referencing permits the user to locate every word quickly and easily. Each word is followed by a pronunciation key in brackets, a concise definition, and a sentence example demonstrating how the word is used in everyday English. Hence, this dictionary enables the reader not only to find sets of easily confused words, but also to discover how the words are pronounced, what they mean, and how to use them in the written or spoken language.

This dictionary is designed to help speakers and writers master the confusing words in the English language. It will also pique (or is it *peak?*) interest in learning more about these pesky problem words.

Acknowledgments

I wish to thank all of my students—past, present, and future—not only for their contributions to this book, but also for making teaching the rewarding profession that it is.

I am also grateful to Jeanne Breaugh, Trudy Carpenter, John McAlear, and Linda Peckham for the support, enthusiasm, and expertise they offered me during this project.

A special thanks to Dr. Larry Standridge who piqued my interest in adult education and gave me yet another homophone.

And finally, I will always be grateful to my family for allowing me to make a dream come true.

Deborah K. Williams

Pronunciation Guide

Each word in the dictionary is followed by a phonetic transcription in the symbols of the International Phonetic Alphabet (IPA). The style of pronunciation reflected here is conversational or informal and is intended to help users *recognize* the word. The transcriptions distinguish between [a] and [ɔ] and between [w] and [ʍ] even though not all Americans do so. In strict IPA fashion, [j] rather than the [y] substitute is used for the initial sound in "yellow." The most prominent syllable in a multisyllabic word is *preceded* by a [ˈ].

The following chart shows the American English values for each of the IPA symbols used in the phonetic transcriptions. To use the chart, first find the large phonetic symbol whose value you want to determine. The three, simple English words to the right of the symbol contain examples of the sound for which the phonetic symbol stands. The letters in boldface type indicate where the sound in question is found in the English word.

[ɑ]	stop, top	[ɚ]	bird, turtle	[ŋ]	bring, thing	[u]	food, blue
[æ]	sat, track	[f]	feel, if	[o]	coat, wrote	[ʊ]	put, look
[ɑʊ]	cow, now	[g]	get, frog	[oɪ]	spoil, boy	[v]	save, van
[ɑɪ]	bite, my	[h]	hat, who	[ɔ]	caught, yawn	[w]	well, wind
[b]	beet, bubble	[i]	feet, leak	[p]	tip, pat	[ʍ]	wheel, while
[d]	dead, body	[ɪ]	bit, hiss	[r]	rat, berry	[z]	fuzzy, zoo
[ð]	that, those	[j]	yellow, you	[s]	sun, fast	[ʒ]	pleasure, treasure
[dʒ]	jail, judge	[k]	can, keep	[ʃ]	fish, sure	[ˈ]	ˈwater, hoˈtel
[e]	date, sail	[l]	lawn, yellow	[t]	top, pot		
[ɛ]	get, set	[m]	family, slam	[tʃ]	cheese, pitcher		
[ə]	but, nut	[n]	new, funny	[θ]	thin, faith		

NTC's Super-Mini Dictionary of EASILY CONFUSED WORDS

A

a while—awhile

- **a while** [ə'ʍaɪl] a short time. ☐ *It might be a while before he returns from his errand.*
- **awhile** [əʍaɪl] for a short time. ☐ *We will rest awhile before continuing our hike.*

acts—axe

- **acts** [ækts] the plural of *act* 'a deed or an action.' ☐ *In the military, acts of heroism are recognized by the presentation of ribbons and medals.*
- **acts** [ækts] the plural of *act* 'one of the main divisions of a musical comedy or a play.' ☐ *Each of the play's three acts ended with a dimming of the stage lights.*
- **acts** [ækts] the present tense, third person singular of *act* 'to behave.' ☐ *Gregory acts quite differently at school than he does at home.*
- **ax(e)** [æks] a hand-held chopping tool, similar to a hatchet. ☐ *One swing of the axe splintered the logs.*
- **ax(e)** [æks] to ask something of someone. (An older, now dialect, form of *ask*. Not considered standard English. Spelling may vary.) ☐ *I want to axe you a question.* ☐ *Did you axe her yet?*

ad—add

- **ad** [æd] an abbreviation of *advertisement* 'a notice of some type, usually published or broadcast.' ☐ *The ad for a part-time farmhand attracted several interested people.*
- **add** [æd] to increase something in amount, number, or size. ☐ *Each year, I add several stamps to my collection.* ☐ *As a child, I found it easier to add than to subtract.*

add See the main entry beginning with *ad.*

addition—edition

- **addition** [ə'dɪʃn] a room or rooms built onto a house or other building. □ *Mr. Smith is building an addition on the back of his house.*
- **addition** [ə'dɪʃn] an increase. □ *The addition of two clerks in the office will lighten everyone's workload.*
- **edition** [ə'dɪʃn] a version of a published book or other document. □ *A later edition of a textbook usually contains some changes to the original.* □ *The morning edition of the newspaper reaches the newsstands very early in the day.*

adds—adze

- **adds** [ædz] the present tense, third person singular of *add* 'to increase the number, size, or amount of something.' □ *Tom usually adds too much salt to the soup.*
- **adze** [ædz] a sharp cutting tool with a curved blade. □ *An adze is one of the tools used by a ship's carpenter.*

adherence—adherents

- **adherence** [əd'hɛɚənts] a steadfast attachment to something. □ *Joe's strict adherence to high moral principles made him an excellent role model.*
- **adherents** [əd'hɛɚənts] the plural of *adherent* 'a person who follows or believes a certain doctrine, person, or plan.' □ *The adherents of the religious leader numbered in the tens of thousands.*

adherents See the main entry beginning with *adherence.*

adze See the main entry beginning with *adds.*

affect—effect

- **affect** [ə'fɛkt] to have an impression, influence, or effect on something. □ *Offers of athletic scholarships could affect Jim's decision on which college to attend.*
- **effect** [ə'fɛkt, ɛ'fɛkt] a result or consequence. □ *Some drugs have the effect of causing sleepiness.*

aid—aide

- **aid** [ed] assistance or help. □ *Several nations sent medical and financial aid to the war-torn country.*
- **aide** [ed] a person who acts as a helper or assistant. □ *A general's personal aide must be completely trustworthy.*

aide See the main entry beginning with *aid.*

ail—ale

- **ail** [el] to be in ill health. ☐ *Many townspeople continued to ail long after the plague swept through their village.*
- **ale** [el] an alcoholic beverage brewed from malt and hops. ☐ *The members of the wedding party raised their steins filled with ale and sang in unison.*

air—err—heir

- **air** [ɛɚ] the compound of various gases and oxygen that we breathe. ☐ *On hot, still days the air above large cities is often filled with smog.*
- **air** [ɛɚ] to broadcast or transmit something. ☐ *The network will air the television special on three consecutive evenings.*
- **air** [ɛɚ] to expose something to the open air. ☐ *I need to air the sleeping bags before we use them again.*
- **air** [ɛɚ] the demeanor or manner of a person. ☐ *He has an aristocratic air about him.*
- **err** [ɛɚ] to make a mistake. ☐ *Sandy did not want to err on her first day on the job.*
- **heir** [ɛɚ] a person who inherits something. ☐ *Charlie is the heir to his father's dry-cleaning business.*

aired—erred

- **aired** [ɛɚd] the past tense and past participle of *air* 'to broadcast or transmit something.' ☐ *One of the news channels aired the conference.*
- **aired** [ɛɚd] the past tense and past participle of *air* 'to expose something to the open air.' ☐ *After Susan aired the house, she closed all of the windows.*
- **erred** [ɚd, ɛɚd] the past tense and past participle of *err* 'to make a mistake.' ☐ *Our accountant erred on a number of points when he figured our taxes last year.*

aisle—I'll—isle

- **aisle** [ɑɪl] a passage or corridor, usually between rows of seats. ☐ *The wedding guests stood when the bride appeared at the head of the aisle.*
- **I'll** [ɑɪl] the contraction of *I will* or *I shall*. ☐ *"I'll never pass this exam if I don't learn these equations," moaned Jane.*
- **isle** [ɑɪl] a small island. ☐ *The author's dream is to live alone on a beautiful tropical isle.*

ale See the main entry beginning with *ail.*

all—awl

- **all** [ɔl] the whole of a number or quantity. ☐ *When making a* *difficult decision, try to consider all aspects of the problem.*

- **awl** [ɔl] a sharp, pointed tool used to puncture or etch. ☐ *To create the fine details in her work, the artist used an awl.*

all ready—already

- **all ready** [ɔl'rɛdi] completely prepared. ☐ *When the runners were all ready, the starter fired his gun to begin the race.*
- **already** [ɔl'rɛdi] previously; beforehand. ☐ *Volunteer firemen were already at the scene of the blaze when the police and ambulances arrived.*

all together—altogether

- **all together** [ɔltə'gɛðɚ] united; gathered. ☐ *When I had my fabric all together, I began the tedious task of sewing.*
- **altogether** ['ɔltəgɛðɚ] thoroughly; totally. ☐ *We were altogether surprised when James showed up uninvited.*

all ways—always

- **all ways** ['ɔl'wez] all of the ways. ☐ *We used a guidebook to study all ways of traveling across the country.*
- **always** ['ɔwɪz] without exception; at all times. ☐ *"Always check for traffic before crossing the street," Aunt Jane reminded him.*

allowed—aloud

- **allowed** [ə'lɑʊd] the past tense and past participle of *allow* 'to permit someone to do something.' ☐ *The child was never allowed to go outside of his fenced yard without one of his parents.*
- **aloud** [ə'lɑʊd] [speaking] audibly. ☐ *To help memorize his speech, the candidate rehearsed his message aloud in front of a mirror.*

allusion—elusion—illusion

- **allusion** [ə'luʒn] an indirect reference to someone or something. ☐ *I caught the speaker's allusion to waste in government, but the rest of the speech was completely confusing to me.*
- **elusion** [ə'luʒn] an evasion or escape. ☐ *His elusion of the uncomfortable situation was obvious.*
- **illusion** [ɪ'luʒn] a misleading image; a mistaken assumption. ☐ *The magician is a master of illusion.* ☐ *I was under the illusion that the doctor was a licensed practitioner, but he was not.*
- **illusion** [ɪ'luʒn] a fine, filmy transparent fabric. ☐ *The model's gown was made of ivory satin with an overlay of illusion.*

aloud See the main entry beginning with *allowed.*

already See the main entry beginning with *all ready.*

altar—alter

- **altar** ['ɔltɚ] a raised platform used in worship or ritual. ☐ *Each Sunday, vases of fresh flowers grace the altar of the church.*
- **alter** ['ɔltɚ] to change something; to make something different. ☐ *Pilots must sometimes alter their flight plans to avoid severe weather.*

alter See the main entry beginning with *altar.*

altogether See the main entry beginning with *all together.*

always See the main entry beginning with *all ways.*

among—between

- **among** [ə'məŋ] situated amidst more than two persons or things; in a grouping of more than two persons or things. ☐ *Among those three poets, Robert Frost is my favorite.*
- **between** [bɪ'twin] adjacent to and separating two persons or things. ☐ *Mary stood between Tim and Paul.*
- **between** [bɪ'twin] involving two persons, groups, or things. ☐ *A fight erupted between the two rival gangs.*

ant—aunt

- **ant** [ænt] a type of tiny insect that lives in a colony and has a complex social system. ☐ *An ant crawled across my plate at the picnic.*
- **aunt** [ænt, ɑnt] the sister of one's mother or father; the wife of one's uncle. (Black English and Boston English. The pronunciation [ɑnt] is Southern American English.) ☐ *My aunt is very proud of the roses in her garden.*

ante—anti—auntie

- **ante** ['ænti] a poker stake made to increase the pot. ☐ *The highest allowable ante in John's poker games is a nickel.*
- **ante** ['ænti] before something; in front of something. (A prefix.) ☐ *The anteroom of the convention hall serves as a foyer.*
- **anti** ['ænti] opposed to someone or something. (A prefix.) ☐ *Anti-war activists protested in front of the memorial all week.*
- **auntie** ['ænti, 'ɑnti] a diminutive of *aunt* 'the sister of one's mother or father.' (The pronunciation ['ɑnti] is Southern American English.) ☐ *In the movie "The Wizard of Oz," Dorothy lived with her Auntie Em and Uncle Henry.*

anti See the main entry beginning with *ante.*

any more—anymore

- **any more** [ɛni'mɔə˞] some more. ☐ *Do you have any more time to donate?*
- **anymore** [ɛni'mɔə˞] at the present time; nowadays. (Often viewed as incorrect if used in the affirmative.) ☐ *The girls do not sit next to each other in class anymore.*

anymore See the main entry beginning with *any more.*

appraise—apprise

- **appraise** [ə'prez] to establish the value of something. ☐ *We let a jeweler appraise the ruby.*
- **apprise [of]** [ə'praɪz] to inform someone of something. ☐ *In the future, please apprise me of the problem earlier.*

apprise See the main entry beginning with *appraise.*

arc—ark

- **arc** [ɑə˞k] an arch; a curve. ☐ *One seldom sees a rainbow's arc touching the horizon at both ends.*
- **ark** [ɑə˞k] a type of ship; the ship built by Noah in the biblical story found in Genesis. ☐ *According to the Bible, Noah led the animals aboard his ark two by two.*

ark See the main entry beginning with *arc.*

ascent—assent

- **ascent** [ə'sɛnt] the act of going up. ☐ *The ascent of a mountain is no less dangerous than the descent.*
- **ascent** [ə'sɛnt] the amount of upward slope. ☐ *The angle of ascent was extremely steep.*
- **assent** [ə'sɛnt] to agree with someone. ☐ *Judge Smith will assent with the other justices on all points except one.*

assent See the main entry beginning with *ascent.*

assistance—assistants

- **assistance** [ə'sɪstn̩ts] help; support; aid. ☐ *Following World War II, the Civilian Conservation Corps (CCC) was a form of public assistance.*
- **assistants** [ə'sɪstn̩ts] the plural of *assistant* 'a helper; an aide.' ☐ *Although the office manager has several assistants, she prefers to do all of the typing herself.*

assistants See the main entry beginning with *assistance.*

ate—eight

- **ate** [et] the past tense of *eat* 'to take in food.' ☐ *After a very difficult practice, the rugby team ate ten large pizzas.*
- **ate** [et] the past tense of *eat* 'to harrass someone; to bother someone.' ☐ *His intense feelings of guilt ate at his conscience.*
- **eight** [et] the number between seven and nine. ☐ *A stop sign has eight sides.*

aught—ought

- **aught** [ɔt] zero; nothing. ☐ *Phil always says aught when he reads a zero.* ☐ *John says his telephone number is two-two-three, aught-aught-four-one.*
- **ought** [ɔt] to be obliged to do something. ☐ *"You ought to decline Bob's invitation before you accept Bill's," Mrs. Smith cautioned her daughter.*

aunt See the main entry beginning with *ant.*

auntie See the main entry beginning with *ante.*

awhile See the main entry beginning with *a while.*

awl See the main entry beginning with *all.*

axe See the main entry beginning with *acts.*

aye—eye—I

- **aye** [ɑɪ] yes. ☐ *"Aye, aye, captain," responded the ship's first mate.* ☐ *When the legislative vote was finally taken, the aye votes outnumbered the nays.*
- **eye** [ɑɪ] the organ of sight. ☐ *The sight in her left eye was lost in an accident.*
- **eye** [ɑɪ] the center of something. ☐ *Compared to the turbulent outer edges of a hurricane, the eye of the storm is calm.*
- **I** [ɑɪ] the first person, singular pronoun. ☐ *"I can't find my favorite teddy bear," whined the sleepy child.*

B

bail—bale

- **bail** ['bel] the security money paid to ensure the appearance of a prisoner in court. □ *Generally, a higher bail is set for more serious crimes than for minor ones.*
- **bail** ['bel] to remove water from a vessel. □ *Before we can go fishing, we must bail out the boat.*
- **bale** ['bel] a large, closely pressed package of material. □ *For clean, comfortable dog bedding, nothing beats a fresh, dry bale of straw.*
- **bale** ['bel] evil or sorrow. □ *The poet often composed verses of intense bale when she was in a dark mood.*

bait—bate

- **bait** [bet] something used to entice or lure an animal or fish. □ *Fisherman often use minnows as bait.*
- **bait** [bet] to nag or tease someone. □ *Joan's brother is forever trying to bait her into an argument.*
- **bate** [bet] to decrease the intensity or force of something. □ *When angered, Fred always tries to bate his temper by counting to ten.*

bald—balled—bawled

- **bald** [bɔld] having no hair. □ *During the winter, the bald man wore a hat to keep his head warm.*
- **bald** [bɔld] bare or unadorned. □ *The Christmas tree appeared bald after we removed all the ornaments.*
- **bald** [bɔld] undisguised. □ *Her bald lie was immediately noted by everyone present.*
- **balled [up]** [bɔld] the past tense and past participle of *ball [up]* 'to form something into a tightly bound mass.' □ *Yards of*

bailer twine balled up inside the jammed machinery.

- **bawled** [bɔld] the past tense and past participle of *bawl* 'to cry out or wail loudly.' ☐ *During the weaning process, the young calf bawled mournfully for its mother.*

bale See the main entry beginning with *bail.*

balled See the main entry beginning with *bald.*

band—banned

- **band** [bænd] something that binds or restricts something. ☐ *A tight rubber band kept John's clock from falling apart.*
- **band** [bænd] a musical group. ☐ *The rock band has a contract to appear nightly at the club for an entire month.*
- **banned** [bænd] the past tense and past participle of *ban* 'to prohibit something.' ☐ *Some cities have banned smoking in public places due to a rising concern over the use and effects of tobacco products.*

banned See the main entry beginning with *band.*

bard—barred

- **bard** [bɑɚd] a composer, singer, or poet who related tales of heroes and their heroic deeds. ☐ *William Shakespeare is considered a bard of unsurpassed talents in English literature.*
- **barred** [bɑɚd] the past tense and past participle of *bar* 'to place something off limits.' ☐ *The public was barred from the courtroom proceedings for security reasons.*
- **barred** [bɑɚd] the past tense and past participle of *bar* 'to fasten with a bar so as to obstruct an entrance or exit.' ☐ *The doors of the abandoned house were barred and the windows boarded to prevent trespassing.*

bare—bear

- **bare** [bɛɚ] plain; unadorned; lacking covering. ☐ *Except for some cacti, the desert landscape was bare.*
- **bare** [bɛɚ] to reveal or uncover something. ☐ *"I swear I will never bare your secrets to a single soul!" exclaimed his confidante.*
- **bear** [bɛɚ] a large mammal belonging to the family Ursidae. ☐ *A bear may seem like an awkward animal, but it can move quickly when alarmed.*
- **bear** [bɛɚ] to carry someone or something; to support someone or something. ☐ *Mike is unable to bear much weight on his injured foot.*
- **bear** [bɛɚ] to endure someone or something. ☐ *I cannot bear to see violent movies.*

baron—barren

- **baron** ['bæɚən] a low-ranking nobleman in various European countries. □ *The woman hoped to marry a baron in order to gain some social standing.*
- **baron** ['bæɚən] a person of powerful influence in some field. □ *The oil baron invested a great deal of money in the project.*
- **barren** ['bæɚən] infertile. □ *Because his wife was barren and could give him no heirs, the king dismissed her.*
- **barren** ['bæɚən] bare. □ *The barren environment of the desert startled Mary, who grew up in the mountains.*

baroness—barrenness

- **baroness** ['bæɚənɛs] the wife or widow of a baron. □ *Contrary to her husband's naive nature, the baroness was a shrewd and cunning woman.*
- **barrenness** ['bæɚənɛs] the lack of productivity. □ *John was fired due to the barrenness of his work.*

barred See the main entry beginning with *bard.*

barren See the main entry beginning with *baron.*

barrenness See the main entry beginning with *baroness.*

base—bass

- **base** [bes] the lower part of something; the bottom and supporting part of something. □ *Standing at the base of the Statue of Liberty, one cannot help but be in awe of its immense size.*
- **base** [bes] a center of operations. □ *The army set up a temporary communications base in the empty warehouse.*
- **base [on]** [bes] to establish a foundation for an idea. □ *I will base my decision on many factors.*
- **bass** [bes] a musical instrument or a person's voice with a low pitch. □ *Debbie plays the bass in the school orchestra.* □ *The small chorus is composed of six sopranos, four altos, two tenors, and a single bass.*

bases—basis

- **bases** ['besɪz] the plural of *base* 'the bottom and supporting part of something.' □ *The bases of the fruit trees were wrapped in tape to prevent damage by small animals and insects.* □ *The bases of all of the stemmed goblets were broken in the dishwasher.*
- **bases** ['besɪz] the plural of *base* 'a center of operations.' □ *Military bases are located all around the country's borders.*
- **bases [on]** ['besɪz] the present tense, third person singular

of *base [on]* 'to establish a foundation for an idea.' □ *She almost always bases her opinions on hearsay.*

- **basis** [ˈbesɪs] a concept on which a reasoned conclusion is based. (The plural is pronounced [ˈbesiz].) □ *Three people will be indicted for the crime on the basis of the woman's testimony.*

basis See the main entry beginning with *bases.*

bass See the main entry beginning with *base.*

bate See the main entry beginning with *bait.*

bawled See the main entry beginning with *bald.*

bazaar—bizarre

- **bazaar** [bəˈzɑɚ] a marketplace or fair for the sale of goods. □ *Multitudes of sights, sounds, and smells filled the bazaar in the village square.*
- **bizarre** [bɪˈzɑɚ] odd; eccentric; out of the ordinary. □ *The detective had a bizarre habit of inviting suspects to dinner.*

be—bee

- **be** [bi] to exist; to live; to occupy space or time. □ *We'll be grateful when winter ends and spring arrives.*
- **bee** [bi] an insect that feeds on pollen and produces honey. □ *A hive can have only one queen bee at a time.*
- **bee** [bi] a gathering for a specific purpose. (Typically a *spelling bee, quilting bee,* or a *[corn] husking bee.*) □ *The entire town turned out to watch the day-long spelling bee.*

beach—beech

- **beach** [bitʃ] a stretch of sandy or rocky area along a water's edge. □ *Such interesting creatures as hermit crabs, brittle stars, and jellyfish can be found on the beach after the tide recedes.*
- **beach** [bitʃ] to run a boat or ship onto the shore. □ *The sailors tried to beach their small vessel during the violent storm.*
- **beech** [bitʃ] a type of hardwood tree characterized by smooth gray bark. □ *The beech in our backyard produces an ample supply of nuts for the deer in winter.*

bear See the main entry beginning with *bare.*

beat—beet

- **beat** [bit] to hit someone or something. □ *I beat the rug in an effort to remove as much dust and dirt from it as possible.*
- **beat** [bit] to overcome someone or something; to defeat someone or something. □ *Our hometown football team is not likely*

to beat its arch rival.

- **beat** [bit] an audible pulsation. □ *The drumbeat accompanied tribal members in their ceremonial dance.*
- **beet** [bit] a garden vegetable with edible leaves and roots. □ *Mom's enormous beet won first prize at the state fair.*

beau—bow

(See also *bough—bow.*)

- **beau** [bo] a boyfriend; a suitor. □ *The attention of each new beau only added to Rita's vanity.*
- **bow** [bo] a ribbon tied in a decorative knot. □ *On his first birthday, the child was interested only in the bow on each present given to him.*
- **bow** [bo] a stick equipped with stretched horsehairs, used to play stringed musical instruments. □ *While his violin is an antique, the bow used to play it is new.*
- **bow** [bo] a curved piece of strong material strung with a cord and used to shoot arrows. □ *The bow and arrows were presented to the young hunter as a gift on his sixteenth birthday.*

beaut—butte

- **beaut** [bjut] an abbreviation of *beauty* 'a beautiful person or thing.' (Slang. Used as an expression of admiration. Often used sarcastically.) □ *Your new car is a real beaut.* □ *"That black eye you have is a real beaut!" exclaimed Jeff.*
- **butte** [bjut] a large, solitary hill with steep sides and a small, flat top. □ *From a distance, the butte appeared to be a rectangular box sitting on the horizon.*

bee See the main entry beginning with *be.*

beech See the main entry beginning with *beach.*

been—bin

- **been** [bɪn] the past participle of *be* 'to exist.' □ *To have been able to sail around the world was, he felt, his greatest opportunity in life.*
- **bin** [bɪn] a storage container. □ *At the end of the harvest, each bin was filled to capacity with corn.*

beer—bier

- **beer** [bɪɚ] a fermented alcoholic beverage. □ *Brewers spend thousands of dollars each year advertising beer on T.V.*
- **bier** [bɪɚ] a platform on which a corpse or a coffin is placed. □ *The body of the chief was set high on a bier in the wilderness.*

beet See the main entry beginning with *beat.*

bell—belle

- **bell** [bɛl] a hollow instrument that produces a ringing sound when struck. □ *Kathleen has a tiny glass bell and a huge antique school bell in her collection.*
- **belle** [bɛl] an attractive, popular woman or girl. □ *Amy felt like the belle of the ball when she was asked to dance five times.*

belle See the main entry beginning with *bell.*

berry—bury

- **berry** ['bɛɚi] the small, sometimes edible fruit of various plants and shrubs. □ *The berry of the currant bush makes a tasty, tart jam.*
- **bury** ['bɛɚi] to conceal something some place; to cover someone or something with earth. □ *To bury one's face in one's hands can be a sign of joy, grief, or disbelief.* □ *We were not permitted to bury our dog in the backyard.*

berth—birth

- **berth** [bɚθ] a platform or bed on a train or ship. □ *My berth in the train's sleeping car was extremely small.*
- **berth** [bɚθ] a place where a ship docks or anchors. □ *Huge oceangoing vessels require a large berth when in port.*
- **berth** [bɚθ] a job. (Figurative.) □ *Although he had hoped to play in the major leagues, James eagerly accepted a berth in an amateur baseball club.*
- **birth** [bɚθ] the process by which an offspring emerges from its mother. □ *The birth of a rare white tiger cub caused quite a stir at the zoo.*
- **birth** [bɚθ] the beginning of something. □ *The birth of the space age spawned a flurry of activity among the world's highly developed nations.*

better—bettor

- **better** ['bɛtɚ] superior, but not the best. □ *While Aaron was an excellent math student, his twin brother Alex was better in science.*
- **bettor** ['bɛtɚ] a person who bets or gambles. □ *The bettor placed his chips nervously on the roulette table.*

bettor See the main entry beginning with *better.*

between See the main entry beginning with *among.*

bier See the main entry beginning with *beer.*

billed—build

- **billed** [bɪld] the past tense and past participle of *bill* 'to present a statement of charges.' □ *The telephone company incorrectly billed us for several long distance calls.*

- **build** [bɪld] to construct something. □ *In order to build a house on that piece of property, a building permit is required.*
- **build** [bɪld] to establish or increase something. □ *The seminar is designed to help people build self-esteem.*

bin See the main entry beginning with *been.*

birth See the main entry beginning with *berth.*

bizarre See the main entry beginning with *bazaar.*

blew—blue

- **blew** [blu] the past tense of *blow* 'to move something about with air.' □ *A warm, southerly wind gently blew the windsocks in the breeze.*
- **blew [about]** [blu] the past tense of *blow [about]* 'to boast or brag about someone or something.' □ *Jeff blew about even his minor accomplishments to anyone who would listen.*
- **blue** [blu] the color of a clear sky. □ *The clear, sparkling water surrounding the atoll was an amazing shade of deep blue.*
- **blue** [blu] depressed; low in spirit. □ *The death of her cat made Mary blue.*

bloc—block

- **bloc** [blɑk] a united group of people or countries acting together for a common purpose. □ *The bloc of coffee-producing nations opposed the trade embargo levied against one of its members.*
- **block** [blɑk] a solid piece of material with one or more flat surfaces. □ *Tim used a large block of wood to prop up the truck.*
- **block** [blɑk] to obstruct someone or something. □ *The iron gate serves to block any unwanted visitors.*
- **block** [blɑk] an obstacle. □ *The school board's refusal to give teachers dental insurance created a block in the negotiations.*
- **block** [blɑk] one of the parcels of land delineated by a grid of streets. (This refers to the square or rectangular parcels of land as well as the distance of one of the sides of the parcels.) □ *New sidewalks were installed around the entire block of our neighborhood.*

block See the main entry beginning with *bloc.*

blue See the main entry beginning with *blew.*

boar—boor—bore—Boer

- **boar** [bɔə˞] a male mammal of some species, usually the swine family. □ *The hunters captured a wild boar in the woods.*

- **boor** [bʊɚ, bɔɚ] a rude, discourteous person. □ *The boor continually disrupted the meeting with his bad behavior.*
- **bore** [bɔɚ] to drill a hole in something. □ *Special metal drill bits are needed to bore through granite.*
- **bore** [bɔɚ] the hollow space in a gun barrel or an engine cylinder. □ *A bullet passes through the bore of a gun when the gun is fired.*
- **bore** [bɔɚ] to make someone uncomfortable or weary through inactivity or by something tedious. □ *Please do not bore us with all of the small details.*
- **Boer** [bɔɚ] a South African of Dutch or Huguenot descent. □ *No one but a Boer had been elected to office in many years.*

board—bored

- **board** [bɔɚd] a plank of wood. □ *Bill had some difficulty rounding a corner while carrying the long board beneath his arm.*
- **board** [bɔɚd] a game table. □ *The board used to play checkers can also be used to play chess.*
- **board** [bɔɚd] a group of governing officers. □ *The board of directors meets once a month on Tuesday evenings.*
- **board** [bɔɚd] to go onto a vessel. □ *No one is allowed to board the ship without first going through a security check.*
- **bored** [bɔɚd] the past tense and past participle of *bore* 'to make someone uncomfortable or weary through inactivity or by something tedious.' □ *After just five minutes with her new doll, the child was utterly bored.*

boarder—border

- **boarder** ['bɔɚdɚ] a person who rents a room, usually in a house or inn. □ *A private entrance is available for the boarder who lives in the upstairs apartment.*
- **border** ['bɔɚdɚ] a boundary; an edge. □ *The border of the natural bird sanctuary is posted with warning signs that read "Please Do Not Feed The Birds."*

Boer See the main entry beginning with *boar*.

bold—bowled

- **bold** [bold] unafraid in the face of danger. □ *Risk-takers tend to be bold in spirit.*
- **bold** [bold] impudent; presumptuous. □ *The girl rejected the advances of the bold young man.*
- **bold** [bold] standing out; prominent. □ *The new vocabulary words in each chapter are printed in bold type.*

- **bowled** [bold] the past tense and past participle of *bowl* 'to roll a ball down a lane in the sport of bowling.' ☐ *Although an amateur, Rachel bowled three perfect games in the tournament.*
- **bowled [over]** [bold] the past tense and past participle of *bowl [over]* 'to overwhelm someone with surprise.' ☐ *I was completely bowled over by his extreme generosity.*

bolder—boulder

- **bolder** ['boldɚ] more fearless than someone or something else. ☐ *Sam's tiny chihuahua has always been bolder than his timid cat.*
- **boulder** ['boldɚ] a large rock, usually detached from surrounding rocky masses. ☐ *The massive boulder that perched above the rustic cabin seemed threatening.*

boll—bowl

- **boll** [bol] the pod of a cotton plant. ☐ *Not a single cotton plant showed signs of its boll being infested with weevils.*
- **bowl** [bol] a rounded dish used for holding liquids and other food. ☐ *A festive bowl of fresh fruit served as the centerpiece on the table.*

boor See the main entry beginning with *boar.*

border See the main entry beginning with *boarder.*

bore See the main entry beginning with *boar.*

bored See the main entry beginning with *board.*

born—borne

- **born** [bɔɚn] the past participle of *bear* 'to give birth to someone or some creature.' ☐ *Migratory animals have often born offspring under difficult conditions.*
- **borne** [bɔɚn] the past participle of *bear* 'to carry or support someone or something.' ☐ *Our pack animals have borne heavy loads of materials on their backs.*
- **borne** [bɔɚn] the past participle of *bear* 'to accept or assume something.' ☐ *Throughout history, great leaders have borne responsibility for their decisions and actions.*
- **borne** [bɔɚn] the past participle of *bear* 'to produce or yield something.' ☐ *The newly developed plants have borne larger yields of fruits in shorter periods of time.*

borne See the main entry beginning with *born.*

borough—burro—burrow

- **borough** ['bɚo] a political division in an urban area. (Particularly in New York City, which has five boroughs.) ☐ *Mr.*

O'Leary was once a police officer in the borough of Queens in New York City.

- **burro** ['bɚo] a donkey. ☐ *When one pictures a gold prospector in the western United States, one almost always imagines a burro as his trusty companion.*
- **burrow** ['bɚo] a hole dug in the ground by an animal for living or hiding. ☐ *The burrow of a groundhog has at least two tunnels for entrance and escape.*
- **burrow** ['bɚo] to excavate a hole or tunnel. ☐ *Many animals that hibernate for the winter burrow under woodpiles or rocks.*

bough—bow

(See also *beau—bow.*)

- **bough** [bɑʊ] the limb of a tree. ☐ *During the violent thunderstorm, a large bough of the maple tree bent to the ground and snapped.*
- **bow** [bɑʊ] to bend forward at the waist, usually as a sign of greeting or deference. ☐ *Gentlemen should always bow when introduced to Britain's queen, and ladies should always curtsey.*
- **bow** [bɑʊ] the forward part of a ship. ☐ *The huge waves washed over the bow of the boat during the violent windstorm.*

bouillon—bullion

- **bouillon** ['buljən] a broth made from beef or chicken stock. ☐ *A cup of hot bouillon tastes good on a cold, wintry evening.*
- **bullion** ['buljɑn] gold or silver that has been formed into bars. ☐ *The buried pirate's chest was stuffed with gold bullion and precious gems.*

boulder See the main entry beginning with *bolder.*

bow See the main entry beginning with *beau* and the main entry beginning with *bough.*

bowl See the main entry beginning with *boll.*

bowled See the main entry beginning with *bold.*

boy—buoy

- **boy** [bɔɪ] a male child. ☐ *In some cultures, boys are preferred over girls.*
- **buoy** ['bui] a floating marker in a lake, river, or ocean. ☐ *When snorkeling or skin diving, a buoy should be anchored near the dive site to alert boaters to divers in the area.*
- **buoy** ['bui] to support someone. ☐ *We tried to buoy his spirits by telling jokes.*

braid—brayed

- **braid** [bred] a type of weaving using three or more strands of something, usually hair. □ *The French braid has gained popularity as both a casual and elegant hair fashion.*
- **braid** [bred] to weave something into a braided pattern. □ *I do not have the patience to braid my daughter's hair every morning.*
- **brayed** [bred] the past tense and past participle of *bray* 'to utter the loud, harsh sound of a donkey or mule.' □ *Each time visitors came near the donkey, it brayed loudly hoping for a carrot or sugar cube.*

braise—brays—braze

- **braise** [brez] to prepare food in its own juices with very little water in a covered pot. □ *I prefer to braise my pot roasts in the oven rather than fix them in a pressure cooker.*
- **brays** [brez] the plural of *bray* 'a loud, harsh sound, as that made by a donkey.' □ *The brays of discordant notes played by the unpracticed band was hardly music to the ears.*
- **brays** [brez] the present tense, third person singular of *bray* 'to utter a loud, harsh sound, like that made by a donkey.' □ *The mule brays loudly each day around feeding time.*
- **braze** [brez] to unite metal objects with solder. □ *Tom used solder to braze the broken hitch together.*

brake—break

- **brake** [brek] to stop a vehicle. □ *He was not able to brake the car in time to avoid hitting the branch in the road.*
- **brake** [brek] a device used to lock the wheels of a vehicle. □ *Do you always set the emergency brake on your car when parking on a hill?*
- **break** [brek] to smash something; to separate something into parts, often by force. □ *If you step on that toy, it will surely break.*
- **break** [brek] an intermission or recess from something. □ *We will take a break halfway through the class.*
- **break** [brek] to violate or disregard a law, rule, or tradition. □ *If you break the law, you must pay the penalty for your wrongdoing.*

brayed See the main entry beginning with *braid*.

brays See the main entry beginning with *braise*.

braze See the main entry beginning with *braise*.

breach—breech

- **breach** [britʃ] a violation or infraction of a law, norm, or obligation. □ *When he failed to live up to the terms of the agreement, the contractor was sued for breach of contract by his employees.*
- **breach** [britʃ] a break, hole, or gap in a structure. □ *The breach in the dam posed a serious threat to the safety of the village.*
- **breach** [britʃ] to leap out of the water. □ *No one knows for certain the reason whales breach.*
- **breech** [britʃ] the part of a firearm nearest the rear of the barrel. □ *The breech of the rifle was damaged when it fell against a rock.*

bread—bred

- **bread** [brɛd] a leavened food made of flour, liquid, and shortening. □ *Some bakeries sell only bread made with all natural ingredients and no preservatives.*
- **bread** [brɛd] money. (Slang.) □ *"I need some bread so I can take my girl to the movies," said Rusty.*
- **bred** [brɛd] the past tense and past participle of *breed* 'to mate so as to produce offspring.' □ *Mares are usually bred on a yearly basis to prevent barrenness.*

break See the main entry beginning with *brake.*

bred See the main entry beginning with *bread.*

breech See the main entry beginning with *breach.*

brewed—brood

- **brewed** [brud] the past tense and past participle of *brew* 'to create a beverage through steeping or fermentation.' □ *Mary always brewed a fresh pot of coffee first thing each morning.*
- **brewed [up]** [brud] the past tense and past participle of *brew [up]* 'to plot or contrive something.' □ *The thieves brewed up a plan to steal the valuable paintings.*
- **brood** [brud] the young offspring of an animal, particularly fowl. □ *The mother hen attentively hovered over her brood of chicks.*
- **brood** [brud] to worry. □ *Don't brood over past mistakes; try to avoid future ones.*

brews—bruise

- **brews** [bruz] the present tense, third person singular of *brew* 'to make a beverage by steeping or fermentation.' □ *Grandma always brews her herbal tea for exactly four minutes.*

- **brews** [bruz] the present tense, third person singular of *brew* 'to form or develop.' ☐ *Trouble often brews when those two mischievous children get together.*
- **bruise** [bruz] a discoloration of the skin. ☐ *The bruise on his arm changed colors before it healed completely.*
- **bruise** [bruz] to inflict an injury or wound on someone. ☐ *Please do not bruise my ego further by criticizing my work.*

bridal—bridle

- **bridal** ['brɑɪdl] having to do with a bride or a wedding. ☐ *Elaborate bridal shows seem to offer everything for the future bride except the groom.* ☐ *The bridal bouquet had roses and tulips in it.*
- **bridle** ['brɑɪdl] the headgear worn by a horse by which the rider controls the animal. ☐ *Just before the race began, the jockey noticed his horse's bridle was broken.*
- **bridle** ['brɑɪdl] to put headgear on a horse. ☐ *After you saddle and bridle the horse, lead it out to the paddock.*
- **bridle** ['brɑɪdl] to curb or restrain someone or something. ☐ *"I wish I could bridle that child's energy," moaned the weary mother.*

bridle See the main entry beginning with *bridal.*

broach—brooch

- **broach** [brotʃ] a sharp, pointed tool. ☐ *When the whiskey is fully mature, a broach is used to tap the casks.*
- **broach** [brotʃ] to open up a topic for discussion. ☐ *It is difficult to broach the subject of his deceased wife without Mr. Jones becoming upset.*
- **brooch** [brotʃ] a large, decorative pin usually worn by women. ☐ *In old photographs, women are often seen wearing a brooch at the throat of their blouse.*

brooch See the main entry beginning with *broach.*

brood See the main entry beginning with *brewed.*

brows—browse

- **brows** [brɑʊz] the plural of *brow* 'the forehead, eyebrow, or browridge.' ☐ *The brows of the committee members wrinkled in anger at the unexpected news.*
- **browse** [brɑʊz] the young, tender plants or trees on which certain animals like to graze. ☐ *Deer browse often consists of acorns, beechnuts, and the young leaves of various plants.*
- **browse** [brɑʊz] to leisurely gaze through, look over, or inspect something. ☐ *To browse casually through a large bookstore is*

one of life's small pleasures.

browse See the main entry beginning with *brows.*

bruise See the main entry beginning with *brews.*

build See the main entry beginning with *billed.*

bullion See the main entry beginning with *bouillon.*

buoy See the main entry beginning with *boy.*

burley—burly

- **burley** ['bɚli] a mild, air-cured tobacco grown primarily in Kentucky. □ *When traveling through the Kentucky countryside in late summer, one can see the open-sided sheds where burley ripens to its peak.*
- **burly** ['bɚli] solidly and strongly built. □ *Despite his burly physique, Kent is extremely mild-mannered.*

burly See the main entry beginning with *burley.*

burro See the main entry beginning with *borough.*

burrow See the main entry beginning with *borough.*

bury See the main entry beginning with *berry.*

bus—buss

- **bus** [bəs] a large, motorized vehicle usually used for public transportation. □ *Group travel by bus or motorcoach is extremely popular today.*
- **bus** [bəs] to transport someone or something by bus. □ *In an effort to integrate their school district, the school board voted to bus students across town.*
- **bus** [bəs] to tidy tables in a restaurant by clearing away dirty dishes and replacing them with clean ones. □ *When he learned that he would have to bus tables as well as wash dishes, Todd decided not to take the restaurant job.*
- **buss** [bəs] a kiss. □ *The tourists were greeted at the airport in Hawaii with a flower lei and a buss on the cheek.*
- **buss** [bəs] to kiss someone or something. □ *Bobby always squirms away from his great-aunt when she tries to buss him.*

buss See the main entry beginning with *bus.*

bussed—bust

- **bussed** [bəst] the past tense and past participle of *bus* 'to transport someone or something by bus.' □ *The stranded travelers were bussed to nearby motels to spend the evening.*

- **bussed** [bəst] the past tense and past participle of *bus* 'to clear away dirty dishes and then replace them with clean ones in a restaurant.' ☐ *Cheryl collected the tips for the waiters as she bussed the tables.*
- **bussed** [bəst] the past tense and past participle of *buss* 'to kiss someone.' (Slang or colloquial.) ☐ *The hostess bussed each of the departing dinner guests on the cheek.*
- **bust** [bəst] a sculpture of the upper part of a human body. ☐ *A bust of William Shakespeare rests on a pedestal in a public garden in Stratford, Ontario.*
- **bust** [bəst] the upper portion of a woman's body or the part of a woman's garment between the neck and waist. ☐ *While the rest of Sheila's gown fit perfectly, the bust was much too tight.*
- **bust** [bəst] to break someone or something; to ruin someone or something. (Colloquial for *break*. Considered slang or nonstandard for *burst*.) ☐ *Those poor management policies will eventually bust the corporation.*
- **bust** [bəst] an arrest by the police; police intervention of a criminal activity. (Slang.) ☐ *The late-night bust of the nightclub resulted in the arrest of several gambling suspects.*
- **bust** [bəst] to hit or punch someone or something. (Slang.) ☐ *Stop making those ugly remarks or I'll bust you in the mouth.*

bust See the main entry beginning with *bussed.*

but—butt

- **but** [bət] except for someone or something; without someone or something. (A conjunction.) ☐ *The motorist knew the stretch of highway was heavily patrolled, but she continued to exceed the speed limit anyway.*
- **butt** [bət] the buttocks of a person or animal. (Colloquial and sometimes considered rude.) ☐ *That type of injection is always given in the butt.*
- **butt** [bət] to push or strike someone or something with the head or horns. ☐ *If you step into the pasture, the ornery ram might butt you.*
- **butt** [bət] to fit or press something end to end; to fit tightly against something. ☐ *The pieces of wood must butt tightly in order to get a good fit.*

butt See the main entry beginning with *but.*

butte See the main entry beginning with *beaut.*

buy—by—bye

- **buy** [baɪ] to purchase something; to hire or bribe someone, usually by a payment of money. □ *I want to buy a new computer in the near future.* □ *My money will buy three hours of the plumber's time.*

- **buy** [bɑɪ] a bargain; the purchase of something at a good price. □ *The lawn-care tools were priced so low that the gardener couldn't pass up such a good buy.*
- **by** [bɑɪ] by means of someone or something; by way of something. □ *We will have to do it by hand.* □ *Ms. Smith seldom travels by highway if she can take a more scenic route.*
- **by** [bɑɪ] past something. □ *My father drove right by me and didn't see me.*
- **by** [bɑɪ] near or close to someone or something. □ *I left my glasses sitting by the telephone book.*
- **bye** [bɑɪ] an abbreviation of good-bye. □ *Mary always says "bye" before hanging up the phone.*
- **bye** [bɑɪ] a situation in a tournament or contest where a player or team has no opponent and advances to the next stage without playing. □ *Drawing a bye in the early rounds of the play-offs allowed the team more time to practice.*

by See the main entry beginning with *buy.*

bye See the main entry beginning with *buy.*

C

cache—cash

- **cache** [kæʃ] a hiding place, often for food, fuel, or money; the contents of a hiding place. ☐ *Few people knew the location of the cache where the excess foodstuffs were stored.* ☐ *The cache of stolen money was hidden deep inside the cave.*
- **cash** [kæʃ] bills or coins; money ready at hand. ☐ *Since I did not have enough cash to pay for my purchase, I had to charge it on my credit card.* ☐ *John paid cash for his groceries because there was not much money in his checking account.*
- **cash** [kæʃ] to exchange a check or bill for cash. ☐ *You may cash your paycheck at the grocery store if it doesn't exceed $300.00.*

caddie—caddy

- **caddie** ['kædi] a wheeled cart used to transport objects. ☐ *The movers used a caddie to take the refrigerator from the house to the moving van.*
- **caddie** AND **caddy** ['kædi] a person who carries clubs and balls for a golfer. ☐ *Tom has spent the past three summers working as a caddie at the local golf course.* ☐ *The caddy could not find Bill's ball.*
- **caddy** ['kædi] a small box or container for storing things. ☐ *Tea bags remain fresh longer if kept in an airtight caddy.*

caddy See the main entry beginning with *caddie.*

callous—callus

- **callous** ['kæləs] hardened. ☐ *Bill developed a callous growth of skin on his thumb from many years of sorting mail.*
- **callous** ['kæləs] devoid of feelings; not caring. ☐ *While the*

tough-minded businesswoman appears to be very callous toward her employees, she is actually kind and considerate.

- **callus** ['kæləs] a hardened or thickened part of the skin. □ *Mary developed a callus on each heel.*

callus See the main entry beginning with *callous.*

can—may

- **can** [kæn] to be capable of or know how to do something. □ *I can find my way around New York City without trouble.*
- **may** [me] to have permission to do something. □ *You may go to a movie after your chores are done.*

cannon—canon

- **cannon** ['kænən] a large artillery gun that shoots lead balls or explosive shells. □ *The large cannon on the courthouse lawn gives a certain ambiance to the village square.*
- **canon** ['kænən] a rule or law of a church or religion. □ *The priest explained the purpose of each canon of the Catholic church to the children.*
- **canon** ['kænən] a generally accepted standard or principle. □ *An unspoken canon in retail business is that the customer is always right.*
- **canon** ['kænən] a musical piece of several parts in which the melody is precisely imitated by successive voices or instruments. □ *The group of children sang the old canon* "Row, Row, Row Your Boat" *with much enthusiasm.*

canon See the main entry beginning with *cannon.*

cant—can't

- **cant** [kænt] the angle or slant of something. □ *The cant of the new roof is not steep enough to shed rainwater.*
- **cant** [kænt] to lean or slope to the side. □ *That sculpture was designed to cant to one side to give it an unusual appearance.*
- **cant** [kænt] words spoken in a sing-song manner. □ *The beggar's cant was almost unintelligible.*
- **can't** [kænt] a contraction of *cannot* 'unable to do something.' □ *If you can't finish your term paper on time, ask your instructor for an extension.*

can't See the main entry beginning with *cant.*

canter—cantor

- **canter** ['kæntɚ] a horse's gait somewhere between a trot and a gallop. □ *Some riders prefer the smooth movement of a canter to a jerky trot.*

- **cantor** ['kæntɚ] an official of a synagogue who sings or chants prayer. □ *The cantor at our synagogue has a wonderful voice.*

cantor See the main entry beginning with *canter.*

canvas—canvass

- **canvas** ['kænvɪs] a closely woven cloth made of cotton or linen, often used for clothing, ships' sails, and oil paintings. □ *Nowadays racing boats use a lightweight fabric for their sails instead of canvas.*
- **canvass** ['kænvɪs] to travel through voting districts in an effort to gain information or support for political candidates and issues. □ *We will canvass our neighborhood to gain support for our candidate.*

canvass See the main entry beginning with *canvas.*

capital—capitol—Capitol

- **capital** ['kæpɪtl] punishable by death. □ *Murder in the first degree is a capital offense in several states.*
- **capital** ['kæpɪtl] principal; main. □ *Our capital concern was the welfare of the children.*
- **capital** ['kæpɪtl] a city that serves as a seat of government. □ *The capital of a state is not necessarily the state's largest city.*
- **capital** ['kæpɪtl] accumulated money or property. □ *Before he could start a business, Martin had to raise capital to finance the venture.*
- **capitol** ['kæpɪtl] the building in which the legislature of a state meets. □ *The capitol of Michigan was designed by the same architect who designed the Texas capitol.*
- **Capitol** ['kæpɪtl] the building in Washington, D.C., where the United States Congress meets. □ *The U.S. Capitol is located on First Street between Constitution and Independence avenues.*

capitol See the main entry beginning with *capital.*

Capitol See the main entry beginning with *capital.*

carat—caret—carrot—karat

- **carat** AND **karat** ['kæɚət, 'kɛɚət] a measurement of weight for precious stones. (*Carat* is the most common form.) □ *Her diamond engagement ring contained a single marquise-shaped stone weighing less than a carat.*
- **caret** ['kæɚət, 'kɛɚət] a V-like symbol pointing to where something is to be inserted into a line of writing or print. □ *The proofreader used a caret to show where Pamela had omitted a word in the sentence.*

- **carrot** ['kæɚət, 'kɛɚət] a common garden vegetable having an edible orange root. ☐ *Put a carrot or two in the stew to add both flavor and color.*
- **carrot** ['kæɚət, 'kɛɚət] a promised but often deceptive reward or advantage. (From the image of a carrot tied to the end of a stick and held out in front of a horse, causing it to move forward in hopes of getting to eat the carrot.) ☐ *To inspire Austin to earn all A's on his report card, his parents coaxed him with a carrot of box seats to the Pirate's opening day game.*
- **karat** ['kæɚət, 'kɛɚət] a unit of pureness of gold in an alloy. ☐ *What karat is the gold in your wedding ring?*

caret See the main entry beginning with *carat.*

carol—carrel

- **carol** ['kæɚəl, 'kɛɚəl] a song usually associated with the Christmas season. ☐ *Their favorite holiday carol is* "God Rest Ye Merry Gentlemen."
- **carrel** ['kæɚəl, 'kɛɚəl] a small, three-sided, desklike enclosure usually found in libraries and other study areas. ☐ *Food, drink, and portable radios are not permitted in any study carrel.*

carrel See the main entry beginning with *carol.*

carrot See the main entry beginning with *carat.*

cash See the main entry beginning with *cache.*

cast—caste

- **cast** [kæst] to throw someone or something. (Usually with an adverb, such as *away, out,* or *off.)* ☐ *The sailor cast the rope around the piling on the dock.*
- **cast** [kæst] to assign roles or parts in a production. ☐ *The director cast an unknown actress in the movie's lead role.*
- **cast** [kæst] to form something in a mold. ☐ *The sculptor cast the statue in bronze.*
- **cast** [kæst] to direct one's sight onto something. ☐ *As Tommy cast his eyes on his new birthday pony, he became very excited.*
- **caste** [kæst] a social rank usually based on birth, wealth, or occupation. ☐ *In some societies, individuals are prohibited from moving out of the caste into which they were born.*

caste See the main entry beginning with *cast.*

cedar—seeder

- **cedar** ['sidɚ] a type of coniferous tree known for its sturdy, aromatic wood. ☐ *The craftsman carefully lined the drawers of the chest with fragrant cedar.*

- **seeder** ['sidɚ] a farm or garden implement used to plant seeds. ☐ *Planting corn is much easier with the help of a seeder.*

cede—seed

- **cede** [sid] to yield, withdraw, or grant something, usually by a formal treaty. ☐ *The terms of the cease-fire included an agreement by the defeated country to cede the disputed strip of land to the victors.*
- **seed** [sid] the ripened germ of a plant. ☐ *The seed sent up a tiny shoot only a week after it was planted.*
- **seed** [sid] to plant or sow seeds. ☐ *If we seed the lawn just before a rain, the grass has a better chance of taking hold.*

ceiling—sealing

- **ceiling** ['silɪŋ] the top of a room. ☐ *A vast mural covers the ceiling of the art room.* ☐ *Her ceiling consists of a swirled plaster stucco.*
- **ceiling** ['silɪŋ] the above-ground height of the lowest layer of cloud cover. ☐ *We delayed our flying lesson yesterday due to the extremely low ceiling.*
- **sealing** ['siliŋ] the present participle of *seal* 'to fasten something with something that must be broken to gain access.' ☐ *After sealing the envelope, Mary placed it in the mailbox.*

cell—sell

- **cell** [sɛl] a small, lockable room or compartment. ☐ *The prisoner's cell had none of the comforts of home.*
- **cell** [sɛl] a small, microscopic unit of living matter. ☐ *Each student looked at his or her own skin cell under the microscope.*
- **cell** [sɛl] the smallest basic unit of an organization. ☐ *The cell of the secret underground group consisted of only four members.*
- **sell** [sɛl] to offer something for sale; to exchange something for money. ☐ *Tom hopes to sell his old car some day soon.* ☐ *The spy was willing to sell government security secrets in exchange for a large sum of money.*

cellar—seller

- **cellar** ['sɛlɚ] a basement or underground storeroom. ☐ *The cellar is nothing but a cold, damp, and unused area of the house.*
- **seller** ['sɛlɚ] a person who offers something for sale. ☐ *The young seller of the baseball card collection was reluctant to part with his treasures.*

censer—censor—censure—sensor

- **censer** ['sɛnsɚ] a container used to burn incense. □ *A pleasant fragrance floated from the censer.*
- **censor** ['sɛnsɚ] a person who examines published or distributed material and makes recommendations for the deletion of objectionable matter. □ *The censor suggested that some of the dialogue be removed from the author's latest novel.*
- **censor** ['sɛnsɚ] to examine published or distributed material with a view to removing objectionable material. □ *The director of the film knew that the commission would censor her work mercilessly.*
- **censure** ['sɛnʃɚ] [for a legislative body] to reprimand one of its members. □ *The legislature voted to censure its most notorious member.*
- **sensor** ['sɛnsɚ] a device that senses movement, light, or heat and reacts to it in some way. □ *A smoke detector contains a sensor that reacts quickly and noisily to both smoke and heat.*

censor See the main entry beginning with *censer.*

censure See the main entry beginning with *censer.*

census—senses

- **census** ['sɛnsəs] a periodic counting of the population by the government. (This is done every ten years in the United States.) □ *The most recent census showed a sizable shift of people from the Midwestern states to the coastal regions.*
- **senses** ['sɛnsəz] the plural of *sense* 'an ability to perceive sound, sight, touch, smell, and taste.' □ *The senses of sight and hearing usually diminish with age.*
- **senses** ['sɛnsəz] a mental state where one is logical or reasonable. □ *I hope Elaine comes to her senses before she does something she'll regret later.*
- **senses** ['sɛnsəz] the present tense, third person singular of *sense* 'to have a feeling or sensation.' □ *Doug often senses when his daughter is upset.*

cent—scent—sent

- **cent** [sɛnt] one penny; one-hundredth of a dollar. □ *"You won't get a cent from me," yelled the angry customer.*
- **scent** [sɛnt] a smell; an odor. □ *The wonderful scent of lilacs was everywhere.* □ *Our dog easily picked up the scent of the quail on the damp ground.*

- **sent** [sɛnt] the past tense and past participle of *send* 'to cause someone or something to go somewhere.' □ *We sent the courier to deliver the message.* □ *The fast-breaking news story was sent through the wire services.*

cents—scents—sense

- **cents** [sɛnts] the plural of *cent* 'one penny; one one-hundredth of a dollar.' □ *Items that once cost a few cents now cost a few dollars.*
- **scents** [sɛnts] the plural of *scent* 'a smell; an odor.' □ *The combination of scents from the different foods was almost sickening.*
- **sense** [sɛnts] a feeling or sensation. □ *We had a definite sense of uneasiness as we approached the dimly lit house.*

cereal—serial

- **cereal** ['sɪɚiəl] a food made of grain and eaten for breakfast. □ *The price of cereal in the supermarket has risen dramatically in the past two years.*
- **serial** ['sɪɚiəl] in or of a series, rank, or order. □ *A new automobile is stamped with a serial number to aid in identification.*
- **serial** ['sɪɚiəl] a publication or program offered in segments at intervals. □ *The new book will appear, in part, as a monthly serial in that magazine.*

cession—session

- **cession** ['sɛʃn] a concession, withdrawal, or yielding to something else. □ *The large cession of land was welcomed by the county that received it.*
- **session** ['sɛʃn] a meeting for the purpose of transacting business. □ *The collective bargaining session lasted into the wee hours of the night.*
- **session** ['sɛʃn] the set period of time in which a legislative body meets before adjournment. □ *Congress will not be in session again until after the holidays.*

chance—chants

- **chance** [tʃænts] a possibility. □ *There is a chance that it will rain tomorrow.*
- **chance** [tʃænts] an opportunity. □ *Next summer, the Boy Scout troop will have the chance to camp on a very remote island.*
- **chance** [tʃænts] by coincidence or accident. □ *Quite by chance I saw a former classmate at the bus depot.*
- **chants** [tʃænts] the plural of *chant* 'a song or statement, sung or spoken in a monotonous tone of voice.' □ *The loud*

chants of the protestors could be heard for several city blocks.

chants See the main entry beginning with *chance.*

chased—chaste

- **chased** [tʃest] the past tense and past participle of *chase* 'to pursue or follow someone or something quickly.' ☐ *The hounds and hunters chased the fox over miles of countryside.*
- **chaste** [tʃest] pure; virginal; unblemished. ☐ *Monks are expected to be chaste in thought, word, and deed.*

chaste See the main entry beginning with *chased.*

cheap—cheep

- **cheap** [tʃip] inexpensive; not costly. ☐ *The garment is made of cheap fabric.*
- **cheap** [tʃip] contemptible or unworthy. ☐ *The unkind remark was a cheap attempt to embarrass him.*
- **cheep** [tʃip] a faint, shrill sound, often associated with birds and fowl. ☐ *The cheep of the newly hatched robin brought its parents to its side immediately.*

cheep See the main entry beginning with *cheap.*

chews—choose

- **chews** [tʃuz] the present tense, third person singular of *chew* 'to grind or crush something with the teeth.' ☐ *Because she chews gum in her classroom, the business teacher allows her students to chew it also.*
- **choose** [tʃuz] to select; to prefer something from among alternatives. ☐ *I usually choose fish or chicken when dining at restaurants.*

chic—sheik

- **chic** [ʃik] elegant; stylish. (Fashion.) ☐ *Why don't ordinary people look as chic wearing the latest styles as fashion models do?*
- **sheik** [ʃik, ʃek] an Arab chief. ☐ *A sheik owns the three new luxury car dealerships in Phoenix.*

Chile—chili—chilly

- **Chile** ['tʃɪle, 'tʃɪli] a country in South America. ☐ *Chile is right next to Argentina.*
- **chili** ['tʃɪli] a hot, spicy traditional Mexican dish consisting of meat, beans, tomatoes, peppers, and spices. ☐ *If you're going to eat spicy chili, be prepared for the results.*
- **chili** ['tʃɪli] a hot, sweet pepper. ☐ *I added a chili to the nachos to give them more flavor.*

- **chilly** ['tʃɪli] cool; cold. □ *The damp, chilly weather made us shiver.*
- **chilly** ['tʃɪli] lacking warmth of feeling. □ *Each political opponent gave the other a chilly stare.*

chili See the main entry beginning with *Chile.*

chilly See the main entry beginning with *Chile.*

choler—collar

- **choler** ['kɑlɚ] anger; temper. □ *She was a woman of high choler.*
- **collar** ['kɑlɚ] a chain or strap worn about the neck. □ *The dog's license, rabies tag, and I.D. are attached to its collar.*
- **collar** ['kɑlɚ] the neckpiece of a garment. □ *The collar on his shirt was frayed from wear.*
- **collar** ['kɑlɚ] to capture someone or something. (Slang.) □ *The policemen hope to collar the suspect as soon as possible.*

choose See the main entry beginning with *chews.*

chorale—coral—corral

- **chorale** [kɔɚ'æl] a chorus. □ *Joe belongs to the university men's chorale.*
- **coral** ['kɔrəl] deep pink. □ *Her flowers were red and coral and complemented her gown perfectly.*
- **coral** ['kɔrəl] the limestone skeletal structures that support various species of marine polyps. □ *They love to go to the warm waters and snorkel amidst the coral reefs.*
- **corral** [kɔɚ'æl] a fenced enclosure for keeping livestock. □ *Those horses in the corral belong to a riding stable.*
- **corral** [kɔɚ'æl] to gather, capture, or confine. □ *I tried to corral the escaped geese by shooing them into a corner of the yard.*

chord—cord

- **chord** [kɔɚd] a harmonious blend of tones. □ *That chord is a difficult one to play on a twelve-string guitar.*
- **chord** [kɔɚd] a straight line connecting two points on a curve. □ *The geometery instructor asked his class to accurately measure the chord of the circle.*
- **cord** [kɔɚd] a strong string or rope woven of several strands. □ *Sam's puppy is tied to the clothesline with a cord.*
- **cord** [kɔɚd] a tubular or ropelike structure. □ *The baby's umbilical cord was wrapped around its neck at birth.*
- **cord** [kɔɚd] a stack of firewood measuring 4' × 4' × 8'. □ *I was tired and thirsty after stacking the cord of wood in the barn.*

- **cord** [kɔɚd] a fabric with raised rows of material. ☐ *Our home economics teacher suggested using a sturdy fabric such as twill, cord, or denim for our project.*

chute—shoot

- **chute** [ʃut] a sloped passageway through which things may be sent. ☐ *A clothes chute leading from the bathroom to the basement is very convenient.*
- **chute** [ʃut] a parachute. (Slang or colloquial.) ☐ *Tom has to pack his own chute when he goes skydiving.*
- **shoot** [ʃut] to discharge a gun or other weapon at someone or something. ☐ *Before you shoot the rifle, make certain you have a clear line of fire.*
- **shoot** [ʃut] to discharge a gun at someone; to release an arrow at someone. ☐ *"Please do not shoot me!" begged the clerk.*
- **shoot** [ʃut] to photograph someone or something. ☐ *The film company making the movie will shoot some scenes along the waterfront.*
- **shoot** [ʃut] a small sprout of new plant growth. ☐ *Warm sunshine and plenty of water will enable the shoot to grow quickly.*

cite—sight—site

- **cite** [sɑɪt] to order someone to appear in court. ☐ *If you get caught speeding, the officer may cite you for a moving violation.*
- **cite** [sɑɪt] to quote something from a published source. ☐ *Her attorney will cite a little-known law when presenting her defense.*
- **cite** [sɑɪt] to recognize someone in commendation. ☐ *During his speech, the speaker will cite the award winner's many accomplishments.*
- **sight** [sɑɪt] the ability to see. ☐ *The child's sight improved greatly following eye surgery.*
- **sight** [sɑɪt] a view or glimpse. ☐ *The Grand Canyon is a magnificent sight.*
- **site** [sɑɪt] a position, place, or scene of something such as a town or building. ☐ *The site for the new veterans memorial has not been decided.*

clause—claws

- **clause** [klɔz] a group of words containing a subject and a verb, used in either a compound or complex sentence. ☐ *'While he tinkered in his workshop all morning' is a dependent clause.*
- **clause** [klɔz] a specific section of a written document. ☐ *The contract contained an escape clause to protect both parties.*

- **claws** [klɔz] the plural of *claw* 'a sharp, curved nail on the toe of an animal.' ☐ *When he decided to keep his cat indoors, Mario had its claws removed.*
- **claws** [klɔz] the plural of *claw* 'the pincherlike appendage like that of a lobster or crab.' ☐ *Some fishmarkets offer crab claws for sale.*

claws See the main entry beginning with *clause.*

click—clique
- **click** [klɪk] a sharp, taplike sound. ☐ *Tom knew someone picked up the extension phone when he heard a click on the line.*
- **click** [klɪk] to make a taplike sound. ☐ *I dislike hearing people click their tongues in disapproval.*
- **click** [klɪk] to fit together or agree. ☐ *Since they both enjoyed classical music, the new roommates knew immediately that they would click.*
- **clique** [klik, klɪk] an exclusive, closely knit group sharing some similar interest, purpose, or view. ☐ *There always seems to be a particular clique to which many high-school students want to belong.*

climb—clime
- **climb** [klɑɪm] to go or move up something. ☐ *Be careful when you climb the ladder.* ☐ *The song's climb to the top of the record charts was quick.*
- **clime** [klɑɪm] a climate. ☐ *Bonnie prefers a warm clime to a cold one.*

clime See the main entry beginning with *climb.*

clique See the main entry beginning with *click.*

close—clothes
- **close** [kloz] to shut something. ☐ *Please close the door before leaving.*
- **close** [kloz] a conclusion; an ending. ☐ *At the close of the speech, the drowsy audience began to stir.*
- **clothes** [kloz, kloðz] garments. ☐ *His clothes always look as if he slept in them.*

clothes See the main entry beginning with *close.*

coarse—course
- **coarse** [kɔɚs] rough or harsh. ☐ *The coarse texture of the garment was irritating to the skin.*

- **coarse** [kɔə·s] of poor quality. □ *The cabin's coarse furnishings were almost unusable.*
- **coarse** [kɔə·s] lacking refinement in skills or manners. □ *His behavior is sometimes coarse and offensive.*
- **course** [kɔə·s] a path of action. □ *The new college students were encouraged to stay on course and not get distracted from their studies.*
- **course** [kɔə·s] a series of lectures or other materials dealing with a given subject. □ *The most difficult course in the curriculum is entitled "Ethics and Issues."*
- **course** [kɔə·s] a pathway over which something moves. □ *The sailboat was blown off its course by strong winds.*

collar See the main entry beginning with *choler.*

collard—collared

- **collard** ['kɑlə·d] a vegetable with smooth leaves belonging to the cabbage family. □ *A pesky rabbit has nibbled every collard in my vegetable garden.*
- **collared** ['kɑlə·d] the past tense and past participle of *collar* 'to fit someone or something with a collar.' □ *High, stiff-collared shirts were a popular men's fashion in the 1800's.*
- **collared** ['kɑlə·d] the past tense and past participle of *collar* 'to catch someone or something; to arrest someone.' (Slang.) □ *I collared the dog and tied it to a tree.* □ *The cops collared the crooks just after the robbery.*

collared See the main entry beginning with *collard.*

colonel—kernel

- **colonel** ['kə·nl] a rank of commissioned military officer higher than lieutenant colonel but lower than brigadier general. □ *Even a colonel must answer to a higher authority.*
- **kernel** ['kə·nl] the soft, inner part of a fruit stone, nut, or seed. □ *The small child planted a kernel of corn in each tiny hole in the earth.*

complement—compliment

- **complement** ['kɑmplɪmənt] something that enhances or completes someone or something. □ *A fine red wine is a nice complement for a meal including red meat.*
- **complement** ['kɑmplɪmənt] the number or quantity needed to make something complete. □ *When the final complement of troops arrived, the unit moved out.*
- **compliment** ['kɑmplɪmənt] to express admiration or respect for something. □ *"I'd like to compliment you on your fine*

achievements," began the speaker.

- **compliment** ['kamplɪmənt] an expression of praise or recognition. ☐ *Some people become very embarrassed when paid a compliment.*

compliment See the main entry beginning with *complement.*

confidant—confident

- **confidant** ['kanfɪdant] a person in whom one confides or trusts. ☐ *The frightened youngster chose an understanding police officer as a confidant.*
- **confident** ['kanfidənt] full of assurance and self-reliance. ☐ *As the ball game progressed, the pitcher grew more confident of herself.*

confident See the main entry beginning with *confidant.*

continence—continents

- **continence** ['kantɪnənts] self-restraint. ☐ *Tom's continence dissolved as the badgering and ridicule of his friends continued.*
- **continence** ['kantɪnənts] the ability to control excretory functions. ☐ *The stroke victim no longer had continence.*
- **continents** ['kantɪnənts] the plural of *continent* 'one of the seven major land masses on the earth.' ☐ *Australia is the smallest of the world's continents.*

continents See the main entry beginning with *continence.*

continual—continuous

- **continual** [kən'tɪnjuəl] on a regular or frequent basis. ☐ *Her continual complaints are annoying.*
- **continuous** [kən'tɪnjuəs] constantly; without an end. ☐ *That machine's continuous knocking sound must be fixed.*

continuous See the main entry beginning with *continual.*

coo—coup

- **coo** [ku] a happy, gurgling sound made by an infant. ☐ *New parents are often thrilled by the first coo made by their offspring.*
- **coo** [ku] the low, soft sound of a pigeon or dove. ☐ *On hot summer mornings the coo of a mourning dove is easily recognizable.*
- **coo** [ku] to utter a soft cooing sound. ☐ *To coo like a baby is usually a sign of contentment.*
- **coup** [ku] a sudden, unexpected, and usually successful action. ☐ *The unseasoned athlete staged a coup against the champion and eventually won the title.*

coop—coupe

- **coop** [kup] a small shed or enclosure, usually used to keep poultry. □ *That pesky raccoon raids the chicken coop almost every night.*
- **coop [up]** [kup] to confine someone or something in close, restricted quarters. □ *"If you don't behave," threatened the baby-sitter, "I'll coop you up in your room for an hour."*
- **coupe** AND **coupé** [kup, ku'pe] a two-door car with a hard roof. □ *While my brother prefers a convertible, I much prefer a sporty coupe.*

cops—copse

- **cops** [kɑps] the plural of *cop* 'a law enforcement officer.' (Slang.) □ *Cops patrol New York City's streets on horseback.*
- **copse** [kɑps] a small, thick growth of trees or bushes. □ *The copse at the back of the farm is a haven for many birds and small animals.*

copse See the main entry beginning with *cops.*

coral See the main entry beginning with *chorale.*

cord See the main entry beginning with *chord.*

core—corps

- **core** [kɔɚ] the center or foundation of something. □ *At the core of the curriculum are eight required courses.*
- **core** [kɔɚ] the center, inedible part of many fruits. □ *Be sure to remove the core of the apple when slicing it for the salad.*
- **core** [kɔɚ] the central meaning of something. □ *The core of the telephone solicitor's pitch was a request for donations.*
- **corps** [kɔɚ] a group of individuals organized and acting together under common direction; an organized subdivision of a military unit. (The pronunciation [kɔrps] is viewed as an error.) □ *While enlisted in the army, Josh was a clerk in the Army Corps of Engineers.* □ *The city's youth corps provides jobs for many disadvantaged young people.*

corps See the main entry beginning with *core.*

corral See the main entry beginning with *chorale.*

correspondence—correspondents

- **correspondence** [kɔɚ-ə'spɑndənts] a relationship of one thing with another. □ *There is a direct correspondence between diet and the general health of a person.*
- **correspondence** [kɔɚ-ə'spɑndənts] an exchange of written communication. □ *Mrs. Smith has carried on a correspondence*

with her French pen pal for more than forty years.
- **correspondents** [kɔə·ə'spɑndənts] people who communicate regularly in writing with one another. ☐ *As correspondents, Kathy and I have enjoyed keeping in touch though we are separated by thousands of miles.*
- **correspondents** [kɔə·ə'spɑndənts] people who serve as news reporters from a distant location. ☐ *During the Persian Gulf War, news correspondents reported events as they happened.*

correspondents See the main entry beginning with *correspondence.*

council—counsel
- **council** ['kaʊnsl] a body of people that meets to consult or make policy. ☐ *Our city council meets once a month.*
- **council** ['kaʊnsl] a federation made up of small, local chapters. ☐ *The council on physical fitness has established guidelines for school-age children's fitness levels.*
- **counsel** ['kaʊnsl] to offer someone advice or consultation. ☐ *Clergymen often counsel young couples preparing for marriage.*
- **counsel** ['kaʊnsl] an attorney hired to advise or represent someone in legal matters. ☐ *"Counsel will refrain from badgering the witness," roared the angry judge.*

counsel See the main entry beginning with *council.*

coup See the main entry beginning with *coo.*

coupe See the main entry beginning with *coop.*

course See the main entry beginning with *coarse.*

coward—cowered
- **coward** ['kaʊə·d] a person who demonstrates fear. ☐ *Susan is a real coward when it comes to flying.*
- **cowered** ['kaʊə·d] the past tense and past participle of *cower* 'to draw away from someone or something in fear.' ☐ *When the dog heard the bathwater running, it cowered in a corner of the bedroom.*

cowered See the main entry beginning with *coward.*

creak—creek
- **creak** [krik] a squeaking or grating noise. ☐ *The creak of the swing on the front porch annoys me.*
- **creak** [krik] to produce a creaking sound. ☐ *That door will creak if you open it slowly.*
- **creek** [krik, krɪk] a natural stream of water usually smaller

than a river. □ *The homesteaders searched for some land with a creek running through it.*

cream—creme

- **cream** [krim] the fatty part of whole milk that rises to the top when milk is left standing. □ *Grandma always adds cream to her tea.*
- **cream** [krim] the best of something or some group. □ *Only the cream of the contestants will go on to the final competition.*
- **cream** [krim] to whip or beat a substance until it becomes smooth. □ *You should cream the sugar and shortening before adding the other ingredients.*
- **creme** AND **crème** [krim, krɛm] a sweet, creamy liqueur. □ *He occasionally likes a splash of crème de menthe over ice for a summer beverage.*

creek See the main entry beginning with *creak.*

creme See the main entry beginning with *cream.*

crewel—cruel

- **crewel** [krul] a loosely twisted yarn used in embroidery. □ *The wall hanging in the foyer was done in crewel by her aunt.*
- **cruel** [krul] causing pain, grief, or injury. □ *Children often utter cruel words to one another in anger.*

crews—cruise

- **crews** [kruz] the plural of *crew* 'a group of people working together in cooperation.' □ *Each of the work crews was assigned a task to be completed by the day's end.*
- **cruise** [kruz] to sail through a geographical location. □ *I would someday like to cruise Alaska's inland passage.*
- **cruise** [kruz] to wander streets randomly. □ *Gangs of youths cruise the streets of the city day and night.*
- **cruise** [kruz] to travel at the most efficient speed. □ *The pilot announced that the aircraft would cruise at an altitude of 33,000 feet.*

cruel See the main entry beginning with *crewel.*

cruise See the main entry beginning with *crews.*

cue—queue

- **cue** [kju] a signal given to someone for a specific purpose. □ *When the director gave him the cue, Ken strutted onto the stage.*
- **cue** [kju] to prompt someone. □ *If you forget your lines in the play, a prompter will cue you from behind the curtain.*
- **cue** [kju] a stick used to strike the balls in pool or billiards.

☐ *For better contact with the ball, put chalk on the end of your cue.*

- **queue [up]** [kju] to line up in a row. ☐ *Concert fans began to queue up for tickets at midnight.*
- **queue** [kju] a line; a row. ☐ *The queue of antique cars at the fair attracted many admirers.*
- **queue** [kju] a braid of hair worn dangling at the back of the neck. ☐ *Mary wore her hair in a queue interwoven with colorful ribbons.*

currant—current

- **currant** [ˈkɚənt] the small, berrylike fruit of several shrubs. ☐ *I ate almost every currant I picked!*
- **current** [ˈkɚənt] up-to-date; presently acceptable or practiced. ☐ *The man prides himself on his knowledge of current world events.* ☐ *The current medical procedure for curing that ailment is really quite simple.*
- **current** [ˈkɚənt] the flow of something in a specific direction. ☐ *Be careful of the strong current in that river.*

current See the main entry beginning with *currant.*

cymbal—symbol

- **cymbal** [ˈsɪmbl̩] a percussion instrument made of brass that produces a loud, crashing sound when struck with a stick or another cymbal. ☐ *To play the cymbal well, one must have perfect timing.*
- **symbol** [ˈsɪmbl̩] something that stands for something else by reason of association or resemblance. ☐ *The dictator's face became a symbol of hatred to the oppressed people.*

D

dam—damn

- **dam** [dæm] a structure in a river or a stream preventing the flow of water. ☐ *The beavers built a dam at the narrowest part of the river.*
- **dam** [dæm] to place a barrier in a river or a stream to restrict the flow of water. ☐ *If we dam the flow of water upstream, we can slow the current here.*
- **dam** [dæm] the female parent of a horse. ☐ *The filly's dam has a strong racing background.*
- **damn** [dæm] to condemn someone to punishment. ☐ *The court chose to damn the traitor to a lifetime of banishment.*
- **damn** [dæm] to bring ruin upon someone or something. ☐ *The defeat of that issue will damn any chance of further school improvements.*
- **damn** [dæm] to condemn someone or something through a curse. ☐ *"Damn the day my curiosity got the best of me!" wailed the woman.*

damn See the main entry beginning with *dam.*

days—daze

- **days** [dez] the plural of *day* 'the period between sunrise and sunset.' ☐ *During the summertime, days are much longer than during the winter.*
- **days** [dez] the plural of *day* 'a twenty-four hour period.' ☐ *You will feel better in a couple of days.*
- **daze** [dez] to stun or disorient someone or some creature. ☐ *Repeated blows to the head began to daze the tired but determined boxer.*
- **daze** [dez] a state of disorientation. ☐ *Severe jet lag seems to*

put some travelers in a daze.

daze See the main entry beginning with *days.*

dear—deer

- **dear** [dɪɚ] highly valued; precious. □ *My grandmother's antique locket is very dear to me.*
- **dear** [dɪɚ] costly; expensive. □ *For some people, the price paid for personal freedom is dear indeed.*
- **dear** [dɪɚ] a loved one. (A term of address.) □ *Now, my dear, what may I do for you?*
- **deer** [dɪɚ] a wild, swift-running animal having hooves and antlers in all males and the females of some species. □ *Each year, the same deer munches on my father's garden.*

deer See the main entry beginning with *dear.*

demur—demure

- **demur** [dɪˈmjɚ] to object; to make an objection. □ *I appreciate your suggestion but I must demur. That is the wrong approach.*
- **demure** [dɪˈmjur] modest; coyly decorous. □ *The demure young priest was very precise in his homily.*

demure See the main entry beginning with *demur.*

dense—dents

- **dense** [dɛnts] thick; closely grown. □ *Although Harold has a dense head of hair, his brother Hank is nearly bald.*
- **dense** [dɛnts] dull; stupid. □ *In the movie, that character is a dense, bumbling door-to-door salesman.*
- **dents** [dɛnts] the plural of *dent* 'an indentation or hollow made by a blow.' □ *The autobody shop was able to repair all of the dents in the car's bumper.*

dental—dentil

- **dental** [ˈdɛntəl] having to do with teeth or dentistry. □ *One of the fringe benefits of that job is a complete dental insurance plan.*
- **dental** [ˈdɛntəl] pronounced with the tip of the tongue against the back of the upper front teeth. □ *The sounds* d *and* t *are said to be dental because of the way they are spoken.*
- **dentil** [ˈdɛntəl] a small, rectangular decorative block projecting below a cornice or overhang on a building. (Architectural.) □ *A dentil had fallen here and there, but the look of the old building was still pleasant.*

dentil See the main entry beginning with *dental.*

dents See the main entry beginning with *dense.*

dependence—dependents

- **dependence** [də'pɛndənts] the state or quality of relying on someone or something else. □ *Children remain in a state of complete dependence on their parents for many years.*
- **dependents** [də'pɛndənts] the plural of *dependent* 'someone who relies upon someone else for support.' □ *How many dependents do you claim on your federal and state income tax?*

dependents See the main entry beginning with *dependence.*

depravation—deprivation

- **depravation** [dɛprə'veʃn] corruption or downfall. □ *Association with the wrong people seemingly caused the depravation of the innocent woman.*
- **deprivation** [dɛprə'veʃn] losing or removing something. □ *Deprivation of food and clothing made their existence miserable.*

deprivation See the main entry beginning with *depravation.*

descension—dissension

- **descension** [də'sɛnʃn] the process of going from a higher rank, status, or altitude to a lower one. □ *The wrestler's sudden descension in the tournament's ranking was a shock to his teammates.*
- **dissension** [də'sɛnʃn, dɪ'sɛnʃn] quarreling; disagreement of opinion. □ *The issue of promotion and seniority caused much dissension among the office workers.* □ *There was little dissension among the Supreme Court justices regarding that case.*

descent—dissent

- **descent** [də'sɛnt] a movement downward. □ *The hikers' descent of the mountainside was slow and tedious.*
- **descent** [də'sɛnt] birth; lineage. □ *Otis MacFarland can trace his descent back many centuries to some very old Scottish families.*
- **dissent** [dɪ'sɛnt] to withhold agreement from someone or something. □ *I will exercise my right to dissent on that particular issue.*
- **dissent** [dɪ'sɛnt] a difference of opinion. □ *The representative's dissent was noted in the minutes.*

desert—dessert

- **desert** ['dɛzɚt] a hot, dry area of land, usually covered with sand. □ *There is hardly any life in the sands of the desert.*
- **desert** [də'zɚt] to leave or abandon someone or something

on purpose. ☐ *Rather than stay and fight, the soldiers chose instead to desert their units.*

- **dessert** [də'zɚt] the last course of a meal, usually something sweet. ☐ *His favorite dessert is black walnut cake.*

dessert See the main entry beginning with *desert.*

dew—do—due

- **dew** [du, dju] the moisture that condenses on a cool surface, usually during the night. ☐ *As temperatures continue to drop, the dew on the grass will soon become frost.*
- **do** [du] to perform something; to carry something out. ☐ *Do your chores first, and then you'll have plenty of time for other activities.*
- **due** [du, dju] owed or owing as a debt, moral obligation, or right. ☐ *The electric bill is due on the 15th of each month.* ☐ *My final paper is due on the last day of class.*

die—dye

- **die** [dɑɪ] to cease to live. ☐ *Certain insects die a day or so after hatching.*
- **die** [dɑɪ] to expire. ☐ *If not acted upon, the bill will die in committee.*
- **die [down]** [dɑɪ] to decrease gradually; to stop. ☐ *I wish the wind would die down so I can rake these leaves.*
- **die** [dɑɪ] a six-sided cube with varying numbers of dots on each side that is used in games. ☐ *With each roll of the die the man's luck seemed to increase.*
- **die** [dɑɪ] a tool or device needed to make shapes, forms, or surfaces. ☐ *The die used for casting that part has cracked and can no longer be used.*
- **dye** [dɑɪ] to change the color of something. ☐ *Everyone will notice if you dye your blond hair black.*
- **dye** [dɑɪ] an agent used to change the color of something. ☐ *The purple dye would not wash off his hands.*

disburse—disperse

- **disburse** [dɪs'bɚs, dɪ'spɚs] to pay out money from a fund. ☐ *Our company will disburse bonus checks at the end of the year.*
- **disburse** [dɪs'bɚs, dɪ'spɚs] to distribute something. ☐ *She requested that her attorney disburse her estate's assets according to her will.*
- **disperse** [dɪ'spɚs] to scatter or break up something. ☐ *Police officers tried in vain to disperse the unruly mob.*
- **disperse** [dɪ'spɚs] to spread or distribute something evenly from a fixed source. ☐ *Prisms disperse sunlight in unusual*

and beautiful patterns.

discreet—discrete

- **discreet** [dɪ'skrit] having the ability to show good judgment, especially in conduct and speech. ☐ *A job that involves handling confidential information requires a discreet employee.*
- **discrete** [dɪ'skrit] distinct or separate. ☐ *Though quite similar in appearance, the twins each have a discrete personality.*

discrete See the main entry beginning with *discreet.*

disinterested—uninterested

- **disinterested** [dɪs'ɪntrɪstɪd] free from personal motive or interest. ☐ *Let's ask a disinterested third party to help settle this dispute.*
- **uninterested** [ən'ɪntrɪstɪd] not interested. ☐ *The bored audience was obviously uninterested in what the speaker was saying.*

disperse See the main entry beginning with *disburse.*

dissension See the main entry beginning with *descension.*

dissent See the main entry beginning with *descent.*

do See the main entry beginning with *dew.*

doe—dough

- **doe** [do] a female deer. ☐ *The doe flicked her ears and tail nervously while her fawns ate nearby.*
- **doe** [do] a female of most species where the male is called a buck. ☐ *Ginny won first prize in the rabbit competition at the fair with her pet doe, Flopsy.*
- **dough** [do] a mixture of flour, liquid, and other ingredients, usually used for breads, cookies, and pie crusts. ☐ *My sister's recipe for homemade bread dough is easy to make.*
- **dough** [do] money. (Slang.) ☐ *"Hey, man, can you give me some dough?" asked the beggar.*

does—doze

- **does** [doz] the plural of *doe* 'a female deer or other female animal where the male is called a buck.' ☐ *In the wild, the number of does outweighs the number of bucks.*
- **does** [dəz] the third person singular of *do* 'to perform an act.' ☐ *He does what he is told.*
- **doze** [dəz] to fall into a light, unintentional sleep. ☐ *I doze in front of the television set each night during the news.*
- **doze** [doz] to bulldoze something. ☐ *A work crew will doze the site of the demolished building.*

done—dun

- **done** [dən] the past participle of *do* 'to perform an act.' ☐ *After you have done the filing, please type this letter.*
- **done** [dən] completed; finished. ☐ *When the candy thermometer reads 250 degrees, you'll know that the mixture is done simmering.*
- **dun** [dən] a horse of a neutral light brown color. ☐ *At the riding stable, Jane was given a dun mare to ride.*
- **dun** [dən] marked by drabness or dullness. ☐ *The dun color of the room wasn't very attractive.*
- **dun** [dən] to hound someone for the payment of a debt. ☐ *If you do not pay your bills, they will dun you until you do.*

dough See the main entry beginning with *doe.*

doze See the main entry beginning with *does.*

draft—draught

- **draft** [dræft] to draw up or design something. ☐ *We were asked to draft a document listing our goals for the projects.*
- **draft** [dræft] capable of pulling a load or doing heavy labor. (Usually said of horses.) ☐ *The team of draft horses strained under the heavy weight of the load.*
- **draft** [dræft] to inhale or swallow something. ☐ *Henry can draft an entire stein of beer in one long gulp.*
- **draft** [dræft] to selectively choose someone or something for a particular purpose. ☐ *The college football coach is hoping to draft some of the top prep players for his team.*
- **draft** [dræft] a current of air entering a closed space. ☐ *The cold draft coming under the door made sitting in the room most uncomfortable.*
- **draught** [dræft] a move in a chess or checkers game. ☐ *As usual, Terry defeated me in chess by a clever draught that I missed.*

draught See the main entry beginning with *draft.*

dual—duel

- **dual** [dul, djul] two; double. ☐ *The hot-rod car has dual exhaust pipes.* ☐ *Psychiatrists spend a good deal of time studying patients with dual personalities.*
- **duel** [dul, djul] a confrontation between two armed combatants, usually to settle an argument. (*Duels* are now illegal.) ☐ *A well-known duel in American history involved Alexander Hamilton and Aaron Burr.*
- **duel** [dul, djul] a conflict of interest, persons, forces, or ideas.

☐ *The two courtroom attorneys were locked in a duel of minds.*

ducked–duct

- **ducked** [dəkt] the past tense and past participle of *duck* 'to push someone or something under water.' ☐ *The children ducked one another during a game in the pool.*
- **ducked** [dəkt] the past tense and past participle of *duck* 'to hide from or avoid someone or something.' ☐ *He ducked before the intended blow landed on his head.*
- **duct** [dəkt] a passageway through which something travels. ☐ *The air duct carries warm air in the winter and cool air in the summer.* ☐ *Julie had to go to the doctor because she had an infection in her left tear duct.*

duct See the main entry beginning with *ducked.*

due See the main entry beginning with *dew.*

duel See the main entry beginning with *dual.*

dun See the main entry beginning with *done.*

dye See the main entry beginning with *die.*

E

earn—urn

- **earn** [ɝn] to receive payment or reward in return for work that one has done. □ *Jenny hopes to earn enough money to pay her own way through college.* □ *Three young men in that scout pack will soon earn the rank of Eagle Scout.*
- **urn** [ɝn] a vessel with a pedestal used for planting flowers or preserving ashes following cremation. □ *The urn on the patio contains geraniums and marigolds.* □ *The urn on the mantle contains the remains of Uncle Herman.*

eave—eve

- **eave** [iv] a low, usually separate border of a roof that overhangs a wall and is designed to funnel off water. □ *When the antenna blew off the roof, it badly dented an eave.*
- **eve** [iv] the evening or day before a special event. □ *On the eve of her wedding, Jane was nervous and jittery.*
- **eve** [iv] the period immediately preceding something. □ *During the eve of the American Civil War, tensions between the North and South steadily increased.*

edition See the main entry beginning with *addition.*

effect See the main entry beginning with *affect.*

eight See the main entry beginning with *ate.*

elicit—illicit

- **elicit** [ə'lɪsɪt] to bring something out; to draw something forth. □ *Will you help me elicit support among your friends for this cause?*
- **illicit** [ɪ'lɪsɪt] illegal; unlawful. □ *The illicit sale of drugs is a*

major problem in many cities.

elusion See the main entry beginning with *allusion.*

eminent—imminent

- **eminent** [ˈɛmɪnənt] noted for position, rank, or achievement. ☐ *The eminent author won many Newbery Awards for his children's books.*
- **eminent** [ˈɛmɪnənt] conspicuous; readily noticeable. ☐ *The comedian ridiculed the politician's eminent nose.*
- **imminent** [ˈɪmɪnənt] soon to happen or take place. ☐ *The prisoner on death row knew his execution was imminent.*

ensure—insure

- **ensure** [ɛnˈʃʊɚ] to guarantee something; to make certain of something. ☐ *I will ensure your safe arrival at your destination.*
- **insure** [ɪnˈʃʊɚ] to acquire or give insurance for; to make certain. ☐ *Be sure to insure your new motorcycle before driving it.* ☐ *I will send the letter first class to insure that it arrives as soon as possible.*

epic—epoch

- **epic** [ˈɛpɪk] long in length or scope. ☐ *The epic novel gave several viewpoints of the conquest of the American West.*
- **epoch** [ˈɛpək] an event or period of time noted as the beginning of a new period or development. ☐ *With Eli Whitney's invention of interchangeable parts, the epoch of industrialization began in earnest.*
- **epoch** [ˈɛpək] a geological time span. ☐ *We studied the Miocene epoch in great depth in my geology class.*

epoch See the main entry beginning with *epic.*

err See the main entry beginning with *air.*

erred See the main entry beginning with *aired.*

eve See the main entry beginning with *eave.*

ewe—yew—you

- **ewe** [ju] a female sheep or related animal. ☐ *It is not at all unusual for a ewe to bear triplets or even quadruplets.*
- **yew** [ju] a type of evergreen tree or shrub that has stiff needles and is often used in landscaping. ☐ *The tiny yew he planted many years ago has grown into a beautiful tree.*
- **you** [ju] the second person pronoun that refers to the person or persons being addressed. ☐ *Would you care to join me for a cup of coffee?*

ewes—use—yews

- **ewes** [juz] the plural of *ewe* 'a female sheep or related animal.' □ *After lambing, the ewes stay close to their young.*
- **use** [juz] to utilize or employ someone or something. □ *That contracting business does not use unskilled laborers.*
- **use** [juz] to expend or consume something. □ *Jeff uses as much solar energy as possible to heat his home.*
- **yews** [juz] the plural of *yew* 'a type of evergreen tree or shrub that has stiff needles.' □ *Don lined the borders of his property with yews to serve as a windbreak.*

eye See the main entry beginning with *aye.*

eyed—I'd

- **eyed** [ɑɪd] the past tense and past participle of *eye* 'to look or glance at someone or something.' □ *The little girl eyed the colorful hair ribbons longingly.*
- **eyed** [ɑɪd] the condition of having eyes. □ *Most of the Dutch children in that community are blue-eyed blondes.*
- **I'd** [ɑɪd] a contraction of *I had, I would,* or *I should.* □ *If I'd known you were coming, I'd have tidied up the house a bit.*

F

facts—fax

- **facts** [fækts] the plural of *fact* 'a piece of information that can be proven.' ☐ *After we examine all the facts, we'll make a decision.*
- **fax** [fæks] an electronic facsimile transmission. ☐ *The realtor agreed to accept the fax of the offer as legal and binding.*
- **fax** [fæks] to transmit a facsimile by wire. ☐ *George's business is much more efficient now that he is able to fax information to his clients.*
- **fax** [fæks] a machine used for electronic facsimile transmissions. ☐ *I decided to buy a fax when they went on sale.*

faint—feint

- **faint** [fent] to lose consciousness. ☐ *Sally will faint at the mere sight of blood.*
- **faint** [fent] feeling weak, dizzy, or lightheaded. ☐ *He felt faint for days after suffering the head injury.*
- **faint** [fent] lacking courage or spirit. ☐ *Skydiving is no hobby for a faint individual.*
- **feint** [fent] a trick; a deception. ☐ *The player's double feint completely caught her opponent off guard.*
- **feint** [fent] to pretend to do something, usually attack, as a means of distraction. ☐ *The battalion will feint at the enemy's left flank but then attack the right.*

fair—fare

- **fair** [fɛɚ] attractive; beautiful. ☐ *The fair maiden caught the eye of the knight in shining armor.*
- **fair** [fɛɚ] honest and impartial. ☐ *That judge is known for his fair decisions.*

- **fair** [fɛɚ] blond or light complexioned. □ *Many Scandinavians are fair and have blue eyes.*
- **fair** [fɛɚ] clear. □ *The weather during our week-long vacation was fair and warm.*
- **fair** [fɛɚ] just and equal. □ *It is important that everyone does his or her fair share of the work.*
- **fair** [fɛɚ] a competitive exhibition. □ *Each year Mary's baked goods win blue ribbons at the fair.*
- **fair** [fɛɚ] a gathering of buyers and sellers. □ *The computer fair was attended by people from all around the world.*
- **fare** [fɛɚ] a range of available food. □ *I know a terrific restaurant that specializes in superb Italian fare.*
- **fare** [fɛɚ] the price charged to transport something or someone. □ *The roundtrip fare was less costly than buying two one-way tickets.*
- **fare** [fɛɚ] to get along; to succeed. □ *Mr. Smith hopes that each of his children will fare well in life.*

fairy—ferry

- **fairy** [ˈfɛɚi] a tiny, mythical being said to possess magical powers. □ *In the movie "Peter Pan," Tinkerbell is a somewhat mischievous fairy.*
- **fairy** [ˈfɛɚi] a male with effeminate mannerisms. (Slang. Usually derogatory.) □ *While some students at school called Dave a fairy, his friends knew him to be quite masculine.*
- **ferry** [ˈfɛɚi] a vessel used to transport goods or people over water; a place where people or objects are transported across water. □ *Visitors can reach the island only by the ferry that crosses the bay twice daily.* □ *At the ferry you can catch a boat that will take you on a sightseeing trip.*
- **ferry** [ˈfɛɚi] to convey or move something or someone from one place to another. □ *Volunteers will ferry the refugees across the border in private vehicles.*

false—faults

- **false** [fɔls] not real or genuine; imitation. □ *Grandpa was always forgetting where he put his false teeth.*
- **false** [fɔls] intentionally misleading or untrue. □ *She purposely made false statements to try to discredit her employer.*
- **false** [fɔls] impermanent. □ *The library contained a false wall that led into a secret room.*
- **faults** [fɔlts] the plural of *fault* 'a weakness, failing, or imperfection.' □ *While Bob's faults may be many, we still think highly of him.*
- **faults** [fɔlts] the plural of *fault* 'a fracture in the earth's

crust.' □ *Most of California's earthquakes occur along one of several faults in the state.*

fare See the main entry beginning with *fair.*

farther—further

- **farther** ['fɑɚðɚ] AND **further** ['fɚðɚ] a greater distance. □ *The trip from the village to the mountain resort was farther than I thought it would be.*
- **further** ['fɚðɚ] additional. □ *I won't bore you with further details.*
- **further** ['fɚðɚ] to help someone or something progress forward. □ *Bill hopes to further his education by attending college.*

faults See the main entry beginning with *false.*

fax See the main entry beginning with *facts.*

faze—phase

- **faze** [fez] to make an impression on or disturb the composure of someone or something. □ *I doubt that a formal reprimand will even faze Thomas.*
- **phase** [fez] a stage or interval in a cycle or development. □ *The next phase of the project involves the approval of the board of commissioners.*
- **phase** [fez] to schedule something to occur or to be performed. □ *The major automobile makers will phase out their poorest selling models.*

feat—feet—fete

- **feat** [fit] a notable deed, especially one involving great skill or courage. □ *The circus elephant accomplished a most difficult feat.*
- **feet** [fit] the plural of *foot* 'the part of the body at the end of the leg.' □ *The wobbly colt was barely able to stay on its feet immediately after being born.*
- **feet** [fit] the plural of *foot* 'the vertical supports of a leg or a chair.' □ *I constantly bump the feet of the chair when I sweep the floor.*
- **feet** [fit] the plural of *foot* 'a unit of length measuring twelve inches.' □ *The board was six feet long.*
- **fete** AND **fête** [fet, fɛt] an elaborate, large party to commemorate or honor someone or something. □ *A fete recognizing his contributions to literature is scheduled for next month.*
- **fete** AND **fête** [fet, fɛt] to honor someone or something. □ *Her co-workers will fete her new sales record at a special luncheon.*

feet See the main entry beginning with *feat.*

feint See the main entry beginning with *faint.*

ferry See the main entry beginning with *fairy.*

fete See the main entry beginning with *feat.*

feudal—futile

- **feudal** ['fjudl] having to do with feudalism, an ancient political system where land tenure is granted in exchange for loyalty or tribute. □ *In feudal England, serfs did most of the farming.*
- **futile** ['fjutl, 'fjudl] useless; hopeless. □ *His futile attempt to catch the falling vase caused him to sprain his back.*

find—fined

- **find** [faɪnd] to discover someone or something. □ *I hope to find some unusual seashells on the beach.*
- **find** [faɪnd] to arrive at or reach something. □ *Labor and management hope to find solutions to their disagreement.*
- **find** [faɪnd] to determine the judicial guilt or innocence of an accused person. □ *We think the jury will find the accused not guilty.*
- **fined** [faɪnd] the past tense and past participle of *fine* 'to charge a sum of money as punishment for an offense.' □ *John was fined fifty dollars for parking illegally in a handicapped parking space.*

fined See the main entry beginning with *find.*

fir—fur

- **fir** [fɚ] a type of coniferous tree, such as the pine or evergreen. □ *The Christmas tree we bought was a beautifully shaped fir.*
- **fir** [fɚ] the wood of a coniferous tree such as a fir or evergreen. □ *Rick made the table out of some planks of discarded fir.*
- **fur** [fɚ] the hairy coat of an animal. □ *Sable pelts are a very valuable fur.*
- **fur** [fɚ] a clothing article made with fur. □ *Jane hung her fur in the cedar-lined closet.*

fisher—fissure

- **fisher** ['fɪʃɚ] a dark brown carnivorous mammal belonging to the weasel family. □ *The strange animal we saw may have been a fisher.*
- **fissure** ['fɪʃɚ] a crack or narrow opening resulting from breakage or separation. □ *That fissure in the sidewalk was probably caused by frost.*

- **fissure** ['fɪʃɚ] a disagreement in viewpoint. ☐ *Because of their fissure on that issue, the men argue constantly.*

fissure See the main entry beginning with *fisher.*

flair—flare

- **flair** [flɛɚ] natural aptitude for something. ☐ *Christy has a real flair for interior design.*
- **flair** [flɛɚ] an odor. ☐ *The flair of the skunk seemed to be apparent for miles around.*
- **flare** [flɛɚ] a blaze or flame of fire or light used as a signal to attract attention. ☐ *Mike has never needed to use the emergency flare he carries in his car.*
- **flare** [flɛɚ] to burn or shine with an unsteady flame or sudden light. ☐ *A fire in the fireplace will sometimes flare up if a sudden draft occurs.*
- **flare** [flɛɚ] to suddenly become angry, excited, or more intense. ☐ *If you mention that incident, Brad's temper will flare.*

flare See the main entry beginning with *flair.*

flaunt—flout

- **flaunt** [flɔnt] to make a gaudy or defiant display of something. ☐ *Even though he is extremely rich, Dr. Shear does not flaunt his wealth.*
- **flout** [flɑʊt] to mock or show disrespect for someone or something. ☐ *The poacher continues to flout the "No Trespassing" signs as he hunts on my property.*

flea—flee

- **flea** [fli] a flightless, bloodsucking insect that feeds on warm-blooded animals. ☐ *The dog wears a special collar to protect it from fleas and other parasites.*
- **flee** [fli] to run away from danger. ☐ *The refugees had to flee their war-torn nation.*

flee See the main entry beginning with *flea.*

flew—flu—flue

- **flew** [flu] the past tense of *fly* 'to move through the air, often on wings.' ☐ *The swallows flew swiftly and gracefully in the air.*
- **flew** [flu] the past tense of *fly* 'to move rapidly or swiftly.' ☐ *The skiers flew down the steep slopes on the new snow.*
- **flew** [flu] the past tense of *fly* 'to operate an airplane.' ☐ *The pilot flew the airplane skillfully.*
- **flu** [flu] influenza. ☐ *The school closed because so many*

children were home sick with the flu.

- **flue** [flu] an enclosed tube, pipe, or passageway used to convey or channel something. □ *The chimney's flue was blocked by a squirrel's nest.*

floe—flow

- **floe** [flo] a large sheet of floating ice on the surface of water. □ *Polar bears will sometimes swim out to a floe to eat or rest.*
- **flow** [flo] to circulate or move about easily. □ *Due to the crowded conditions in the building, air does not flow as it should.* □ *Traffic does not flow smoothly during rush hour.*
- **flow** [flo] to move in a stream or flood, especially water. □ *The river will flow much faster after the snow melts in the mountains.*

flounder—founder

- **flounder** ['flaʊndɚ] to make awkward attempts to move or gain balance; to move clumsily or in confusion. □ *I hated to see the beached dolphin flounder about on the shore.* □ *Turn on the lights so we don't flounder about in the darkness.*
- **flounder** ['flaʊndɚ] a flat-bodied fish often used for food. □ *Jack ordered stuffed flounder for dinner.*
- **founder** ['faʊndɚ] a person who founds or establishes something. □ *Mr. Brown was the founder of the local historical society.*
- **founder** ['faʊndɚ] to give way, collapse, or become disabled. □ *The weight of its pack caused the mule to founder.*
- **founder** ['faʊndɚ] to sink beneath the surface of water. □ *Several ships began to founder during the terrible storm.*

flour—flower

- **flour** ['flaʊɚ] a finely ground grain meal used for baking or cooking. □ *Sarah uses whole wheat flour to make her homemade bread braids.*
- **flour** ['flaʊɚ] to cover something in flour. □ *Be sure to grease and flour the bottom and sides of the baking dish.*
- **flower** ['flaʊɚ] a plant usually grown for its blossoms. □ *The flower in his lapel was a red carnation.*
- **flower** ['flaʊɚ] to produce flowers. □ *Most desert cacti flower in late spring.*
- **flower** ['flaʊɚ] to flourish or develop. □ *Despite her tomboy appearance, Casey will eventually flower into a young lady.*

flout See the main entry beginning with *flaunt.*

flow See the main entry beginning with *floe.*

flower See the main entry beginning with *flour.*

flu See the main entry beginning with *flew.*

flue See the main entry beginning with *flew.*

foaled—fold
- **foaled** [fold] the past tense and past participle of *foal* 'to give birth to a newborn horse, donkey, or mule.' □ *The racehorse foaled last year.*
- **fold** [fold] a flock of sheep or an enclosure for such. □ *The fold has never been attacked by coyotes.*
- **fold** [fold] one part of something laid over another part. □ *The fold of her skirt concealed the torn seam.*
- **fold** [fold] to intertwine the fingers of both hands. □ *Fold your hands and bow your head when saying grace at the dinner table.*
- **fold** [fold] to bring to an end or to fail. □ *Without further financial support, the company will surely fold.*

fold See the main entry beginning with *foaled.*

for—fore—four
- **for** [fɔɚ] a preposition indicating purpose or function. □ *The outside fork at a place setting is for the meal while the inside fork is for dessert.*
- **for** [fɔɚ] to be in support of someone or something. □ *Uncle Ray is always for any type of law that favors small businesses.*
- **for** [fɔɚ] representing someone or something. (A preposition.) □ *The speaker said, "I am here for Senator Young who was unable to attend this evening."*
- **fore** [fɔɚ] occupying a front or leading position. (A prefix.) □ *The dining car is located in the forepart of the train.*
- **fore** [fɔɚ] "Look out!" (A golf term used to warn other players that a ball is being struck, possibly in their direction.) □ *Marilyn yelled "fore" when she saw that her tee shot was headed toward the golfers ahead of her.*
- **four** [fɔɚ] the number between three and five. □ *"Can we play euchre with more than four people?" asked Pete.*

fore See the main entry beginning with *for.*

foreword—forward
- **foreword** ['fɔɚwɚd] the introductory remarks of a writer or speaker. □ *In the foreword of the safety manual, the writers explain the purpose of the text.*
- **forward** ['fɔɚwɚd] being near or at the front of something.

☐ *The foot soldiers were forward of the medical and supply units.*

- **forward** [ˈfɔɚwɚd] unabashed; brash. ☐ *He has always been a forward young man.*
- **forward** [ˈfɔɚwɚd] to advance or send something along. ☐ *I hope the post office will forward this letter if the address has changed.*
- **forward** [ˈfɔɚwɚd] getting ready for or relating to the future. ☐ *Matt's forward thinking has saved his company a great deal of money.*
- **forward** [ˈfɔɚwɚd] an offensive player on various types of sports teams. ☐ *The team's forward set a new school point record at last Friday night's basketball game.*

formally–formerly

- **formally** [ˈfɔɚməli] carried out in a ceremonial fashion. ☐ *The pioneering scientist will formally receive her award in three months.*
- **formerly** [ˈfɔɚmɚli] in times past. ☐ *Our neighbors were formerly stationed in Bangkok, Thailand, before being reassigned to San Diego, California.*

formerly See the main entry beginning with *formally.*

forth–fourth

- **forth** [fɔɚθ] onward or outward in time, place, or order. ☐ *Step forth into the light where I can see you better.*
- **fourth** [fɔɚθ] the ordinal number between third and fifth. ☐ *The huge jumbo jet was fourth in line to take off on the runway.*
- **fourth** [fɔɚθ] one quarter of a whole. ☐ *Almost a fourth of her newly planted garden was eaten by rabbits.*

forward See the main entry beginning with *foreword.*

foul–fowl

- **foul** [fɑʊl] offensive to the senses. ☐ *When we entered the room, we detected a foul odor.*
- **foul** [fɑʊl] profane; obscene. ☐ *That coach will not tolerate foul language from his players.*
- **foul** [fɑʊl] treacherous. ☐ *Due to the foul weather, we cancelled the dinner cruise aboard the yacht.*
- **foul** [fɑʊl] an infringement of the rules in a game or sport. ☐ *Neither Donald nor Russell committed a single foul during the basketball game.*
- **fowl** [fɑʊl] a member of the bird family, usually used for food. ☐ *The wild turkey is an interesting fowl to observe.*

- **fowl** [fɑʊl] the meat of birds eaten as food. ☐ *While Mr. Smith prefers red meat, his wife would rather eat fowl.*

founder See the main entry beginning with *flounder.*

four See the main entry beginning with *for.*

fourth See the main entry beginning with *forth.*

fowl See the main entry beginning with *foul.*

frays—phrase

- **frays** [frez] the plural of *fray* 'a raveled or worn area of fabric.' ☐ *Trim the frays off the edge of that material before mending it.*
- **frays** [frez] the present tense, third person singular of *fray* 'to cause a strain on something; to wear at something.' ☐ *Helen is such a sensitive person that even an unkind remark frays her self-esteem.*
- **phrase** [frez] a grammatical sequence of words. ☐ *An overused, trite phrase is called a cliché.* ☐ *The first sentence of the novel began with the phrase, "To dream the dream of kings . . . ."*
- **phrase** [frez] to form an utterance. ☐ *Be careful how you phrase your questions.*

frees—freeze—frieze

- **frees** [friz] the present tense, third person singular of *free* 'to liberate someone or something.' ☐ *Not having to work on Saturday frees Sam to spend time on his hobbies.*
- **freeze** [friz] to use cold to cause a liquid to solidify or a solid to harden. ☐ *You must freeze water to make ice cubes.*
- **freeze** [friz] to become chilled with cold. ☐ *"Let's hurry inside before we freeze," said Sandy.*
- **freeze** [friz] to become fixed or motionless. ☐ *When the suspect began running away, the police officer yelled "Freeze!"*
- **freeze** [friz] a weather condition marked by cold temperatures. ☐ *The late spring freeze ruined the citrus crop.*
- **frieze** [friz] a coarse, durable fabric made with wool and other fibers. ☐ *A sweater made of frieze may not be attractive, but it certainly is warm.*
- **frieze** [friz] an ornamental, usually sculptured, trim on a building. ☐ *The frieze around the mansion's entryway was typical of the 1920's.*

freeze See the main entry beginning with *frees.*

friar—fryer

- **friar** [ˈfrɑɪɚ] a male member of some types of religious orders.

☐ *Why do we usually picture a friar wearing a long, dark, hooded cloak?*

- **fryer** [ˈfrɑɪɚ] a young chicken. ☐ *While a fryer is usually a young bird, a stewing chicken is normally older and tougher.*
- **fryer** [ˈfrɑɪɚ] a cooking pot or pan used to fry foods. ☐ *Pat slowly simmered the meat and vegetables in the fryer.*

frieze See the main entry beginning with *frees.*

fryer See the main entry beginning with *friar.*

fur See the main entry beginning with *fir.*

further See the main entry beginning with *farther.*

futile See the main entry beginning with *feudal.*

G

gait—gate

- **gait** [get] a manner of walking or moving on foot. □ *He moves in an easy, natural gait, never hurrying but never dallying either.*
- **gait** [get] one of the four foot movements or strides of a horse. □ *I prefer riding a horse whose gait is a canter.*
- **gait** [get] to lead a show dog before a judge to display its form and movement. □ *In showmanship classes, each dog handler is asked to gait his animal in front of the judges.*
- **gate** [get] a doorlike closure for an opening in a wall or fence; a place of entrance or exit. □ *The rickety fence gate has almost fallen off its hinges.* □ *To find the concession stand at the park, go through the front gate and turn left.*
- **gate** [get] the total number of spectators or admission receipts at a sporting event. □ *The gate at the final game of the World Series set a new attendance record.*

gamble—gambol

- **gamble** ['gæmbl] to play a game for money or some other stakes. □ *Don't gamble away your life's savings at the casino.*
- **gamble** ['gæmbl] to wager or venture that something will or will not happen. □ *He was willing to gamble that his ideas would succeed.*
- **gamble** ['gæmbl] something risky or chancy. □ *The rescuers knew their daring lifesaving attempt was a gamble.*
- **gambol** ['gæmbl] to play, romp, or move about in a frisky manner. □ *It was fun to watch the new calves gambol about in the pasture.*

gambol See the main entry beginning with *gamble.*

gate See the main entry beginning with *gait.*

gel—jell

- **gel** [dʒɛl] to congeal in a more solid form but not become solid. ☐ *As the soup cools, the fat in it will begin to gel.*
- **gel** [dʒɛl] a substance having a gelatinlike consistency. ☐ *That medication comes in both a lotion and a gel.*
- **jell** AND **gel** [dʒɛl] to solidify into jelly or gelatin. ☐ *The dessert is about to gel.* ☐ *We put the dessert mix in the refrigerator to jell.*
- **jell** [dʒɛl] to become established and certain. ☐ *In order for the plan to work, everything must jell at precisely the right time.*

genes—jeans

- **genes** [dʒinz] the plural of *gene* 'the part of a chromosome that contains hereditary characteristics.' ☐ *Genes that determine brown eyes are dominant over genes that determine blue eyes.*
- **jeans** [dʒinz] blue jeans; denim trousers of any color, constructed to resemble blue jeans. (Originally from *Genoa* 'a cotton denim or twill fabric.') ☐ *Almost every student wore jeans to the picnic.*

gild—guild

- **gild** [gɪld] to cover something with a thin layer of gold. ☐ *The goldsmith thought he should gild the piece of jewelry to make it brighter and more attractive.*
- **gild** [gɪld] to wrongly give an attractive appearance to something. ☐ *The crooked politicians tried to gild the poor financial status of their city.*
- **guild** [gɪld] a group of people with common interests or aims. ☐ *The potter's guild puts on a show and sale each year.*

gilt—guilt

- **gilt** [gɪlt] a young female swine. ☐ *The hog farmer has an especially fine gilt for sale.*
- **gilt** [gɪlt] a layer of gold or gold paint on something. ☐ *At the plant, we saw a machine apply gilt to the edges of books.*
- **gilt** [gɪlt] covered with gold or a goldlike substance. ☐ *Don bought an unusual gilt picture frame at the antique auction.*
- **guilt** [gɪlt] a feeling of blame for an offense. ☐ *She felt both guilt and shame for having lied to her mother.*
- **guilt** [gɪlt] culpability; the fact of having done something wrong. ☐ *The defendant's guilt could not be proven beyond a reasonable doubt.*

gnu—knew—new

- **gnu** [nu] a large African antelope. ☐ *On her photo safari, Barb took a picture of a huge gnu.*
- **knew** [nu, nju] the past tense of *know* 'to sense or perceive something; to be aware of the truth or facts.' ☐ *I knew I should have stayed home during the bad storm.* ☐ *The students knew almost all of the answers on their test.*
- **knew** [nu, nju] the past tense of *know* 'to be acquainted with someone or something.' ☐ *She knew the famous actor when he was still working at a local restaurant.* ☐ *I knew the taste of bitter almonds and quickly spat out the bite I had taken.*
- **new** [nu, nju] recently made or completed. ☐ *I got a new paint job on my car.*
- **new** [nu, nju] unfamiliar; unaccustomed. ☐ *We hope to see some new sights on our next visit to the city.* ☐ *Because he was new to the job, Greg felt a bit uneasy at first.*

golf—gulf

- **golf** [gɔf, gɔlf] a game played with a ball and clubs on a grassy course. ☐ *His dream is to one day play golf at St. Andrews in Scotland.*
- **gulf** [gəlf] a part of an ocean or sea reaching into land. ☐ *The boats sailing in the gulf sparkled in the sunlight.*
- **gulf** [gəlf] a gap, hole, or distance. ☐ *Such a gulf exists between their beliefs that an agreement is not possible.*

gored—gourd

- **gored** [gɔɚd] the past tense and past participle of *gore* 'to cut or make something into a triangular shape.' ☐ *The swirl skirt was gored with several large pieces of fabric.*
- **gored** [gɔɚd] the past tense and past participle of *gore* '[for an animal] to stab someone or something with its horn or tusk.' ☐ *The bulls sometimes gore spectators during the annual Corrida de Toros in Pamplona, Spain.*
- **gourd** [gɔɚd] the edible fruit of certain vine families. ☐ *The Hubbard squash is a type of gourd that can reach huge proportions.*

gorilla—guerrilla

- **gorilla** [gəˈrɪlə] the biggest member of the ape family, found in Africa. ☐ *The gorilla has a gentle, kind nature despite its huge size.*
- **gorilla** [gəˈrɪlə] a thug; a large-bodied criminal; a criminal's bodyguard. (Slang.) ☐ *The boss never went anywhere without a gorilla to protect him.*

- **guerrilla** [gɛˈrɪlə] a person who engages in warfare for hire. ☐ *Each guerrilla carried his own simple weapons.*
- **guerrilla** [gɛˈrɪlə] having to do with irregular warfare by independent bands. ☐ *Guerrilla fighting between warring clans broke out in Somalia.*

gourd See the main entry beginning with *gored.*

grade—grayed

- **grade** [gred] a level or stage in school. ☐ *Cindy moved to a different school after completing fifth grade.*
- **grade** [gred] a naval or military rank. ☐ *An admiral is a naval officer of very high grade.*
- **grade** [gred] a class indicating the size or quality of goods for sale. ☐ *A recipe may call for a certain grade of eggs.*
- **grade** [gred] the angle or degree of a slope. ☐ *The steep grade of the mountainside made traveling dangerous in bad weather.*
- **grade** [gred] having to do with an animal of mixed parentage; a purebred animal crossed with an ordinary animal. ☐ *Stacey wanted a purebred horse but could only afford a grade animal.*
- **grayed** [gred] the past tense and past participle of *gray* 'to become gray.' ☐ *Although none became bald, all of the men in our family grayed at an early age.*

grate—great

- **grate** [gret] a framework of bars designed to prevent the passage of someone or something. ☐ *Each hallway was fitted with an iron grate at its entrance.*
- **grate** [gret] an iron cradle used in stoves and fireplaces to hold what is to be burned. ☐ *Sweep the ashes from under the grate before you build another fire.*
- **grate [on]** [gret] to bother someone; to irritate someone's nerves. ☐ *Her annoying habits grate on my nerves.* ☐ *Your loud voice grates on me!*
- **grate** [gret] to make a harsh, scratching, or grinding sound. ☐ *When the machinery isn't working properly, the moving parts grate noisily.*
- **grate** [gret] to reduce something to pieces by rubbing it with something coarse. ☐ *Let's grate the cheese before putting it on the pizza.*
- **great** [gret] large; big. ☐ *The huge emperor shifted his great form with much difficulty.* ☐ *Great numbers of people appeared at the grand opening ceremony.*
- **great** [gret] remarkable; famous; distinguished. ☐ *The salesman went to great lengths to please his customers.* ☐ *Many*

great athletes never become professional players.

- **great** [gret] a generation removed in a family relationship. ☐ *My great-grandmother was a Chippewa Indian.*

grayed See the main entry beginning with *grade.*

grays—graze

- **grays** [grez] the present tense, third person singular of *gray* 'to become gray; to become dull or colorless.' ☐ *A white shirt grays if it is not washed regularly in hot water with bleach.*
- **grays** [grez] the plural of *gray* 'a gray horse.' ☐ *The pair of grays looked smart pulling the old-fashioned carriage.*
- **graze** [grez] to feed randomly on grasses. ☐ *Sheep require a lot of open land on which to graze.*
- **graze** [grez] to touch something lightly in passing. ☐ *Do not graze your shirt sleeves on the freshly painted walls.* ☐ *The bullet did no more than graze the surface of the skin.*

graze See the main entry beginning with *grays.*

great See the main entry beginning with *grate.*

greave—grieve

- **greave** [griv] a piece of armor worn below the knee. ☐ *The knight lost a greave during the joust.*
- **grieve** [griv] to feel a sense of sorrow, distress, or suffering. ☐ *It is normal to grieve over the loss of a loved pet.*

grieve See the main entry beginning with *greave.*

grill—grille

- **grill** [grɪl] a cooking surface on which food is exposed to direct heat. ☐ *Tom cooked our steaks on the grill.*
- **grill** [grɪl] to cook on a grill. ☐ *I like to grill hamburgers and hot dogs outside in the summertime.*
- **grill** [grɪl] a restaurant that serves broiled foods. ☐ *The gas station that once stood on the corner is now a bar and grill.*
- **grill** [grɪl] to question someone heatedly. ☐ *We will grill the suspect until we arrive at the truth.*
- **grille** [grɪl] a lattice work; a grate that forms a barrier or screen of some type. ☐ *Ken damaged the grille on the front of his new car when he hit the mailbox post.* ☐ *An iron grille covers the front door of the mansion.*

grille See the main entry beginning with *grill.*

grisly—grizzly

- **grisly** ['grɪzli] gory; horrible. ☐ *Even the seasoned police officers were sickened at the grisly scene.*

- **grizzly** [ˈgrɪzli] a large, powerful North American bear known for its ferocity. □ *It is wise to use extreme caution when confronted by a grizzly in the wild.*

grizzly See the main entry beginning with *grisly.*

groan—grown
- **groan** [gron] to utter a moaning sound indicating pain, annoyance, or grief. □ *The student let out a groan when the teacher announced yet another quiz.*
- **grown** [gron] the past participle of *grow* 'to develop in maturity, size, or stature.' □ *Sara has grown into a fine young woman.*
- **grown** [gron] the past participle of *grow* 'to become or to cause something to develop or mature.' □ *The economy has grown sluggish in recent years.* □ *Chris is no longer a boy but a grown man.* □ *In order for coffee to be successfully grown, soil and climate conditions must be just right.*

grown See the main entry beginning with *groan.*

guerrilla See the main entry beginning with *gorilla.*

guessed—guest
- **guessed** [gɛst] the past tense and past participle of *guess* 'to form an answer with little or no evidence.' □ *The student guessed the answer and was correct.*
- **guest** [gɛst] a person invited to some place. □ *Our dinner guest should arrive shortly after six.* □ *A well-known celebrity appears as a guest on the popular talk show each evening.*
- **guest** [gɛst] a patron of a hotel or restaurant. □ *Every guest at the inn is personally greeted by the innkeeper herself.*

guest See the main entry beginning with *guessed.*

guild See the main entry beginning with *gild.*

guilt See the main entry beginning with *gilt.*

guise—guys
- **guise** [gɑɪz] a manner or style of dress. □ *The actress's guise is eccentric.*
- **guise** [gɑɪz] [someone's] outward appearance; a disguise. □ *The undercover agent's guise was that of a beggar.*
- **guys** [gɑɪz] the plural of *guy* 'a man or boy; a person.' (*Guys* can refer to persons of either sex when used in the plural.) □ *Those guys always hang around together at the arcade.*

- **guys** [gɑɪz] the plural of *guy* 'a length of rope, wire, or chain used as a brace or guide.' □ *Be sure to note the location of the guys on the television antenna.*

gulf See the main entry beginning with *golf.*

guys See the main entry beginning with *guise.*

H

hail—hale

- **hail** [hel] rain frozen into balls of ice. ☐ *Hail the size of golf balls pelted the spectators during the sudden cloudburst.*
- **hail** [hel] a shower of something. ☐ *A hail of confetti rained down from the tall buildings during the parade.*
- **hail [(up)on]** [hel] to pour down like hail. ☐ *Strong criticism will probably hail upon the coach if his team loses another game.*
- **hail** [hel] to call for someone or something. ☐ *You can hail a cab from almost any hotel or restaurant in town.*
- **hail [from]** [hel] to come from some place. ☐ *All of my college roommates hail from the Midwest.*
- **hale** [hel] healthy; sound. ☐ *Even at age ninety, our next-door neighbor is as hale as he was twenty years ago.*

hair—hare

- **hair** [hɛɚ] the external body covering of an animal; the threadlike strands that grow out of the human head. ☐ *Some animals grow thick coats of coarse hair during long, harsh winters.* ☐ *As a child, Mary had blond, curly hair.*
- **hair** [hɛɚ] the width of a hair. ☐ *We defended our bed race championship by winning this year's contest by a hair.*
- **hare** [hɛɚ] a type of large rabbit known for its long ears and large hind legs. ☐ *The hare circled around trying to put off the pursuing hounds.*

hale See the main entry beginning with *hail.*

hall—haul

- **hall** [hɔl] a lobby or entryway off which other rooms open.

☐ *A dimly lit hall can be frightening to a young child.*

- **hall** [hɔl] a large room used for public meetings. ☐ *The great hall in the convention center is the site of many formal receptions.*
- **hall** [hɔl] a building on a university or college campus. ☐ *A university may name a hall after a famous professor.*
- **haul** [hɔl] to transport a burden, usually using a vehicle. ☐ *We haul all of the building supplies in a flatbed truck.* ☐ *A tractor was used to haul the heavy logs.*
- **haul** [hɔl] to pull something; to redirect something. ☐ *The captain ordered the helmsman to haul the bow of the ship into the wind.*

halve—have

- **halve** [hæv] to divide something into two equal parts; to reduce something by one half. ☐ *If I halve this submarine sandwich, would you like part of it?* ☐ *The girls agreed to halve whatever profits they made selling their baked goods.* ☐ *The business owner is hoping to halve the number of shoplifting incidents in his store next year.*
- **have** [hæv] to own or possess someone or something. ☐ *They have a cottage on the smaller of the two lakes.* ☐ *We have numerous friends living in New England.* ☐ *Jerry said, "I have some terrific news to share with you."* ☐ *While my siblings all have dark locks, I have blond hair.*
- **have [to]** [hæv] to have an obligation or feel a necessity to do something. ☐ *I have to go to my great-aunt's birthday party next Sunday.*
- **have** [hæv] to bear offspring. ☐ *The couple hopes to have a child in the near future.*

handmade—handmaid

- **handmade** ['hænd'med] made by hand, not machined. ☐ *As a housewarming gift, she gave the couple a handmade bed quilt.*
- **handmaid** ['hændmed] a female servant or attendant. ☐ *The princess has a handmaid to attend to her every whim.*

handmaid See the main entry beginning with *handmade.*

hangar—hanger

- **hangar** ['hæŋɚ] a shed or building where aircraft are housed and repaired. ☐ *Security is tight around the hangar where the president's aircraft are kept.*
- **hangar** ['hæŋɚ] to put something in a hangar. ☐ *We'd better hangar the plane before the storm hits.*
- **hanger** ['hæŋɚ] something that is used to hang or suspend

something else. ☐ *After locking his keys inside, Fred used a wire coat hanger to open his car door.*

hanged—hung

- **hanged** [hæŋd] the past tense and past participle of *hang* 'to put a person to death by suspending the person by the neck.' ☐ *The judge sentenced the convicted murderer to be hanged.*
- **hung** [həŋ] the past tense of *hang* 'to suspend or fasten something.' ☐ *Millie hung a portrait of her mother above the fireplace.*

hanger See the main entry beginning with *hangar.*

hare See the main entry beginning with *hair.*

hart—heart

- **hart** [hɑɚt] a mature male deer, especially of the red deer species. ☐ *The hart bounded across the meadow.*
- **heart** [hɑɚt] the muscular organ that maintains blood circulation. ☐ *The patient received a new heart during the transplant surgery.*
- **heart** [hɑɚt] the center or most important part. ☐ *Rather than skirt the issue, the council members wanted to get to the heart of the matter.*
- **heart** [hɑɚt] a playing card bearing red hearts. ☐ *I trumped his card with a higher heart.*
- **heart** [hɑɚt] the center of feeling and sincerity. ☐ *She always speaks from the heart.*

haul See the main entry beginning with *hall.*

have See the main entry beginning with *halve.*

hay—hey

- **hay** [he] a mixture of grasses grown for animal feed. ☐ *The second cutting of hay is always a bit richer than the first.*
- **hay** [he] to feed an animal with hay. ☐ *Be sure you hay the horses twice a day.*
- **hay** [he] a bed. (Slang. Always found in the idiom *hit the hay.*) ☐ *"Let's all hit the hay early tonight," suggested Dad.*
- **hey** [he] an expression used to get someone's attention; a greeting. ☐ *"Hey, wait a minute!" cried Louise.* ☐ *"Hey, Fred! What's happening?"*

hays—haze

- **hays** [hez] the plural of *hay* 'a mixture of grasses grown for animal feed.' ☐ *Many different hays were exhibited at the state fair.*

- **haze** [hez] a cloud of fine particles in the air that reduces visibility. □ *The early morning haze promised that a sultry day lay ahead.*
- **haze** [hez] a vagueness of mental perception. □ *A severe reaction to the prescription left Joe's mind in a haze.*
- **haze** [hez] to harass and humiliate someone deliberately. □ *Many fraternities no longer haze new initiates.*

haze See the main entry beginning with *hays.*

heal—heel—he'll

- **heal** [hil] to cure something; to make something whole. □ *It may take some time for that nasty cut to heal.* □ *One cannot always heal hurt feelings immediately.* □ *Some economists believe the economy should be left alone to heal itself.*
- **heel** [hil] the back of the human foot. □ *Bob bruised his heel playing soccer.*
- **heel** [hil] the bottom, rear, or low part of some structure. □ *Set the heel of the cabinet down and get a better grasp on the sides.*
- **heel** [hil] the crusty end of a loaf of bread. □ *My brother and I always fought over who would get the heel of the bread.*
- **heel** [hil] to follow closely behind or beside someone. □ *The woman made her dog heel before she crossed the busy street.*
- **he'll** [hil] the contraction of *he will.* □ *If Doug waits in front of the shop, he'll see us when we arrive.*

hear—here

- **hear** [hɪɚ] to perceive something by ear; to listen to someone or something. □ *On a summer's night you can hear the croaking of frogs in the distant swamp.* □ *Be sure you hear the teacher's test directions.*
- **hear** [hɪɚ] to gain information by hearing; to learn something by hearing. □ *I hear what you're saying, and I understand the problem you face.*
- **here** [hɪɚ] this place; this location. □ *Here in Michigan, winters can alternately be mild or severe.* □ *"Come here at once," scolded the naughty child's father.*
- **here** [hɪɚ] an affirmative reply in a roll call. □ *Please reply "here" when your name is called.*

heard—herd

- **heard** [hɚd] the past tense and past participle of *hear* 'to perceive something by ear; to listen to someone or something; to learn something by hearing.' □ *I distinctly heard him say he would not be able to attend the seminar.* □ *The group heard the* *speaker as she related her personal safari experiences.* □ *We heard that there will be numerous layoffs at the plant before the year's end.*

- **herd** [hɚd] a group animals of the same species, usually hoofed animals. □ *The cattle herd will soon be driven to market.* □ *The noise made by the thundering herd of wildebeest was almost deafening.*
- **herd** [hɚd] an unthinking mass of people. (Figurative.) □ *At the moment the stadium gates opened, the herd of spectators swarmed in.*
- **herd** [hɚd] to assemble things or people into a group. (Literal for animals. Figurative for people.) □ *Try to herd the sheep into a corner of the pen.* □ *The usher herded my friends and me into the first row.*

heart See the main entry beginning with *hart.*

he'd—heed
- **he'd** [hid] the contraction of *he had* or *he would.* □ *If he'd studied for the test, he surely would have passed it.* □ *I'm sure he'd do it if you would ask him.*
- **heed** [hid] to take notice of someone or something. □ *I hope Tom will heed my warning about the drop-off in the lake.*
- **heed** [hid] caution; care. (Almost always with *give* or *take.*) □ *Take heed when pulling out into a busy intersection.* □ *Give heed to my warning.*

heed See the main entry beginning with *he'd.*

heel See the main entry beginning with *heal.*

heir See the main entry beginning with *air.*

he'll See the main entry beginning with *heal.*

herd See the main entry beginning with *heard.*

here See the main entry beginning with *hear.*

heroin—heroine
- **heroin** ['hɛɚoɪn] a strongly addictive narcotic. □ *Cocaine is now more widely used than heroin.*
- **heroine** ['hɛɚoɪn] a female hero. □ *The heroine in that story is a young poverty-stricken girl.* □ *Mother Theresa is a heroine in most parts of the world.*

heroine See the main entry beginning with *heroin.*

hew—hue

- **hew** [hju] to cut, fell, or give form to something with heavy, cutting blows. □ *To hew a canoe from a single log is no small task.*
- **hue** [hju] a shade of color. □ *Her favorite hue of blue is azure.*
- **hue** [hju] aspect. □ *Most of Poe's poetry is of a somber hue.*

hey See the main entry beginning with *hay.*

hi—high

- **hi** [hɑɪ] an informal greeting or salutation. □ *"Hi, Grandma. This is Jennifer," whispered the little girl into the telephone.*
- **high** [hɑɪ] raised; elevated. □ *The high fence kept curiosity seekers from looking in.*
- **high** [hɑɪ] sharp; shrill. □ *Joan always speaks rapidly and in a high voice when she's irritated or frightened.*
- **high** [hɑɪ] noble or noteworthy. □ *He is a man of high principles.*
- **high** [hɑɪ] strong; forceful. □ *High winds and the sea battered the barrier islands.*

high See the main entry beginning with *hi.*

higher—hire

- **higher** [hɑɪɚ] the comparative form of *high* 'at a greater height.' □ *The higher he climbed on the ladder, the more nervous he became.*
- **hire** [hɑɪɚ] to take someone into employment; to engage the personal services of someone. □ *Shall we hire a cab to take us home after the play?*

him—hymn

- **him** [hɪm] the third person singular, objective, masculine pronoun. □ *Give him that invoice to check against the shipment.*
- **hymn** [hɪm] a song of joy, praise, or thanksgiving, usually sung in worship services. □ *Mama's favorite hymn was "Rock of Ages."*

hire See the main entry beginning with *higher.*

hoard—horde

- **hoard** [hoɚd] a concealed supply or cache of something. □ *The crow stashed a hoard of small sparkling items in its nest.*
- **hoard** [hoɚd] to hide a supply or cache of something. □ *It is not safe to hoard valuables in likely hiding places.*
- **horde** [hoɚd] a swarm or throng. □ *A horde of people waited in line all night for the concert tickets.*

- **horde** [hoəd] a group of nomadic people, particularly of Mongolian ancestry. ☐ *The pastoral horde wandered the region for decades.*

hoarse—horse
- **hoarse** [hoəs] harsh, grating, or rough in sound. ☐ *Following a bout with bronchitis, Tom's voice was very hoarse.*
- **horse** [hoəs] a four-legged animal with a flowing mane and tail. ☐ *The horse I was given at the riding stable was a gentle mare.*
- **horse** [hoəs] a gymnastic apparatus consisting of a padded framework mounted on legs. ☐ *One of Steve's strongest events is the horse.*
- **horse** [hoəs] to move something by force. ☐ *Be careful not to horse that antique desk around when you move it.*

hoes—hose
- **hoes** [hoz] the plural of *hoe* 'a garden tool used to break up the earth.' ☐ *The hoes are in the shed with the rest of the garden equipment.*
- **hose** [hoz] a flexible, hollow tube used to convey liquids. ☐ *I need to replace the water hose in my car.*
- **hose** [hoz] socks or stockings. ☐ *The splintered chair leg caused a run in Sally's hose.*
- **hose [down]** [hoz] to wash or spray something with a hose. ☐ *You must hose down the tumbler of the cement truck after each delivery.*

hold—holed
- **hold** [hold] to possess something. ☐ *She holds a degree in economics.*
- **hold** [hold] to contain someone or something; to support someone or something. ☐ *Will this box hold all the books?* ☐ *I don't believe this little chair will hold me.*
- **hold** [hold] to maintain a grasp on someone or something. ☐ *Hold the kite string tightly or the wind will blow the kite away.*
- **holed [up]** [hold] the past tense of *hole [up]* 'to hide; to retire in a place.' ☐ *The crooks holed up in a deserted building for a week.*

holed See the main entry beginning with *hold.*

hole—whole
- **hole** [hol] a depression or opening. ☐ *The meteorite left a huge hole in the earth when it hit the ground.*
- **hole** [hol] a fault or flaw. ☐ *The burglar discovered a hole in*

the security system of the building.

- **hole** [hol] an awkward position. ☐ *The sudden departure of three valuable employees left the company in a hole.*
- **whole** [hol] entire or unbroken. ☐ *Let's look at the whole picture.* ☐ *The vase remained whole even though I dropped it.*
- **whole** [hol] the complete number or sum of something. ☐ *The whole list had eleven chores on it.*
- **whole** [hol] a system of parts working together as a single unit. ☐ *As a whole, our fire department provides excellent service.*

holy—wholly

- **holy** ['holi] sacred; godly; that which evokes or merits reverence or respect. ☐ *The woman devoted her life to the holy service of God.* ☐ *People of all faiths observe certain days that are considered holy.*
- **holy** ['holi] used to express intensity. (Idiomatic.) ☐ *That unruly child is a holy terror!*
- **wholly** ['holi] completely. ☐ *We are wholly in agreement on that issue.*
- **wholly** ['holi] solely, to the exclusion of others. ☐ *No one person is wholly responsible for what happened.*

hoop—whoop

- **hoop** [hup] a ring. ☐ *The circus tiger fearlessly jumped through the hoop of fire.*
- **hoop** [hup] a flexible, rounded framework used to expand a skirt. ☐ *Dresses with hoop skirts are becoming fashionable again for formal wear.*
- **whoop** [ʍup, wup] a sudden, loud sound emitted in enthusiasm or eagerness. ☐ *With a whoop, the crowd rose to its feet.*
- **whoop** [ʍup, wup] to utter a loud and enthusiastic sound. ☐ *"I'll whoop for joy if I pass that exam!" exclaimed Carlos.*

horde See the main entry beginning with *hoard.*

horse See the main entry beginning with *hoarse.*

hose See the main entry beginning with *hoes.*

hostel—hostile

- **hostel** ['hastl] a supervised lodging provided for young people when traveling. ☐ *The college students met interesting people at each hostel.*
- **hostile** ['hastl, 'hastaɪl] antagonistic or unfriendly; relating to the enemy. ☐ *Joan is such a hostile person that none of her co-workers like her.* ☐ *The troops encountered hostile snipers*

on the far side of the river.

hostile See the main entry beginning with *hostel.*

hour—our

- **hour** [ɑʊɚ] a period of sixty minutes. ☐ *Each swimming lesson lasts an hour.*
- **hour** [ɑʊɚ] the time of day indicated by a timepiece. ☐ *"Could you please tell me the hour?" inquired the man at the bus stop.*
- **hour** [ɑʊɚ] a particular time. ☐ *At the appointed hour and place, the two intelligence agents met secretly.*
- **our** [ɑʊɚ] first person, plural possessive pronoun. ☐ *Yesterday our car got a flat tire.*

hue See the main entry beginning with *hew.*

humerus—humorous

- **humerus** [ˈhjumɚəs] the long, heavy bone of the upper arm or forelimb extending from the shoulder to the elbow. ☐ *The humerus of Jacob's left arm was fractured when the scaffolding fell on him.*
- **humorous** [ˈhjumɚəs] characterized by humor or wit. ☐ *Generally there is a humorous side to any embarrassing situation.*

humorous See the main entry beginning with *humerus.*

hung See the main entry beginning with *hanged.*

hymn See the main entry beginning with *him.*

I

I See the main entry beginning with *aye.*

I'd See the main entry beginning with *eyed.*

idle—idol—idyll

- **idle** ['aɪdl] lacking purpose or worth. □ *All that talk about going on strike is just idle rumor.*
- **idle** ['aɪdl] not employed or occupied. □ *The autoworkers were idle due to a shutdown of production lines.*
- **idle** ['aɪdl] not being used appropriately. □ *Mischief often results from idle time.*
- **idol** ['aɪdl] something or someone that is worshipped or idolized. □ *That culture has a sunlike symbol as an idol.*
- **idol** ['aɪdl] a person or object of passionate devotion. □ *The teenager was devoted to the rock-and-roll idol.*
- **idyll** ['aɪdl] a simple, descriptive poem or writing depicting the virtues of the peaceful, rustic out-of-doors. □ *The short idyll painted images of a blissful shepherd's life.*

idol See the main entry beginning with *idle.*

idyll See the main entry beginning with *idle.*

I'll See the main entry beginning with *aisle.*

illicit See the main entry beginning with *elicit.*

illusion See the main entry beginning with *allusion.*

imminent See the main entry beginning with *eminent.*

imply—infer

- **imply** [ɪm'plaɪ] to suggest something without saying it specifically. □ *Do you mean to imply that I made a mistake?*

- **infer** [ɪnˈfɚ] to come to a conclusion about something. □ *Since the jury is deadlocked, we can infer that no decision will be reached.*

in—inn

- **in** [ɪn] inside; within; into. (A preposition.) □ *Someday I would like to fly in the Concorde SST.* □ *Please come in out of the rain.*
- **inn** [ɪn] a public lodging for travelers that usually provides food and drink. □ *The inn just outside the village provides comfortable beds and good food.* □ *The men stop each night for a beer at the inn.*

incite—insight

- **incite** [ɪnˈsɑɪt] to stir up or move someone or something to action. □ *The speaker failed to incite the crowd to action.*
- **insight** [ˈɪnsɑɪt] the ability to see or understand something intuitively. □ *Our physics teacher has great insight into how to motivate uninterested students.*

infer See the main entry beginning with *imply.*

inn See the main entry beginning with *in.*

innocence—innocents

- **innocence** [ˈɪnəsənts] guiltlessness or purity. □ *Throughout the trial, the accused proclaimed her innocence.*
- **innocents** [ˈɪnəsənts] the plural of *innocent* 'a person who is blameless or without fault.' □ *In any war it seems the innocents pay the dearest price.*

innocents See the main entry beginning with *innocence.*

insight See the main entry beginning with *incite.*

instance—instants

- **instance** [ˈɪnstənts] circumstance, example, or case. □ *In that particular instance, you probably should have kept quiet.*
- **instants** [ˈɪnstənts] the plural of *instant* 'a moment; a second; a split second.' □ *During those few frightening instants, we didn't know what would happen.*

instants See the main entry beginning with *instance.*

insure See the main entry beginning with *ensure.*

intense—intents

- **intense** [ɪnˈtɛnts] strong; extreme. □ *Tom felt intense relief after his solo performance.*

- **intense** [ɪnˈtɛnts] deeply feeling, usually by temperament or nature. ☐ *Sam is an intense person at all times.*
- **intents** [ɪnˈtɛnts] the plural of *intent* 'a purpose or an intention.' ☐ *Our intents have always had your best interests in mind.*

intents See the main entry beginning with *intense.*

isle See the main entry beginning with *aisle.*

its–it's
- **its** [ɪts] the possessive form of *it.* ☐ *The kitten licked its paws after walking through the puddle of water.*
- **it's** [ɪts] the contraction of *it is* or *it has.* ☐ *It's always exciting to have a birthday party—no matter how old you are.*

it's See the main entry beginning with *its.*

J

jam—jamb

- **jam** [dʒæm] to press or wedge something into a tight position. ☐ *Do not try to jam too many clothes into the suitcase.*
- **jam** [dʒæm] an obstruction or congestion. ☐ *The traffic jam on the highway caused us to miss our plane.*
- **jam** [dʒæm] a difficult predicament. ☐ *Whenever Mary gets in a jam, she calls her parents for help.*
- **jam** [dʒæm] a condiment made with fruit and sugar. ☐ *Homemade peach jam is my favorite.*
- **jamb** [dʒæm] an upright structure or piece forming the side of an opening. ☐ *Not a single door jamb in the building was straight.*

jamb See the main entry beginning with *jam.*

jeans See the main entry beginning with *genes.*

jell See the main entry beginning with *gel.*

jinks—jinx

- **[high] jinks** [dʒɪŋks] pranks. ☐ *"I will not put up with any high jinks while you're here," scolded Grandmother.*
- **jinx** [dʒɪŋks] someone or something that brings bad luck or misfortune. ☐ *Eddie was a jinx to our team's winning streak.*
- **jinx** [dʒɪŋks] to bring bad luck to someone. ☐ *Mary is so superstitious that she believes a passing black cat will jinx her.*

jinx See the main entry beginning with *jinks.*

K

karat See the main entry beginning with *carat.*

kernel See the main entry beginning with *colonel.*

key—quay

- **key** [ki] a metal piece used to open a lock. □ *I lost my car key and had to call a locksmith.*
- **key** [ki] the solution to a problem; the explanation for something complicated. □ *The key to the mystery was the fingerprints that the police found on the doorknob.*
- **key** [ki] a lever used to play a piano or an organ. □ *I pressed one key after another and nothing happened!*
- **key** [ki] major; principal. □ *Ted is a key figure in the negotiations.*
- **key** [ki] a particular musical scale. □ *The entire sonata was in the key of C major.*
- **quay** [ki] a wharf. □ *Our ship docked at the quay and the passengers got off quickly.*

kill—kiln

- **kill** [kɪl] to deprive someone or something of life; to murder or slay someone or something. □ *My brother will not even kill a mosquito.*
- **kill** [kɪl] to put an end to something; to stop something. □ *Another loss will kill the team's hopes of post-season play.* □ *Kill the engine so we don't run out of gas.*
- **kill** [kɪl] to destroy the vitality of something or someone. □ *Don't kill her enthusiasm by being too critical.*
- **kill** [kɪl] to let something elapse. □ *We have some time to kill before the movie begins.*

- **kill** [kɪl] to exhaust someone or something. ☐ *"If we have to run another mile, it will just kill me," complained Gary.*
- **kill** [kɪl] something killed. ☐ *The hunter's kill consisted of two rabbits and three squirrels.*
- **kill** [kɪl] the act of killing something or someone. ☐ *When the wounded zebra staggered, the lions moved in for the kill.*
- **kiln** [kɪl, kɪln] a heated enclosure used to dry substances. ☐ *The owner of the ceramic shop has just purchased a new kiln.*

kiln See the main entry beginning with *kill.*

knead—kneed—need

- **knead** [nid] to form or shape something into a mass with the hands; to rub or squeeze something with the hands. ☐ *It is best to knead and punch the bread dough twice before letting it rise for the final time.* ☐ *A massage therapist will knead the muscles in your neck.*
- **kneed** [nid] the past tense and past participle of *knee* 'to strike someone with one's knee.' ☐ *Sam was upset when the person sitting behind him kneed him in the back.*
- **need** [nid] to be in want of something or someone. ☐ *I need more time to think over my options.*
- **need** [nid] a lack of something necessary, useful, or desirable. ☐ *His need for steady employment is pressing.*
- **need** [nid] an obligation or duty. ☐ *There is no need to arrive early.*

kneed See the main entry beginning with *knead.*

knew See the main entry beginning with *gnu.*

knickers—nickers

- **knickers** ['nɪkɚz] short, loose-fitting pants gathered at the knee. ☐ *Knickers were once the men's fashion rage in golf.*
- **nickers** ['nɪkɚz] the plural of *nicker* 'the neigh or whinny of a horse.' ☐ *From the barn we could hear the impatient pony's nickers.*

knight—night

- **knight** [nɑɪt] in feudal society, a man-at-arms serving a superior noble. ☐ *The knight in shining armor rescued the princess from the castle tower.*
- **knight** [nɑɪt] to bestow knighthood upon someone. ☐ *The king will knight the two men who saved his life.*
- **knight** [nɑɪt] a chess piece, usually in the shape of a horse bust. ☐ *In chess, a knight is a higher-ranking piece than a pawn.*

- **night** [nɑɪt] darkness. ☐ *Nocturnal animals are able to see at night.* ☐ *Night covered the campsite and one by one we turned on our flashlights.*
- **night** [nɑɪt] evening. ☐ *Last night I spotted a shooting star in the sky.*

knit–nit

- **knit** [nɪt] to interlace yarn or thread in a series of connected loops using needles. ☐ *Mom always liked to knit rather than crochet.*
- **knit** [nɪt] to form, tie, or link something closely together. ☐ *The new trade agreement will knit the nations.*
- **knit** [nɪt] to contract something into wrinkles. ☐ *Father used to knit his brow when he was upset or worried.*
- **nit** [nɪt] a young, parasitic insect or the egg of a young, parasitic insect. ☐ *Head lice are a type of nit.*

knob–nob

- **knob** [nɑb] a rounded handle. ☐ *To open the front door, you must twist the knob.*
- **knob** [nɑb] a small, isolated hill or mountain. ☐ *The knob would make a perfect ski slope.*
- **knob** [nɑb] a lump. ☐ *The sharp blow raised a knob on his head.*
- **nob** [nɑb] the head. (Slang.) ☐ *You'll have a bump on your nob from that nasty insect bite.*
- **nob** [nɑb] in cribbage, a jack of the same suit as the starter that scores a point for the holder. ☐ *A nob in cribbage is similar to the "right" or "left" in euchre.*

knock–nock

- **knock** [nɑk] to hit something with a sharp blow. ☐ *Please knock on the door before entering the office.*
- **knock** [nɑk] to collide with something or someone. ☐ *Be careful not to knock over the figurines.*
- **knock** [nɑk] to wander about. ☐ *Ken wants just to knock around for awhile after he graduates from high school.*
- **knock** [nɑk] a setback or misfortune. ☐ *Losing the game in the final moments was a hard knock.*
- **knock** [nɑk] to find fault with someone or something. ☐ *Don't knock my earnest attempts.*
- **knock** [nɑk] an abnormal noise originating from the engine of a car or truck. ☐ *Richard detected an engine knock in his new car.*
- **nock** [nɑk] a notch in a bow used to hold the bowstring or

the arrow. □ *The craftsman carefully cut a nock into each end of the bow.*

- **nock** [nɑk] the rear notched part of the arrow that is fitted to the bowstring and holds it in place. □ *The archer's aluminum arrow is fitted with a plastic nock.*
- **nock** [nɑk] to fit an arrow to a bowstring. □ *Upon seeing the bear, the frightened hunter was able to nock his bow quickly.*

knot—naught—not

- **knot** [nɑt] an interlacing of string, twine, or rope. □ *I was unable to untangle the knot in my fishing line.*
- **knot** [nɑt] a hard-to-solve problem or dilemma. □ *That issue put a knot in the discussion.*
- **knot** [nɑt] a bond of union, especially marriage. (Always in the idiom *tie the knot.*) □ *The couple has finally decided to tie the knot.*
- **knot** [nɑt] one nautical mile per hour. □ *The tugboat chugged out of the harbor at a single knot.*
- **naught** [nɔt, nɑt] nothing. (Typically with *for.*) □ *All his hard work was for naught.*
- **not** [nɑt] a word indicating *no* or negation. □ *We are not hungry at the moment.*

knotty—naughty

- **knotty** ['nɑti] having many knots, as with hair, rope, or string. □ *After a day in the wind, my hair was all knotty.*
- **knotty** ['nɑti] having many knots, as with lumber containing the bases of many branches. □ *I can't use this board because it is too knotty.*
- **naughty** ['nɔti, 'nɑti] ill-behaved; disobedient. □ *If you are naughty, I will have to send you to bed.*

know—no

- **know** [no] to understand or discern something; to be sure of the truth or certainty of something. □ *Charley does not know how to solve that problem.* □ *I know that she is an honest person.*
- **no** [no] none or not any. □ *There is no other way to the top of the tower other than the steep staircase.*
- **no** [no] a negative reply or denial. □ *No, I don't care for any more coffee.*

knows—nose

- **knows** [noz] the present tense, third person singular of *know* 'to understand or perceive something; to be aware of a fact.' □ *The boy knows he will be punished severely for coming home* *late.* □ *Mary knows a surprise party is being planned in honor of her retirement.*

- **knows** [noz] the present tense, third person singular of *know* 'to be acquainted with someone or something.' □ *She knows the shortest route to that town.* □ *Mary knows Bob very well.*
- **nose** [noz] the organ of smell. □ *The actress's nose is her most distinguishing feature.*
- **nose** [noz] to detect or sense something or someone by smell. □ *His dog can nose a rabbit out of any briar patch.*
- **nose** [noz] to pry or meddle in something. □ *You have no right to nose about in other people's business.*
- **nose** [noz] the front part of a structure, vehicle, or craft. □ *As it took off, the nose of the jet seemed to be pointed straight up.*

L

lacks—lax

- **lacks** [læks] the present tense, third person singular of *lack* 'to be in need of something.' □ *That wine lacks a full, fruity flavor.*
- **lax** [læks] loose; slack. □ *Hoist the sails up fully so they are not lax.*
- **lax** [læks] not strict or stringent. □ *Fred is very lax about his personal appearance.*

ladder—latter

- **ladder** ['lædɚ] a structure of two vertical side poles and numerous horizontal rungs that is used for climbing up and down. □ *Jake refuses to walk underneath any ladder.*
- **ladder** ['lædɚ] something that resembles a ladder or functions like a ladder. □ *A fish ladder was constructed to help the salmon swim upstream to spawn.*
- **latter** ['lædɚ, 'lætɚ] referring to the second of two things mentioned. □ *Though Lindsay and Marina are both smart, the latter is the better student.*
- **latter** ['lædɚ, 'lætɚ] the last; the end. □ *In the latter stages of the conflict, the war-weary soldiers wanted to give up.*

lain—lane

- **lain** [len] the past participle of *lie* 'to rest or recline in a horizontal position.' □ *She has lain on the sofa so often that it sags in some places.*
- **lain** [len] the past participle of *lie* 'to occupy a place; to be in a place.' □ *The two rusty plows have lain next to each other in the field for years.*
- **lane** [len] a narrow path or road; a marked path or route; an

ocean route for sea going vessels. ☐ *The country lane is lined with wildflowers in the spring.* ☐ *Jessica was disqualified from the race because she stepped out of her lane on the backstretch.* ☐ *Jane threw her bowling ball so forcefully that it landed in the next lane.*

lam—lamb

- **lam** [læm] a hurried or sudden flight from the law. ☐ *Since the prison escape, the convict has been on a lam.*
- **lamb** [læm] a young sheep. ☐ *The white, fluffy lamb frolicked in the pasture with its mother.*
- **lamb** [læm] a person as weak or gentle as a lamb. ☐ *Despite his huge size, Bob is a real lamb.*
- **lamb** [læm] the meat of a young sheep. ☐ *One of the house specialties at this restaurant is lamb chops with mint sauce.*

lamb See the main entry beginning with *lam.*

lane See the main entry beginning with *lain.*

laps—lapse

- **laps** [læps] the plural of *lap* 'the top of the thighs of a seated person.' ☐ *The baby-sitters held the twins on their laps while reading them bedtime stories.*
- **laps** [læps] the plural of *lap* 'a loose panel or flap of fabric or skin.' ☐ *A current style of women's trousers has billowy laps of fabric along the legs.*
- **laps** [læps] the plural of *lap* 'one circuit, often around a racecourse or swimming pool.' ☐ *Our gym teacher always makes the losing relay team run laps around the track.*
- **laps** [læps] the present tense, third person singular of *lap* 'to drink liquid using the tongue.' ☐ *The kitten always laps its water noisily.*
- **laps** [læps] the present tense, third person singular of *lap* 'to move in small, gentle waves.' ☐ *It is peaceful and relaxing to walk along the beach as the water gently laps the shoreline.*
- **lapse** [læps] a gap or break in some time period or activity; a discontinuance. ☐ *There was a temporary lapse in the electrical service to the neighborhood.* ☐ *During a lapse in the flow of customers, Vince ran out for a quick bite to eat.*
- **lapse** [læps] an error; a slip. ☐ *During a lapse in manners, Dad talked with his mouth full.*
- **lapse** [læps] to backslide or fall into error. ☐ *Now that he has reached his desired weight, Ron hopes that he doesn't lapse into poor eating habits.*

lapse See the main entry beginning with *laps.*

latter See the main entry beginning with *ladder.*

lax See the main entry beginning with *lacks.*

lay—lei

(See also *lay—lie.*)

- **lay** [le] to place or set someone or something down. ☐ *Lay the tools on the workbench.*
- **lay** [le] to wager or bet something. ☐ *I will not lay odds on the outcome of that football game.*
- **lay** [le] to impose as an obligation, reproach, burden, or punishment. ☐ *The government will lay a heavy tax on those imports.*
- **lay** [le] to plan or conceive something. ☐ *Let's lay a plan to make the police think we have disappeared.*
- **lay** [le] a person not of the clergy; a person not belonging to a certain profession. ☐ *Guenter Schmidt is a lay reader at his church.* ☐ *Many computer manuals are written for a lay audience.*
- **lay [down]** [le] the past tense of *lie [down]* 'to rest or recline in a horizontal position.' ☐ *He lay down to rest and fell asleep.*
- **lay** [le] the past tense of *lie* 'to occupy a place; to be situated some place.' ☐ *At one time those two old sheds lay near the main barn.*
- **lei** [le] a wreath or necklace of flowers or similar material. ☐ *The flight attendant placed a lei around Mary's neck when her plane arrived in Hawaii.*

lay—lie

- **lay** [le] to place someone or something onto something. ☐ *Lay the tools over on the workbench, please.* ☐ *Now I lay me down to sleep.*
- **lie** [lɑɪ] to rest or recline in a horizontal position. ☐ *I think you should lie here and rest.*

lays—laze—leis

- **lays** [lez] the present tense, third person singular of *lay* 'to place or set something down.' ☐ *Peter always lays his shoes right where they will get stepped on.*
- **lays** [lez] the present tense, third person singular of *lay* 'to place a bet.' ☐ *Each time she goes to the racecourse, Susan lays a bet on her favorite horse.*
- **lays** [lez] the present tense, third person singular of *lay* 'to contrive a plan.' ☐ *When he doesn't feel like going to school,*

Casey lays a plan to pretend he is ill.

- **laze** [lez] to pass time in relaxation or idleness. ☐ *Summertime affords some students time to laze the days away.*
- **leis** [lez] the plural of *lei* 'a wreath or necklace of flowers or similar material.' ☐ *The prettiest leis are those made of orchid blossoms.*

laze See the main entry beginning with *lays.*

leach—leech

- **leach** [litʃ] to pass something through or out of something by percolation. ☐ *If we first leach this compound, there won't be as much sediment in the liquid that is left.*
- **leech** [litʃ] a bloodsucking worm usually found in fresh, slow-moving water. ☐ *We found a leech in the stagnant pond.*
- **leech** [litʃ] a hanger-on who seeks to gain favor or position by association. ☐ *The leech hoped he would gain favors from the new mayor.*
- **leech** [litʃ] to remove blood from patients, as a treatment for various diseases. (Not widely practiced any longer.) ☐ *Doctors used to leech patients to rid them of disease.*

lead—led

- **lead** [lɛd] a heavy, soft metal that can be formed into shapes. ☐ *Fishing sinkers are usually made of lead.*
- **lead** [lɛd] a thin rod of a marking material found in pencils and pens. ☐ *Jeff broke his pencil lead twice during the exam.*
- **led** [lɛd] the past tense and past participle of *lead* 'to guide, direct, or aim someone or something.' ☐ *The scout led the pioneers into the wilderness.*
- **led** [lɛd] the past tense and past participle of *lead* 'to serve as a leader; to be ahead of or in front of someone.' ☐ *The famous scientist led the team of experts.* ☐ *Scott led his team in rebounds this year.*

leak—leek

- **leak** [lik] a crack or hole that unintentionally allows an escape of something. ☐ *A leak in the water pipe caused the basement to flood.*
- **leak** [lik] to give out information secretly. ☐ *Let's not leak this material to the newspapers ahead of schedule.*
- **leek** [lik] an edible garden herb known for its somewhat pungent taste. ☐ *Since his wife does not like the flavor of leek, Ted leaves it out of his Chinese dishes.*

lean—lien

- **lean** [lin] having little or no fat. ☐ *The circus performer was* *lean and wiry.* ☐ *He eats only lean red meat.*

- **lean** [lin] to rely upon someone or something for support. ☐ *It's nice to have someone to lean on in times of trouble.*
- **lean** [lin] to bend from a vertical position. ☐ *Since Sally is almost deaf, she must lean forward to listen when someone speaks.*
- **lean** [lin] to incline toward something in opinion, taste, or desire. ☐ *My taste in clothing tends to lean toward classic styles.*
- **lien** [lin] a legal charge upon personal property to offset or satisfy some debt or duty. ☐ *The lien on our neighbor's farm must be settled before the bank will approve a new loan.*

leased—least

- **leased** [list] the past tense and past participle of *lease* 'to rent something for one's use, usually real estate or an automobile, for a specified period of time.' ☐ *Last year more companies leased business vehicles than ever before.*
- **least** [list] the superlative form of *less.* ☐ *Of Mary's three children, the youngest boy is the least prone to catching colds.*
- **least** [list] the smallest degree, amount, or size possible. ☐ *I'm not the least bit worried about what he thinks.*

least See the main entry beginning with *leased.*

led See the main entry beginning with *lead.*

leech See the main entry beginning with *leach.*

leek See the main entry beginning with *leak.*

lei See the main entry beginning with *lay.*

leis See the main entry beginning with *lays.*

lend—loan

- **lend** [lɛnd] to give something to someone with an understanding that what was given (or something equal to it) will be returned. ☐ *I'll lend you some of my water goblets for your dinner party.*
- **loan** [lon] something given to a borrower temporarily. ☐ *The loan of Peter's wrench was a great help.* ☐ *Has the loan for your new house been approved?*

lends—lens

- **lends** [lɛn(d)z] the present tense, third person singular of *lend* 'to make a loan of something to someone.' ☐ *Henri often lends Kip his car repair tools.* ☐ *My credit union lends money* *just as most banks do.*

- **lens** [lɛnz] a glass or other substance used to focus or direct light rays. ☐ *The lens of that camera was badly scratched.* ☐ *A piece of metal was imbedded in the lens of her left eye.*

lens See the main entry beginning with *lends.*

lessen—lesson

- **lessen** ['lɛsən] to reduce something in size, number, or degree. ☐ *Aspirin will lessen the pain of your toothache.*
- **lesson** ['lɛsən] a piece of instruction or something to be learned, especially by a student. ☐ *Today's lesson dealt with right triangles.*
- **lesson** ['lɛsən] a rebuke. ☐ *That incident taught us an important lesson about honesty.*
- **lesson** ['lɛsən] a portion of sacred writing read during a worship service. ☐ *"Our lesson for this day is from the book of Acts," announced the minister.*

lesson See the main entry beginning with *lessen.*

lets—let's

- **lets** [lɛts] the third person singular of *let* 'to permit someone to do something.' ☐ *She lets the children stay up late on weekends.*
- **let's** [lɛts] the contraction of *let us*. ☐ *Let's go now.*

let's See the main entry beginning with *lets.*

levee—levy

- **levee** ['lɛvi] a dike or embankment of some type used to prevent flooding. ☐ *The levee was under much stress due to the heavy rainfall.*
- **levee** ['lɛvi] a reception for a particular or important person. ☐ *An afternoon levee was held in honor of the visiting poet.*
- **levy** ['lɛvi] to impose or collect an assessment, tax, or something else by legal means. ☐ *In the future, the court will levy stiffer fines for traffic offenses.*
- **levy** ['lɛvi] to wage or carry something on, as if in war. ☐ *Those two countries continue to levy war on one another.*
- **levy** ['lɛvi] to conscript or draft persons into the military. ☐ *The army needs to levy more troops to increase its numbers.*

levy See the main entry beginning with *levee.*

liar—lyre

- **liar** ['lɑɪɚ] a person who does not tell the truth. ☐ *Though* *she has trouble telling the truth, Liz does not consider herself a liar.*

- **lyre** ['lɑɪɚ] a stringed musical instrument similar to a harp. ☐ *In the ancient drawing a lyre appears in the hands of a servant girl.*

lie—lye

- **lie** [lɑɪ] an untruth that is told deliberately. (See also the entry beginning with *lay.*) ☐ *The child told a lie to avoid punishment.*
- **lie** [lɑɪ] to tell something that is not true in order to deceive someone. ☐ *Please do not lie to me.*
- **lie** [lɑɪ] to rest or recline in a horizontal position. ☐ *I think you should lie down here and rest.*
- **lie** [lɑɪ] to hide. ☐ *The burglars will lie in wait in the shadows before entering the house.*
- **lie** [lɑɪ] to occupy a position in relation to something else. ☐ *The villages lie on opposite sides of the valley.*
- **lye** [lɑɪ] a strong, alkaline solution that comes from wood and is used to make soap. ☐ *Lye can burn your skin if it is too concentrated.*

lien See the main entry beginning with *lean.*

light—lite

- **light** [lɑɪt] something that illuminates to make vision possible. ☐ *Turn on the porch light before you leave.* ☐ *We need some light to be able to see what we are doing.*
- **light** [lɑɪt] truth or enlightenment. ☐ *Casey finally saw the light about the importance of studying hard.*
- **light** [lɑɪt] having little pigment. ☐ *Many red-haired people have light complexions.*
- **light** [lɑɪt] easy. ☐ *Mary is carrying a light class load this term.*
- **light** [lɑɪt] cheerful; jovial. ☐ *The quartet played a light, classical piece of music.*
- **light** [lɑɪt] dizzy; giddy. ☐ *I felt a bit light after hitting my head on the door.*
- **lite** [lɑɪt] containing fewer calories; containing less of some ingredient. ☐ *My wife insists on buying lite bread, margarine, and cottage cheese.*

lightening—lightning

- **lightening** ['lɑɪtnɪŋ] the present participle of *lighten* 'to make someone or something lighter.' ☐ *After lightening the load in my backpack, I was able to keep up with the other hikers.*

☐ *His lightening of my bad mood made me feel much better.*

- **lightening** [ˈlɑɪtnɪŋ] the present participle of *lighten* 'to make something brighter.' ☐ *After the storm we saw a lightening of the sky almost immediately.*
- **lightning** [ˈlɑɪtnɪŋ] a sudden, bright electrical charge from one cloud to another or from a cloud to earth. ☐ *The thunder clapped and the lightning lit up the sky as if it were daytime.*
- **lightning** [ˈlɑɪtnɪŋ] sudden; very fast; having great speed. ☐ *Carl was well-known on the track team for his lightning sprint.*

lightning See the main entry beginning with *lightening.*

links—lynx

- **links** [lɪŋks] the plural of *link* 'a segment of a chain.' ☐ *Because her new watchband was too big, Stella had two links taken out of the band.*
- **links** [lɪŋks] the plural of *link* 'a connection.' ☐ *The police could find no links between the suspects and the crime.*
- **links** [lɪŋks] the plural of *link* 'a piece of jewelry used to fasten the cuffs on a long-sleeved shirt or blouse.' ☐ *Orlando lost one of his cuff links at the dance.*
- **links** [lɪŋks] the plural of *link* 'a tubular segment of sausage.' ☐ *They ate pancakes, eggs, and sausage links for breakfast.*
- **links** [lɪŋks] the present tense, third person singular of *link* 'to join people or things together.' ☐ *The evidence strongly links her to the rumor.*
- **links** [lɪŋks] a golf course. ☐ *Every Saturday morning you can find Mary on the links at the country club.*
- **lynx** [lɪŋks] a wildcat resembling a bobcat but with tufted ears and larger, padded feet. ☐ *Some trappers hunt lynx for their valuable fur.*

lite See the main entry beginning with *light.*

load—lode—lowed

- **load** [lod] something carried by a person or animal. ☐ *The heavy load was too much for the young child to carry.*
- **load** [lod] a mass or weight borne by something. ☐ *There are load limit restrictions on these roads during the springtime.*
- **load** [lod] the amount of work a person is expected to do. ☐ *As a new employee, Stella will carry a lighter load for the first two weeks.*
- **load** [lod] the full sight or story about someone or something; an earful or an eyeful. ☐ *"Wait until you get a load of this!" exclaimed Chuck.*
- **load** [lod] to put someone or something in or on something.

☐ *You load the groceries into the car and I'll drive home.* ☐ *Let's load the trailer before it gets dark.*

- **load** [lod] to increase the weight of something. ☐ *The salt bags will load down the back of the car.*
- **lode** [lod] an abundant store of something. ☐ *Jerry received a lode of money when he won the lottery.*
- **lode** [lod] a mineral deposit within certain boundaries. ☐ *The old prospector bragged about the size of the silver lode he had discovered.*
- **lowed** [lod] the past tense and past participle of *low* '[for cattle] to make a soft, moaning sound.' ☐ *The restless cows lowed softly in the pasture.*

loan—lone

(See also the main entry beginning with *lend.*)

- **loan** [lon] something given for a borrower's temporary use. ☐ *The buyer decided not to apply for a loan to buy the new lawn tractor.* ☐ *I was grateful for the loan of Joe's computer.*
- **lone** [lon] alone, sole, only, isolated. ☐ *The lone Canada goose flew across the darkening sky.*

loath—loathe

- **loath** [loθ] reluctant; unwilling. ☐ *I am loath to sit next to that obnoxious person for even one more minute!*
- **loathe** [loð] to hate someone or something. ☐ *Not only does he loathe the sight of cooked spinach, he also refuses to eat it.*

loathe See the main entry beginning with *loath.*

loch—lock

- **loch** [lɔh, lɔk] a bay or arm of a sea nearly surrounded by land, especially in Scotland. ☐ *There is a famous loch in Scotland where a monster presumably lives.*
- **lock** [lɑk] a security device operated by a key, combination, or electrical circuit and used to restrict entrance to or exit from a place. ☐ *My new key did not fit the lock properly.*
- **lock** [lɑk] a tress of hair; a group of human hairs. ☐ *Mother keeps a lock of our hair in each of our baby books.*
- **lock** [lɑk] an enclosure used for raising and lowering vessels from one water level to another. ☐ *The ship must pass through the lock to enter Lake Superior.*
- **lock** [lɑk] to fasten, join, or hold something together. ☐ *The wrestlers must lock hands before beginning a match.*
- **lock** [lɑk] to secure something with a lock. ☐ *Be sure to lock the door when you leave.*

lock See the main entry beginning with *loch.*

locks–lox

- **locks** [lɑks] the plural of *lock* 'a security device operated by a key, combination, or electrical circuit and used to restrict entrance to or exit from a place.' ☐ *As a safety measure, Sam had the locks on all of the doors changed.*
- **locks** [lɑks] the plural of *lock* 'a tress of hair; a group of human hairs.' ☐ *Her golden locks were the envy of all of her friends.*
- **locks** [lɑks] the plural of *lock* 'an enclosure used for raising and lowering vessels from one water level to another.' ☐ *Most locks do not operate in the winter.*
- **locks** [lɑks] the present tense, third person singular of *lock* 'to fasten, join, or hold something together.' ☐ *A computer automatically locks the gates in the prison.* ☐ *Grandpa never locks his house at night.*
- **lox** [lɑks] smoked salmon. ☐ *Her favorite items on the buffet table are the lox and bagels.*

lode See the main entry beginning with *load.*

lone See the main entry beginning with *loan.*

loot–lute

- **loot** [lut] something taken illegally, often by force, especially in war; spoils of war. ☐ *The soldiers carried the loot into their camp.*
- **loot** [lut] money. (Slang.) ☐ *"Where should we hide the loot?" asked one of the bank robbers.*
- **loot** [lut] illegal gains by public officials. ☐ *No one was aware of the loot skimmed out of the public treasury by top city officials.*
- **loot** [lut] to take something illegally by force or violence. ☐ *Rioters continued to loot the ravaged city day after day.*
- **lute** [lut] a pear-shaped, stringed musical instrument resembling and played like a guitar. ☐ *The wandering minstrel played a lute.*

lowed See the main entry beginning with *load.*

lox See the main entry beginning with *locks.*

lute See the main entry beginning with *loot.*

lye See the main entry beginning with *lie.*

lynx See the main entry beginning with *links.*

lyre See the main entry beginning with *liar.*

M

made—maid

- **made** [med] the past tense and past participle of *make* 'to create something; to manufacture something.' ☐ *Those lanterns were made in Hong Kong.* ☐ *Timothy made a cage for his gerbils.*
- **made [up]** [med] the past tense and past participle of *make [up]* 'to invent a story.' ☐ *She made up a story that was too silly to believe.*
- **made** [med] the past tense and past participle of *make* 'to complete something; to succeed at something.' ☐ *Bill has made his career in politics.*
- **maid** [med] a female servant. ☐ *Mrs. Smith's maid gets every other weekend off.*
- **maid** [med] a young, unmarried girl or woman. (Used only in older stories and fairy tales.) ☐ *A lovely maid captured the young king's heart.*

maid See the main entry beginning with *made*.

mail—male

- **mail** [mel] letters, packages, and other postal material. ☐ *A former roommate of mine was once a mail carrier in California.*
- **mail** [mel] to send something by post or mail. ☐ *Ruth promised to mail the letter in the morning.*
- **mail** [mel] armor made from metal links or plates. ☐ *The knight wore heavy mail during the battle.*
- **mail** [mel] the hard, protective covering of some animals. ☐ *Such animals as the armadillo are covered with mail.*
- **male** [mel] a human, plant, or animal of the masculine gender. ☐ *The test determined that at least one of the unborn twins*

is a male.

- **male** [mel] bearing masculine characteristics. ☐ *A male apple tree is needed to pollinate the female trees.*

main—mane

- **main** [men] chief; essential. ☐ *The main idea of the poem was hard to figure out.*
- **main** [men] physical force or strength. (Always in the idiom *might and main.*) ☐ *Julio pushed the stalled car with all of his might and main.*
- **main** [men] a major duct, pipe, or circuit responsible for feeding lesser branches of a utility system. ☐ *A bulldozer accidently hit a water main while digging at the site.*
- **mane** [men] long, heavy hair growing from the neck of some mammals, especially horses and lions. ☐ *When I lost my grip on the bridle rein, I grabbed a handful of the horse's mane.*
- **mane** [men] the heavy tresses of a person's head. ☐ *Susan has the most beautiful mane of shiny black hair.*

maize—maze

- **maize** [mez] a type of corn. ☐ *Maize was one of the food staples for many North American Indian tribes.*
- **maze** [mez] a complex, confusing network of passageways; a confused or bewildered state. ☐ *The mouse was able to find its way out of the maze.* ☐ *My mind was in a maze after the long study session.*

male See the main entry beginning with *mail.*

mall—maul

- **mall** [mɔl] a mallet. ☐ *He hit the sheet of steel with a rubber mall.*
- **mall** [mɔl] a large, enclosed shopping center. ☐ *A popular place for teenagers to hang out is at the mall.*
- **mall** [mɔl] a public walkway often lined with shade trees. ☐ *Many couples stroll along the mall in the evening.*
- **maul** [mɔl] to molest, mangle, or handle roughly. ☐ *Do not allow that young child to maul those tiny kittens.*
- **maul** [mɔl] a heavy hammer used to drive wedges. ☐ *We'll need a maul to split the wood.*

mane See the main entry beginning with *main.*

manner—manor

- **manner** ['mænɚ] a characteristic way of acting or behaving. ☐ *His manner has always been kind and gentle.*
- **manner** ['mænɚ] sort or kind. ☐ *What manner of person*

would do such a thing?

- **manor** ['mænɚ] the house or mansion of an estate. ☐ *The manor sits at the end of a long, winding drive.*
- **manor** ['mænɚ] a piece of land in which the tenants pay a user's fee either in money or in goods produced on that land. ☐ *The serfs worked the manor in exchange for a portion of their crop.*
- **manor** ['mænɚ] in England, a rural territorial unit or organization. ☐ *That manor is made up mostly of small villages.*

manor See the main entry beginning with *manner.*

mantel—mantle

- **mantel** ['mæntl] a shelf above a fireplace. ☐ *The couple chose an antique barn beam for the mantel in their new home.*
- **mantel** ['mæntl] a structure that supports the masonry above a fireplace. ☐ *The bricklayer first built the mantel and then laid up the fireplace facial brick.*
- **mantle** ['mæntl] a cloak. ☐ *The actor wore a black mantle throughout the play.*
- **mantle** ['mæntl] something that encloses or covers something. ☐ *The captives escaped under a mantle of darkness.*
- **mantle** ['mæntl] the back, shoulders, and wings of a bird. ☐ *The feathers on the mantle of the exotic bird were orange and green.*
- **mantle** ['mæntl] part of the shell of a mollusk. ☐ *We found an oyster mantle that had washed up on the shore.*
- **mantle** ['mæntl] part of the earth's surface just above the central core. ☐ *Do scientists know the depth of the earth's mantle?*
- **mantle** ['mæntl] to cover or spread over something as with a mantle. ☐ *Birds of prey will often mantle their kill with their wings.*

mantle See the main entry beginning with *mantel.*

mare—mayor

- **mare** [mɛɚ] a female horse, donkey, or mule, especially one of breeding age. ☐ *The horse that caught the judges' eyes was a flashy mare with spirit.*
- **mare** [mɛɚ] a supernatural being that causes nightmares. ☐ *She dreamed that an evil mare flew into her bedroom.*
- **mare** [mɛɚ] a large, dark patch on the surface of Mars or the moon. ☐ *The mare on the full moon's surface was visible with the naked eye.*

- **mayor** [mɛɚ, meɚ] the elected chief officer of a city or borough. ☐ *Our city's mayor is very active in local activities.*

marquee—marquis—marquise

- **marquee** [mɑrˈki] a canopy or signboard that projects over the entrance of a theater or other building and consists of metal, lights, and glass. ☐ *The bright yellow lights around the border of the marquee flashed on and off.*
- **marquee** [mɑrˈki] a large tent set up for an outdoor gathering. ☐ *The band will perform under a marquee at the wedding reception.*
- **marquis** [mɑrˈki] a nobleman of inherited rank in some countries. ☐ *The heroine in that romance novel refused to marry the evil marquis.*
- **marquise** [mɑrˈkis] a gemstone or ring setting in the shape of a long oval with pointed ends. ☐ *Donna's diamond engagement ring is a brilliant marquise.*

marquis See the main entry beginning with *marquee.*

marquise See the main entry beginning with *marquee.*

marry—merry

- **marry** [ˈmæɚi, ˈmɛɚi] to join two people in matrimony as husband and wife. ☐ *The rabbi will marry the couple on Friday evening.*
- **marry** [ˈmæɚi, ˈmɛɚi] to take someone as a spouse. ☐ *John will marry Ellen when he finishes college.*
- **marry** [ˈmæɚi, ˈmɛɚi] to unite two things in a close relationship. ☐ *The merger will marry two of the largest airlines in the world.*
- **merry** [ˈmɛɚi] jovial, lighthearted, or festive. ☐ *Everyone attending the festival had a merry time.*

marshal—martial

- **marshal** [ˈmɑrʃl] a person who directs and oversees ceremonial gatherings. ☐ *A celebrity is usually chosen to act as the grand marshal of the annual parade.*
- **marshal** [ˈmɑrʃl] a federal official in charge of prisoners or having certain judicial duties. ☐ *The fugitive surrendered to the marshal.*
- **marshal** [ˈmɑrʃl] an administrative head of a city's fire or police department. ☐ *The local fire marshal inspected the house that was destroyed in the blaze.*
- **martial** [ˈmɑrʃl] pertaining or relating to war, combat, or army or military life. ☐ *She is taking a course in the martial*

arts as a hobby.

marten—martin

- **marten** ['mɑrtn] any of several small, meat-eating mammals belonging to the weasel family that live in semi-forested areas. ☐ *The pine marten is making a comeback in some areas of Michigan.*
- **martin** ['mɑrtn] a shiny, blue-black bird belonging to the swallow family known for its ability to eat large numbers of insects. ☐ *The students put up a birdhouse in the school's nature area in hopes of attracting a martin or two.*

martial See the main entry beginning with *marshal.*

martin See the main entry beginning with *marten.*

massed—mast

- **massed** [mæst] the past tense and past participle of *mass* 'to form or collect something into a body.' ☐ *The shoreline was littered with debris massed in clumps.*
- **mast** [mæst] a long, vertical pole in a ship's deck, used to support rigging, sails, and booms. ☐ *Strong winds threatened to rip apart both the sails and the mast of the ship.*
- **mast** [mæst] edible nuts accumulated on the forest floor and eaten by animals. ☐ *Acorns and beechnuts are a favorite mast of whitetail deer.*
- **mast** [mæst] a naval disciplinary hearing in which the commanding officer listens to and decides cases or charges against his men. ☐ *Following the mast, the charges against the two enlisted sailors were dropped.*

mast See the main entry beginning with *massed.*

mat—matte

- **mat** [mæt] a border around a picture but inside a frame. ☐ *A large mat around a small picture is overwhelming.*
- **mat** [mæt] to make or provide a picture with a mat. ☐ *I would like to mat his portrait in a bright color.*
- **mat** [mæt] to become entangled. ☐ *The cat's fur tends to mat easily.*
- **mat** [mæt] a piece of closely woven coarse fabric used as a covering for a table or floor. ☐ *In some places, a mat instead of a bed is used for sleeping.*
- **mat** [mæt] a small rug used at a door for cleaning shoes. ☐ *Be sure to wipe your feet on the mat before going into the house.*
- **mat** [mæt] a thick, padded cushion used in such sports as wrestling, gymnastics, and tumbling. ☐ *The gymnast fell off*

the balance beam and onto the mat beneath it.
- **matte** [mæt] having a nonglossy or rough, grainy surface. ☐ *Ellen decided to use a paint that gives a matte finish.*

matte See the main entry beginning with *mat.*

maul See the main entry beginning with *mall.*

may See the main entry beginning with *can.*

mayor See the main entry beginning with *mare.*

maze See the main entry beginning with *maize.*

meat–meet–mete
- **meat** [mit] the flesh of an animal used as food. ☐ *Grandfather always liked meat and potatoes for Sunday dinner.*
- **meat** [mit] the edible part of a fruit, nut, or vegetable. ☐ *We'll only use the meat of ripe nuts for the pecan pie.*
- **meet** [mit] to approach or come into contact or the presence of someone or something. ☐ *They agreed to meet for lunch at noon.* ☐ *I often meet defeat when I try to program the VCR.*
- **meet** [mit] to settle with or pay something in full. ☐ *John cannot meet this month's bills because of his recent illness.*
- **meet** [mit] a gathering for some specific activity or competition. ☐ *Chris won the two-mile event in last week's track meet.*
- **mete** [mit] to assign or allot something by measure. ☐ *Her mother does not like to mete out punishment for the children's misbehavior.*

meatier–meteor
- **meatier** ['mitijɚ] the comparative form of *meaty* 'having more meat or substance than something else.' ☐ *I hope the next novel I read has a meatier plot than the last.*
- **meteor** ['mitijɚ, 'mitiɔr] a piece of falling matter from the solar system that becomes visible when it enters the earth's atmosphere. ☐ *The meteor shower was visible only for an instant.*

medal–meddle
- **medal** ['mɛdl] an ornamental metal disk bearing a picture or engraving that remembers a person or event or is rewarded for achievement or excellence. ☐ *It was a great honor to be awarded a medal by the President of the United States.*
- **meddle** ['mɛdl] to interfere in something without permission or right. ☐ *I wish Carl would not meddle in other people's affairs.*

meddle See the main entry beginning with *medal.*

meet See the main entry beginning with *meat.*

merry See the main entry beginning with *marry.*

metal–mettle

- **metal** ['mɛtl, 'mɛdl] a chemical element that is lustrous, opaque, and fusible. □ *Copper is a soft, easily handled metal.*
- **mettle** ['mɛtl, 'mɛdl] spirit or stamina. □ *The Boston Marathon is enough to test the mettle of any serious long-distance runner.*

mete See the main entry beginning with *meat.*

meteor See the main entry beginning with *meatier.*

mettle See the main entry beginning with *metal.*

mews–muse

- **mews** [mjuz] the plural of *mew* 'a soft sound usually associated with cats.' □ *The mournful mews of the trapped kitten brought everyone running to the tree.*
- **mews** [mjuz] the plural of *mew* 'a gull.' □ *Mews swooped above the harbor docks, hoping for a handout of fresh fish.*
- **muse** [mjuz] a state of distraction or deep thought. □ *He was in a muse for days trying to decide what to do.*
- **muse [over]** [mjuz] to think about something reflectively. □ *Grandma likes to muse over times past.*
- **muse** [mjuz] one of a group of nine goddesses in Greek mythology. □ *A muse was believed to bring inspiration to an artist.*

might–mite

- **might** [mɑɪt] a word used to express possibility or probability. □ *The current officeholder might be reelected next year.*
- **might** [mɑɪt] strength, power, or authority wielded by someone or something. □ *Despite his great might, the weight lifter was unable to lift the barbell.*
- **mite** [mɑɪt] a kind of tiny insect known to infest plants, animals, and foods. □ *The dog was pestered by a mite in its ear.*
- **mite** [mɑɪt] a very tiny creature or object. □ *"Mike learned to fish when he was just a little mite," reflected his mother.*
- **mite** [mɑɪt] a small bit of something. □ *I'm so hungry that I want to taste a mite of everything on the buffet table.*

mil–mill

- **mil** [mɪl] a unit of length equal to 1/1000 of an inch. □ *The* *wire required for that circuit was so tiny that it had to be measured to the exact mil.*

- **mill** [mɪl] a unit of monetary value equal to 1/1000 of a United States dollar. ☐ *The school board is requesting an additional mill for operating costs in the special election.*
- **mill** [mɪl] a building used to house cutting or grinding machinery. ☐ *The old lumber mill has shut down.*
- **mill** [mɪl] to grind grain into a powder, meal, or flour. ☐ *People in many cultures still mill their grains using primitive equipment.*
- **mill** [mɪl] to move about in a collective mass. ☐ *The crowd of curious people continued to mill around the accident scene.*

mill See the main entry beginning with *mil.*

mince—mints

- **mince** [mɪnts] to chop or cut something into very tiny pieces. ☐ *Mince the onion and garlic finely when you make that recipe.*
- **mince** [mɪnts] to speak in a restrained manner within boundaries of decorum. ☐ *Bob is very straightforward and does not like to mince words.*
- **mints** [mɪnts] the plural of *mint* 'a place where coins are manufactured.' ☐ *One of the six United States mints is located at Fort Knox, Kentucky.*
- **mints** [mɪnts] the plural of *mint* 'a huge sum of money.' (Colloquial.) ☐ *Those antique cars are worth mints.*
- **mints** [mɪnts] the plural of *mint* 'an aromatic plant used in flavoring and cooking.' ☐ *The leaves of two different types of mints are used to make that tea.*
- **mints** [mɪnts] candy flavored with mint. ☐ *The hostess had dishes filled with nuts and mints sitting on the tables.*
- **mints** [mɪnts] the present tense, third person singular of *mint* 'to stamp coins or money out of metal.' ☐ *Darlene operates a machine that mints new pennies.*

minds—mines

- **minds** [mɑɪndz] the plural of *mind* 'the brain's memory and consciousness; that with which people think and reason.' ☐ *Our minds went blank when we were asked to recall something that happened a long time ago.* ☐ *The top students in the class have excellent academic minds.*
- **minds** [mɑɪndz] the plural of *mind* 'a highly intellectual or scientific person.' ☐ *Some of the best medical minds in the world are searching for a cure for cancer.*
- **minds** [mɑɪndz] the present tense, third person singular of

mind 'to obey someone.' ☐ *That child always minds her parents.*

- **minds** [maɪndz] the present tense, third person singular of *mind* 'to be careful of something.' ☐ *Jimmy always minds the traffic before crossing the street.*
- **minds** [maɪndz] the present tense, third person singular of *mind* 'to take charge of someone or something.' ☐ *The oldest child minds the younger ones when their parents are away.*
- **minds** [maɪndz] the present tense, third person singular of *mind* 'to be concerned with something; to object to something.' ☐ *Dave minds the fact that some people call him by a nickname.*
- **mines** [maɪnz] the plural of *mine* 'a place in the earth from which mineral deposits are taken.' ☐ *Most of the mines in West Virginia contain coal.*
- **mines** [maɪnz] the plural of *mine* 'an explosive device; a stationary bomb.' ☐ *Specially trained experts removed all unexploded mines in the area.*
- **mines** [maɪnz] the present tense, third person singular of *mine* 'to dig for metal or ore.' ☐ *The company mines both silver and copper in several western states.*
- **mines** [maɪnz] the present tense, third person singular of *mine* 'to place explosive mines in strategic positions.' ☐ *In times of war, a country sometimes mines harbors and other important waterways to discourage enemy use.*

miner—minor

- **miner** ['maɪnɚ] a person who mines. ☐ *Like his father and grandfather before him, Dave is a miner in the Pennsylvania coal mines.*
- **minor** ['maɪnɚ] a person who is under legal age. ☐ *It is illegal to sell alcohol and tobacco products to a minor.*
- **minor** ['maɪnɚ] unimportant; inferior in degree, status, number, or size. ☐ *Linda was disappointed that she received only a minor part in the play.*
- **minor** ['maɪnɚ] not involving risk to health or life. ☐ *The man sustained a minor cut to his hand.*
- **minor** ['maɪnɚ] an academic subject requiring fewer courses to earn a degree than a major. ☐ *Peter has a major in American literature and a minor in social studies.*
- **minor** ['maɪnɚ] a musical key. ☐ *Play the recital piece in D minor.*

mines See the main entry beginning with *minds.*

minor See the main entry beginning with *miner.*

mints See the main entry beginning with *mince.*

missed—mist

- **missed** [mɪst] the past tense and past participle of *miss* 'to feel the absence of someone or something.' □ *Lori missed her parents while she was away at summer camp.*
- **missed** [mɪst] the past tense and past participle of *miss* 'to fail to obtain, hit, reach, or make contact with someone or something.' □ *The batter swung at the ball but missed.*
- **missed** [mɪst] the past tense and past participle of *miss* 'to fail to attend something.' □ *Larry missed his first class because he overslept.*
- **missed** [mɪst] the past tense and past participle of *miss* 'to fail to experience, sense, or understand something.' □ *I think I missed the point he was trying to make.*
- **mist** [mɪst] very light, falling, or floating water particles, not as heavy as drizzle or rain. □ *The morning mist covered everything with moisture.* □ *We were unable to see the far side of the pond due to the mist of steam rising from the water.*
- **mist** [mɪst] to spray or cover something with fine water particles. □ *Mist the fern plants every day rather than watering them once a week.*

mist See the main entry beginning with *missed.*

mite See the main entry beginning with *might.*

moan—mown

- **moan** [mon] a wail; a groan. □ *The accident victim uttered a moan when the rescue workers lifted her onto the stretcher.*
- **moan** [mon] to utter a wail or groan. □ *The winds seem to moan down in the valley on breezy nights.*
- **mown** [mon] the past participle of *mow* 'to cut down standing grass or weeds.' (Also *mowed.*) □ *Even after I had mown the grass, dandelions appeared everywhere.*
- **mown [down]** [mon] the past participle of *mow [down]* 'to kill or destroy people in large numbers without mercy; to cut down standing grass or weeds.' □ *The artillery had mown down all opposition in a matter of minutes.* □ *After the grass had been mown down, I raked it up.*

mode—mowed

- **mode** [mod] a specific form, style, or variety of something. □ *The bicycle is a popular mode of transportation in Japan.*
- **mode** [mod] a manner of doing something. □ *The burglar repeatedly used the same mode of operation to gain entry into houses.*

- **mode** [mod] the most frequent value in a frequency distribution. □ *The instructor asked her students to find the mode in the data she provided.*
- **mowed** [mod] the past tense of *mow* 'to cut down standing grass or weeds.' □ *The farmer mowed his hay field four times last year.*
- **mowed [down]** [mod] the past tense of *mow [down]* 'to kill or destroy large numbers of something without mercy.' □ *The ruthless soldiers mowed down every living thing in sight.*

moor—more
- **moor** [mɔɚ, muɚ] a wasteland of low, boggy ground. □ *Peggy often found it peaceful to walk along the moor at night.*
- **moor** [mɔɚ, muɚ] to secure something with anchors or lines, particularly a boat. □ *We had better moor the boat in the cove until this storm passes.*
- **more** [mɔɚ] a greater number, amount, or degree. □ *Nowadays more people live in urban areas than in rural ones.*

moose—mousse
- **moose** [mus] a large grass-eating mammal that belongs to the deer family and lives in forested parts of North America. □ *While driving along a Canadian highway, we spotted a cow moose and her calf drinking from a lake.*
- **mousse** [mus] an airy, sweet dessert made of gelatin and whipped cream. □ *Our hostess served raspberry mousse for dessert.*

more See the main entry beginning with *moor.*

morning—mourning
- **morning** ['mɔɚnɪŋ] the part of the day from midnight or dawn until noon. □ *He prefers to jog early in the morning when it's cooler.*
- **mourning** ['mɔɚnɪŋ] the present participle of *mourn* 'to express grief and sorrow about something, such as a person's death.' □ *Mourning clothes are traditionally black.* □ *The players are still mourning the death of their beloved coach.*
- **mourning** ['mɔɚnɪŋ] a period of grief following a death. □ *The widow continues to wear black to show that she is still in mourning.*

mourning See the main entry beginning with *morning.*

mousse See the main entry beginning with *moose.*

mowed See the main entry beginning with *mode.*

mown See the main entry beginning with *moan*.

muscle–mussel

- **muscle** ['məsl] a body tissue that controls motion. □ *The long jumper pulled a muscle in her lower leg.*
- **muscle** ['məsl] brawn; muscular strength. □ *It will take a lot of muscle to move that large piece of equipment.*
- **mussel** ['məsl] a marine or freshwater bivalve mollusk. □ *While walking along the shoreline, we found a mussel that had washed up on the beach.*

muse See the main entry beginning with *mews*.

mussed–must

- **mussed** [məst] the past tense and past participle of *muss* 'to mess up or make someone or something untidy.' □ *The ride in the convertible certainly mussed her hairdo.*
- **must** [məst] to be compelled to do something by a person, circumstance, or law. □ *We must try to obey the law at all times.*
- **must** [məst] an essential item. □ *A small, compact camera is a must when vacationing.*
- **must** [məst] an imperative need. □ *Complete confidentiality is a must when dealing with private matters.*

mussel See the main entry beginning with *muscle*.

must See the main entry beginning with *mussed*.

mustard–mustered

- **mustard** ['məstɚd] a condiment made of powdered mustard seed and other ingredients. □ *Do you like mustard on your hot dogs?*
- **mustard** ['məstɚd] a pungent yellow powder from the mustard plant used in medicine and chemicals. □ *Grandma used to recommend a mustard plaster for chest colds.*
- **mustard** ['məstɚd] zest; vigor. (Slang.) □ *Though in his eighties, that man still has a great deal of mustard.*
- **mustered** ['məstɚd] the past tense and past participle of *muster* 'to collect, gather, or call something forth.' □ *Todd mustered all of his courage before stepping up to the podium to speak.*
- **mustered** ['məstɚd] the past tense and past participle of *muster* 'to enlist or rouse someone.' □ *Troops were mustered from all over the colonial countryside.*

mustered See the main entry beginning with *mustard*.

N

naught See the main entry beginning with *knot.*

naughty See the main entry beginning with *knotty.*

naval—navel

- **naval** ['nevl] involving or relating to ships, shipping, or a navy. ☐ *While on vacation, we visited the naval facility at Pearl Harbor on Oahu, Hawaii.*
- **navel** ['nevl] a depression or scar in the center of the abdomen where the umbilical cord was once attached. ☐ *The belly dancer wore a gemstone in her navel as part of her costume.*
- **navel** ['nevl] a particular variety of orange. ☐ *There is no orange sweeter than a large, juicy navel.*

navel See the main entry beginning with *naval.*

nay—neigh

- **nay** [ne] a negative reply or vote; a person who votes no. ☐ *When the vote was tallied, there were four yeas and one nay.*
- **nay** [ne] not only this but also. (Formal, stilted, or jocular.) ☐ *"Nay, there were other misdeeds committed by this individual," continued the speaker.*
- **neigh** [ne] the loud, long utterance of a horse, donkey, or mule. ☐ *We could hear the wild horse's neigh across the wide valley.*
- **neigh** [ne] to make the utterance of a donkey, horse, or mule. ☐ *Our donkey will neigh if he hears a loud, piercing noise.*

need See the main entry beginning with *knead.*

neigh See the main entry beginning with *nay.*

new See the main entry beginning with *gnu.*

nickers See the main entry beginning with *knickers.*

night See the main entry beginning with *knight.*

nit See the main entry beginning with *knit.*

no See the main entry beginning with *know.*

nob See the main entry beginning with *knob.*

nock See the main entry beginning with *knock.*

none—nun

- **none** [nən] not any; not a single one. ☐ *I looked for some ripe avocados at the grocery store, but there were none.*
- **none** [nən] not at all; by no means. ☐ *Our band director was none too happy with our recent performance.*
- **nun** [nən] a woman of a religious order, especially one who vows poverty, chastity, and obedience. ☐ *The young Catholic girl thought that one day she might become a nun.*

nose See the main entry beginning with *knows.*

not See the main entry beginning with *knot.*

nun See the main entry beginning with *none.*

O

oar—o'er—or—ore

- **oar** [ɔɚ] a long-handled paddle with a flat, broad blade at one end used to propel a boat through water. ☐ *In his excitement to land the great bass, the fisherman accidentally knocked an oar into the water.*
- **o'er** [ɔɚ] over. ☐ *The rugged pioneers pushed o'er the mountains, valleys, plains, and deserts in their quest for a better life.*
- **or** [ɔɚ] a word suggesting an alternative. ☐ *We can leave now to beat the rush, or we can wait and watch the final minutes of the game.*
- **ore** [ɔɚ] a mineral containing a valuable metallic or other element for which it is mined. ☐ *The discovery of iron ore reshaped many aspects of human existence.*

ode—owed

- **ode** [od] a lyrical song or poem of varying length and complexity, usually addressing a person or event. ☐ *The haunting song "Ode to Billy Joe" was once very popular.*
- **owed** [od] the past tense and past participle of *owe* 'to be indebted to someone or something.' ☐ *Sally finally paid me the ten dollars she owed me.*

o'er See the main entry beginning with *oar*.

oh—owe

- **oh** [o] an expression of various emotions, including surprise, pain, and fear. ☐ *"Oh, my goodness! I've won the lotto jackpot!" exclaimed Andy.*
- **oh** [o] an introductory word used in a direct address. ☐ *"Oh, Marie, I really don't care to see that movie," said Jill in disgust.*

- **oh** [o] zero. □ *Both his house address and his telephone number end in "oh."*
- **owe** [o] to be indebted to someone or something. □ *Since I am as much at fault as you, you do not owe me an apology.*

one—won
- **one** [wən] the number between zero and two. □ *Connie's jersey for the relay team has the number one on it.*
- **one** [wən] a single unit or thing. □ *He doesn't have one item that he can call his own.* □ *One type of woodwind instrument is the clarinet.*
- **one** [wən] any individual indicated in a vague sense. □ *I was the first one to misspell a word in the spelling bee.* □ *One really should not do that!*
- **one** [wən] united; acting or thinking in union. □ *We are one in our belief that we should preserve our environment.*
- **won** [wən] the past tense and past participle of *win* 'to gain the highest honor or best prize in a contest.' □ *Rita won the fudge-making contest.*
- **won** [wən] the past tense and past participle of *win* 'to earn or obtain something.' □ *Her kind ways and sense of fairness won his respect.*

or See the main entry beginning with *oar.*

ordinance—ordnance
- **ordinance** ['ɔɚd(n)nənts] a municipal law or order. □ *A public ordinance prohibits loitering on city streets.*
- **ordnance** ['ɔɚd(n)nənts] military supplies. □ *The ordnance supply included guns and ammunition.*

ordnance See the main entry beginning with *ordinance.*

ore See the main entry beginning with *oar.*

ought See the main entry beginning with *aught.*

our See the main entry beginning with *hour.*

overdo—overdue
- **overdo** [ovɚ'du] to do or use something to excess. □ *Don't try to overdo things on your first day home from the hospital.* □ *I tend to overdo the pot roasts I prepare.* □ *Don't overdo it with those painkillers.*
- **overdue** [ovɚ'du, ovɚ'dju] delayed beyond an appointed time. □ *Carol's baby was three weeks overdue.* □ *My library books are always overdue by the time I return them.*
- **overdue** [ovɚ'du, ovɚ'dju] remaining unpaid when due to be

paid. □ *Last month's mortgage payment is overdue.*

- **overdue** [ovɚ'du, ovɚ'dju] more than ready. □ *James felt he was long overdue for a pay raise.*

overdue See the main entry beginning with *overdo.*

overseas—oversees

- **overseas** [ovɚ'siz] across or beyond the sea. □ *The journalist's next assignment will be somewhere overseas.*
- **oversees** [ovɚ'siz] the present tense, third person singular of *oversee* 'to supervise someone or something.' □ *The office manager oversees the work of all of the clerical and support staff.*

oversees See the main entry beginning with *overseas.*

owe See the main entry beginning with *oh.*

owed See the main entry beginning with *ode.*

P

paced—paste

- **paced** [pest] the past tense and past participle of *pace* 'to establish a reasonable rate of movement or progress.' □ *We paced ourselves to work at a steady rate so we wouldn't tire before the job was done.*
- **paced [off]** [pest] the past tense and past participle of *pace [off]* 'to mark off a unit of distance based on the length of a human stride.' □ *The umpire paced off the distance between the pitcher's mound and the batter's box.*
- **paced** [pest] the past tense and past participle of *pace* '[for a horse] to travel so that the legs on the same side of its body move alternately back and forth at the same time.' □ *The horse paced around the track in record time.*
- **paste** [pest] a wet, sticky mixture used as glue. □ *The preschoolers like to use colored paste on their art projects.*
- **paste** [pest] to cause something to stick to someone or something. □ *Let's paste these drawings up on the walls all around the room.*
- **paste** [pest] to hit someone hard. (Slang.) □ *If you say something to anger Terry, he is likely to paste you.*

packed—pact

- **packed** [pækt] the past tense and past participle of *pack* 'to gather something into a compact form and place it in a container.' □ *The children packed their own suitcases before leaving for camp.*
- **packed** [pækt] the past tense and past participle of *pack* 'to carry a gun.' (Slang.) □ *The police officer always packed his .357 magnum while on duty.*

- **packed** [pækt] the past tense and past participle of *pack* '[for one] to arrange a deck of cards in such a way as to give one a fraudulent advantage.' ☐ *Carl liked to win at cards, so he packed the deck in his favor whenever possible.*
- **packed** [pækt] full of something. ☐ *Our favorite restaurant is always packed with people on Saturday night.*
- **pact** [pækt] a contract; an agreement. ☐ *The neighborhood children formed a pact to meet every day after lunch.*
- **pact** [pækt] a treaty; a contract. ☐ *Six countries signed the pact declaring peace.*

pail—pale

- **pail** [pel] a bucket or other container equipped with a handle and used to carry liquids. ☐ *Our cow kicked over a full pail of milk.*
- **pale** [pel] pallid. ☐ *We knew Henry didn't feel well when he suddenly became very pale.*
- **pale** [pel] not bright or brilliant. ☐ *She painted the room a pale shade of yellow.*
- **pale** [pel] to become less important. ☐ *All of the other girls pale in comparison to Rosa's great beauty.*
- **pale** [pel] one of the stakes or pickets of a fence. ☐ *One pale in the stockade fence is broken and should be replaced.*

pain—pane

- **pain** [pen] distress; suffering; discomfort. ☐ *The pain became so unbearable that Emily finally agreed to see a doctor.*
- **pain** [pen] to cause someone or something to feel pain. ☐ *It will pain us to see you move so far away.*
- **pain** [pen] to cause oneself or another trouble or exertion. ☐ *Do not pain yourself to stand up when you feel so ill.*
- **pane** [pen] a framed piece of glass found in windows and doors. ☐ *During the furious storm, a pane of glass blew out of the large picture window.*

pair—pare—pear

- **pair** [pɛɚ] two corresponding things designed to be used together; two associated or similar things. ☐ *Now what have I done with that pair of socks?* ☐ *Jim needs to buy a pair of shirts to take on his trip.*
- **pair** [pɛɚ] two sweethearts. ☐ *That young pair will probably marry someday.*
- **pair** [pɛɚ] two playing cards of the same value or denomination. ☐ *All she had was a pair of kings in her hand.*
- **pair** [pɛɚ] a matched set. ☐ *The buggy was pulled by a pair*

of matched bays.

- **pair** [pɛɚ] to set or arrange something in groups of two. ☐ *The graduates will pair up to march into the auditorium.*
- **pare** [pɛɚ] to peel or remove the skin or covering from something; to cut something away. ☐ *Will you please pare the potatoes for dinner?* ☐ *We need to pare our budget by several thousand dollars.*
- **pear** [pɛɚ] a fleshy, somewhat gritty fruit of a tree belonging to the rose family. ☐ *The pear was juicy and tasty.*

palate—pallet

- **palate** [ˈpælət] the roof of the mouth. ☐ *The dentist had to numb his patient's palate before he could remove the front tooth.*
- **palate** [ˈpælət] an intellectual taste or enjoyment. ☐ *That author's writing style does not suit my palate.*
- **pallet** [ˈpælət] a lightweight, portable framework on which materials in factories and warehouses can be stored or transported. ☐ *The bags of cement were stacked on a pallet while awaiting shipment.*
- **pallet** [ˈpælət] a sleeping tick or mattress. ☐ *A pallet, though not very comfortable, makes an adequate sleeping surface.*
- **pallet** [ˈpælət] an instrument used for forming or mixing clay or colors. ☐ *The artist used a pallet to combine several different colors for the portrait.*

pale See the main entry beginning with *pail.*

pallet See the main entry beginning with *palate.*

pane See the main entry beginning with *pain.*

pare See the main entry beginning with *pair.*

passed—past

- **passed** [pæst] the past tense and past participle of *pass* 'to move by and beyond someone or something.' ☐ *We passed many vacationing families on the highway.*
- **passed [away]** [pæst] the past tense and past participle of *pass [away]* 'to die.' ☐ *Her great-aunt passed away recently.*
- **passed** [pæst] the past tense and past participle of *pass* 'to hand or transfer someone or something from one person to another person.' ☐ *The relay team members passed the baton smoothly from one to another.* ☐ *After her parents died, Tess was passed from relative to relative.*
- **passed** [pæst] the past tense and past participle of *pass* '[for a vote] to win approval from a legislative body.' ☐ *The bill narrowly passed both houses of the state congress.*

- **past** [pæst] in a previous time period; ago. □ *In years past, life seemed so much simpler.* □ *Grandpa was a spritely, spirited man a long time past.*
- **past** [pæst] after. □ *The clock chimed at half past midnight.*
- **past** [pæst] beyond. □ *Go past the entrance and turn left at the second door.*

past See the main entry beginning with *passed.*

paste See the main entry beginning with *paced.*

patience–patients

- **patience** [ˈpeʃənts] having the capacity to be steadfast, calm, or uncomplaining. □ *Kindergarten teachers must have a great deal of patience.*
- **patients** [ˈpeʃənts] the plural of *patient* 'a person undergoing medical treatment.' □ *The doctor treats all of her patients with care and interest.*

patients See the main entry beginning with *patience.*

pause–paws

- **pause** [pɔz] a temporary break or stop. □ *After a brief pause, the speaker continued.*
- **pause** [pɔz] to stop or linger for a time. □ *Let's pause at the fountain and toss in a coin.*
- **paws** [pɔz] the plural of *paw* 'the foot of some warm-blooded terrestrial animal having claws.' □ *A lynx has huge paws.*
- **paws** [pɔz] the plural of *paw* 'a large, clumsy human hand.' (A figurative use of the previous sense.) □ *"Get your paws off me!" shouted the boy.*
- **paws** [pɔz] the present tense, third person singular of *paw* 'to touch someone rudely or amorously.' □ *Henry, it seems, paws every girl who goes out with him.*
- **paws** [pɔz] the present tense, third person singular of *paw* 'to grab at something repeatedly.' □ *The inexperienced mountain climber paws the air wildly each time he loses his footing.*
- **paws** [pɔz] the present tense, third person singular of *paw* 'to bat or hit at something with a paw.' □ *Each time the cat catches a mouse, it paws its victim pitilessly.* □ *When restless, the stallion paws the stall floor.*

paws See the main entry beginning with *pause.*

peace–piece

- **peace** [pis] a state of security, tranquility, or order between individuals, groups, or countries. □ *A war-torn nation knows* *no peace.* □ *The feuding brothers have finally made peace.*

- **peace** [pis] a freedom from mental or emotional upheaval. □ *His cabin in the woods offers him a haven of peace.*
- **peace** [pis] quiet; silence. □ *With five children in the house, the harried housewife has no peace.*
- **piece** [pis] a portion of a whole. □ *May I please have the last piece of pie?*
- **piece** [pis] an artistic or literary composition. □ *The composer's piece for the piano won the competition.* □ *That piece of artwork was the first ever to be sold by the artist.*
- **piece** [pis] something regarded as an example of a unit of a kind or class. □ *Mary does a piece of work at a time at the garment factory.*
- **piece** [pis] to patch someone or something together; to complete something by adding pieces. □ *We might be able to piece together a quilt from these scraps.* □ *It was difficult to piece together the jigsaw puzzle.*
- **piece** [pis] a handgun; a revolver. (Police and underworld slang.) □ *The robber carried his piece in a shoulder holster.*

peak—peek—pique

- **peak** [pik] a prominent, pointed top or end of something. □ *The mountain peak was covered with snow.*
- **peak** [pik] the highest level; the greatest degree. □ *He reached the peak of his music career at age thirty.*
- **peak** [pik] to reach a summit or maximum of something. □ *The physical condition of the racehorse should peak around the date of the race.*
- **peek** [pik] to glance secretly at something or someone. □ *Children are sometimes tempted to peek at their birthday presents.*
- **peek** [pik] to take a brief look at someone or something. □ *Out of curiosity she wanted to peek at every room in the house.*
- **pique** [pik] a fit of irritation or resentment. □ *In a pique of anger, the child broke her favorite toy.*
- **pique** [pik] to arouse anger or resentment. □ *Try not to pique his wrath by upsetting him.*
- **pique** [pik] to provoke someone or something by a challenge or rebuff. □ *The coach's pep talk served to pique his team's desire to win.*

peal—peel

- **peal** [pil] a loud ringing of bells, especially church bells. □ *Every Sunday morning the peal of the church bell summons people to worship.*

- **peal** [pil] a loud sound or succession of sounds. □ *Her peal of laughter was heard throughout the house.*
- **peel** [pil] to remove or strip off an outer layer of something. □ *I had to peel the apples before I could make the cobbler.*
- **peel** [pil] to remove clothing from a body. □ *Let's peel off those wet clothes before you get a chill.*
- **peel** [pil] the skin or rind of a fruit. □ *The orange peel was easy to remove.*

pear See the main entry beginning with *pair.*

pearl—purl
- **pearl** [pɚl] the lustrous round growth found in the shell of some mollusks and used as a gem in jewelry. □ *The diver found a small pearl in the oyster.*
- **pearl** [pɚl] something resembling a pearl in color, value, or physical qualities. □ *Dad always said he got a real pearl when he married Mom.*
- **pearl** [pɚl] to form in tiny droplets. □ *The light rain began to pearl on the newly waxed surface.*
- **purl** [pɚl] gold or silver thread. □ *Her gown was sewn with silvery purl.*
- **purl** [pɚl] to embroider with gold or silver thread. □ *My aunt taught me to purl delicate handmade doilies.*
- **purl** [pɚl the looped stitch on the edge of lace. □ *The purl on Jane's lace collar caught on her necklace and ripped.*
- **purl** [pɚl] the soft murmur of a gentle, swirling stream. □ *The purl of the slowly flowing brook was barely audible.*
- **purl** [pɚl] to make a murmur. □ *The two streams purl quietly where they meet.*

pedal—peddle—petal
- **pedal** ['pɛdl] a foot-operated lever. □ *The gas pedal on her car got stuck.*
- **pedal** ['pɛdl] to move or propel something by foot, especially a bicycle. □ *Let's pedal up to the corner drugstore for an ice-cream cone.* □ *The tiny toddler was not able to pedal his new tricycle.*
- **pedal** ['pɛdl] relating to or involving a pedal. □ *That antique sewing machine is pedal-driven.*
- **peddle** ['pɛdl] to sell wares from place to place or door to door. □ *The vagrant tried to peddle small items to earn money.*
- **peddle** ['pɛdl] to seek to distribute something; to deal out something. □ *Since you can't go to the football game, why don't you try to peddle your tickets at work?*

- **petal** [ˈpɛdl, ˈpɛtl] a colorful segment of a flower's blossom. ☐ *The petal of the orchid is an unusual color.*

peddle See the main entry beginning with *pedal.*

peek See the main entry beginning with *peak.*

peel See the main entry beginning with *peal.*

peer—pier
- **peer** [pɪɚ] of equal standing with another. ☐ *A peer jury will decide the fate of the accused woman.*
- **peer** [pɪɚ] one of the ranks of the British peerage system. ☐ *Sir Arthur George is a peer of high rank.*
- **peer** [pɪɚ] a companion, friend, or age-mate. ☐ *The students will join their peer after school for a game of soccer.*
- **peer** [pɪɚ] to look carefully or curiously at something not easily discernible. ☐ *If you peer through a beach telescope in Key West, you might be able to see Cuba.*
- **pier** [pɪɚ] a vertical support between two openings. ☐ *To enlarge the room, we'll remove the center pier.*
- **pier** [pɪɚ] a structural landing place extending into water. ☐ *Fishermen can be seen fishing off the pier at any time of day.*
- **pier** [pɪɚ] a structure used to form or protect a harbor for vessels. ☐ *The long rock pier has a lighthouse on its point.*

petal See the main entry beginning with *pedal.*

phase See the main entry beginning with *faze.*

phrase See the main entry beginning with *frays.*

pi—pie
- **pi** [pɑɪ] the ratio of the circumference of a circle to its diameter. ☐ *The students were asked to memorize the formula for figuring pi.*
- **pi** [pɑɪ] the symbol denoting the ratio of a circumference of a circle to its diameter. ☐ *Helen correctly wrote the pi symbol on her math homework.*
- **pi** [pɑɪ] the sixteenth letter of the Greek alphabet. ☐ *Greek letters, such as pi, look so much different than English letters.*
- **pie** [pɑɪ] a food dish made up of a crust and such filling as fruit or meat. ☐ *The topping on the banana cream pie was stiff.*
- **pie** [pɑɪ] a cake layer sliced horizontally and filled with custard, fruit, or cream. ☐ *Tommy wanted a Boston cream pie for dessert.*
- **pie** [pɑɪ] a multi-colored animal, usually with irregular markings. ☐ *The unusually marked horse was a pie.*

pidgin—pigeon

- **pidgin** [ˈpɪdʒən] a simplified manner of speech used to communicate between people of different languages. ☐ *Where more than one language is commonly used, people often choose to speak in pidgin.*
- **pigeon** [ˈpɪdʒən] a fairly stout, usually domesticated bird resembling, but larger than, a dove. ☐ *A fake owl was set on the rooftop to discourage the local pigeon population from landing there.*
- **pigeon** [ˈpɪdʒən] a dupe; an easy mark. ☐ *The con artists thought they could find a pigeon to help carry out their scheme.*
- **pigeon** [ˈpɪdʒən] a spherical, molded shape of clay used for target shooting. ☐ *The young shooter hit every clay pigeon that was thrown into the air.*

pie See the main entry beginning with *pi.*

piece See the main entry beginning with *peace.*

pier See the main entry beginning with *peer.*

pigeon See the main entry beginning with *pidgin.*

pique See the main entry beginning with *peak.*

pistil—pistol

- **pistil** [ˈpɪstl] the part of a seed plant that bears the ovule needed for reproduction. ☐ *On some flowers the pistil is more noticeable than on others.*
- **pistol** [ˈpɪstl] a small, hand-held firearm. ☐ *She keeps a licensed pistol for personal protection.*

pistol See the main entry beginning with *pistil.*

plain—plane

- **plain** [plen] simple; unadorned. ☐ *The house is very plain both inside and out.*
- **plain** [plen] common; ordinary. ☐ *She has rather plain features.*
- **plain** [plen] evident. ☐ *It was plain that Kevin would not change his mind.*
- **plain** [plen] unobstructed. ☐ *The hotel on the hill was in plain view of the surrounding area.*
- **plain** [plen] an extensive, unbroken expanse of flat or rolling treeless countryside. ☐ *The empty plain looks bare and unwelcoming.*
- **plane** [plen] a tool used for smoothing or shaving a wood surface. ☐ *The craftsman used a small plane for his detail work.*

- **plane** [plen] to make something even, level, or smooth. ☐ *I'll plane the tabletop before sanding and restaining it.*
- **plane** [plen] a flat or level surface. ☐ *That piece of equipment must rest on a plane so it doesn't tip over.*
- **plane** [plen] an airplane. ☐ *Passengers should board the plane through gate six.*
- **plane** [plen] to skim across the water or soar on the wind. ☐ *The sailboats plane across the bay easily on windy days.*

plait—plate

- **plait** [plet] a braid made of hair, straw, or some other material. ☐ *Her long hair was arranged in an elaborate plait for the celebration.*
- **plait** [plet] to interweave or braid something. ☐ *If we plait these bundles of straw, they'll be easier to carry.*
- **plate** [plet] a flat, smooth, thin piece of material. ☐ *The surgeon placed a small steel plate in his patient's head during the operation.*
- **plate** [plet] a piece of table service. ☐ *Please do not use the cracked plate when we have guests for dinner.*
- **plate** [plet] a thin layer of a precious metal, usually gold or silver. ☐ *The serving tray had a silver plate.*
- **plate** [plet] a printing surface of some type. ☐ *Carefully arrange the items to be copied on the plate.*
- **plate** [plet] to cover or coat something with some kind of metal. ☐ *The jeweler will plate the inexpensive metal ring with gold to make it look shiny.*
- **plate** [plet] the slab of rubber behind which a baseball or softball catcher squats and next to which the batter stands. ☐ *The umpire cleaned off the plate after the runner slid in.*
- **plate** [plet] a partial denture fitting. ☐ *He wears a small upper plate.*

plane See the main entry beginning with *plain*.

plate See the main entry beginning with *plait*.

pleas—please

- **pleas** [pliz] the plural of *plea* 'in a hearing or trial, the defendant's answer to the plaintiff's charges.' ☐ *Since the defendants stood mute, pleas of "not guilty" were entered for them.*
- **pleas** [pliz] the plural of *plea* 'an appeal or entreaty.' ☐ *Nobody heeded the woman's pleas for help.*
- **please** [pliz] to give pleasure, satisfaction, or gratification to someone. ☐ *It is not hard to please Jack.*

- **please** [pliz] to be willing to do something. □ *If you would please be quiet, we can begin.*
- **please** [pliz] an expression that makes a request or command more polite. □ *Please be seated.*

please See the main entry beginning with *pleas.*

plum—plumb

- **plum** [pləm] a purplish-red, smooth-skinned fruit. □ *Mom packed a sandwich, a plum, and some cheese and crackers in my lunch.*
- **plum** [pləm] any of several trees or shrubs bearing such fruit. □ *Our trees did not bear a single plum last summer.*
- **plum** [pləm] something superior or excellent. □ *Jill's upbeat solo performance was quite the plum.*
- **plum** [pləm] the color of plums. □ *The designer suggested accenting her plum decor with forest green.*
- **plumb** [pləm] a lead weight attached to a line used to indicate vertical position. □ *The plumb showed that the window opening was slightly crooked.*
- **plumb** [pləm] straight up and down. □ *The walls need to be plumb with the ceiling.*
- **plumb** [pləm] to measure depth with a lead weight attached to a line. □ *The students are required to plumb the depths of the different soil levels.*
- **plumb** [pləm] to supply or install plumbing in something. □ *The workers will plumb the new house next week.*

plumb See the main entry beginning with *plum.*

pole—Pole—poll

- **pole** [pol] a long, slender shaft. □ *A pole is used to reach the apples in the tops of the trees.*
- **pole** [pol] the inside position on a racecourse. □ *The fastest qualifying time wins the racecar driver the pole.*
- **pole** [pol] either extremity of an axis of a sphere. □ *Neither pole of the planet Earth is inhabited by people.*
- **pole** [pol] either of two opposites. □ *His opinion on the subject takes the opposite pole from his best friend's.*
- **Pole** [pol] a person of the Polish nationality. □ *Edgar's father was a Pole and his mother a Swede.*
- **poll** [pol] the casting and recording of votes by a body of persons. □ *The final results of the poll show that neither candidate won a majority of the votes.*
- **poll** [pol] to question or canvass people randomly. □ *Some voters do not admit in an exit poll how they really voted.*

- **poll** [pol] to shear or cut hair, wool, treetops, or cattle horns. ☐ *As a safety precaution, the farmers poll all of their cattle's horns.*

poll See the main entry beginning with *pole.*

poor—pore—pour

- **poor** [pɔɚ, puɚ] having few material possessions. ☐ *As a child, he was very poor.*
- **poor** [pɔɚ, puɚ] inferior in value or quality. ☐ *An old pickup truck is a poor substitute for a luxury car when it comes to driving comfort.*
- **poor** [pɔɚ, puɚ] eliciting pity or sympathy. ☐ *I feel sorry for poor Betsy with all of her troubles.*
- **poor** [pɔɚ, puɚ] unproductive; fruitless. ☐ *This year's corn crop was very poor.*
- **pore** [poɚ] a tiny opening in the surface of a membrane through which materials pass. ☐ *An infected skin pore can be painful.*
- **pore** [poɚ] to read or study something attentively. ☐ *Mark used to pore over any book dealing with jets.*
- **pore** [poɚ] to reflect on or ponder something. ☐ *Let me pore over your suggestion before making a decision.*
- **pour** [poɚ, puɚ] to cause something to flow steadily. ☐ *Pour the milk slowly so you don't spill it.*
- **pour** [poɚ, puɚ] to produce something freely in large supply or quantity. ☐ *Most parents pour love and affection onto their children.*
- **pour** [poɚ, puɚ] to rain hard. ☐ *The weatherman said it will pour for the next three days.*

populace—populous

- **populace** ['pɑpjələs] the general population of a given locale. ☐ *The populace of any large city is in a constant state of flux.*
- **populace** ['pɑpjələs] masses of people. ☐ *A huge populace showed up to support their leader.*
- **populous** ['pɑpjələs] crowded; densely populated. ☐ *Tokyo is an excellent example of a populous city.*

populous See the main entry beginning with *populace.*

pore See the main entry beginning with *poor.*

pour See the main entry beginning with *poor.*

praise—prays—preys

- **praise** [prez] to commend, glorify, or worship someone or something. ☐ *"Let us praise the Lord for our blessings," began the minister.*

- **praise** [prez] to express a favorable opinion or evaluation of someone or something. ☐ *My boss is not afraid to praise a job well done.*
- **praise** [prez] an act of praise. ☐ *A little praise goes a long way.*
- **prays** [prez] the present tense, third person singular of *pray* 'to speak to God or a deity.' ☐ *The little girl prays every night before going to sleep.* ☐ *The couple prays that their lost son will soon be found.*
- **preys** [prez] the plural of *prey* 'an animal hunted by another for food.' ☐ *The favorite preys of wolves are deer and moose.*
- **preys** [prez] the plural of *prey* 'a target of evil; someone or something that is helpless or unable to fend off attack.' ☐ *The preys of child molesters are often young, isolated children.*
- **preys [on]** [prez] third person singular of *prey* '[for an animal] to feed on another animal as a matter of preference or habit.' ☐ *Our snake preys on mice.*
- **preys [(up)on]** [prez] third person singular of *prey* 'to take advantage of someone or something; to have an ill effect on someone or something.' ☐ *Mary always preys on my kindness.* ☐ *Pneumonia preys on people who are already weak from other illnesses.*

prays See the main entry beginning with *praise.*

precedent–president

- **precedent** ['prɛsədənt] an example, rule, or judgment that may later serve as a basis for decisions in similar cases. ☐ *In this judicial case, there is no precedent indicating how the problem might be handled.*
- **precedent** ['prɛsədənt] a prior occurrence of a similar type that provides an example. ☐ *The teacher's behavior set a precedent for her student's behavior.*
- **president** ['prɛzədənt] any presiding officer of an organization; a chief official or executive; a chief of state. ☐ *As president of the art guild, Lois has many duties and responsibilities.* ☐ *In the United States, a president is elected every four years.*

presence–presents

- **presence** ['prɛzənts] attendance. ☐ *Your presence at the hearing is required.*
- **presence** ['prɛzənts] an individual's immediate space or vicinity. ☐ *Don't talk like that in the presence of children.*

- **presence** [ˈprɛzənts] the bearing or air of a person, usually involving poise and rapport with others. ☐ *The queen has an unmistakable presence about her.*
- **presents** [ˈprɛzənts] the plural of *present* 'a gift.' ☐ *All of the presents given to him were gag gifts.*

presents See the main entry beginning with *presence.*

president See the main entry beginning with *precedent.*

preys See the main entry beginning with *praise.*

pride—pried

- **pride** [prɑɪd] the feeling, quality, or state of being proud. ☐ *Bob's parents felt a great deal of pride in his accomplishments.*
- **pride** [prɑɪd] extreme self-esteem; conceit. ☐ *Do not let foolish pride keep you from making an apology.*
- **pride** [prɑɪd] acceptable or reasonable self-respect. ☐ *She takes pride in doing her job well.*
- **pride** [prɑɪd] to indulge in the feeling, quality, or state of being proud. ☐ *They pride themselves on having the nicest lawn on the street.*
- **pride** [prɑɪd] a group [of lions]. ☐ *In a pride of lions, the females are the hunters.*
- **pried [into]** [prɑɪd] the past tense and past participle of *pry [into]* 'to delve or inquire into something.' ☐ *She always pried into other people's business.*
- **pried** [prɑɪd] the past tense and past participle of *pry* 'to open or move something with a tool.' ☐ *The thieves pried the window open with a crowbar.*
- **pried [apart]** [prɑɪd] the past tense and past participle of *pry [apart]* 'to separate people or things, usually with some difficulty.' ☐ *The principal pried the fighting boys apart.*

pried See the main entry beginning with *pride.*

pries—prize

- **pries [into]** [prɑɪz] the present tense, third person singular of *pry [into]* 'to inquire into something; to try to find out information about something.' ☐ *Jane thinks her mother pries into her personal affairs too much.* ☐ *If he pries too closely into the material, he may discover the truth.*
- **pries [open]** [prɑɪz] the present tense, third person singular of *pry [open]* 'to use a tool to open something.' ☐ *Each morning, he pries open the stuck drawer to get to his socks.*
- **prize** [prɑɪz] a reward offered to the winner of a contest or

game. □ *His prize in the hot dog-eating contest was a watermelon.*

- **prize** [prɑɪz] something very desirable. □ *The girl he has decided to marry is quite a prize.*
- **prize** [prɑɪz] to value something or someone highly. □ *Employers prize honesty as an important quality.*
- **prize** [prɑɪz] wartime bounty or booty. □ *The soldiers captured an important airstrip as a prize following the fierce fighting.*

prince–prints

- **prince** [prɪnts] a male member of a royal family, especially the son of a king or queen. □ *The prince is tutored privately at the castle.* □ *The heir to the king's throne is the eldest prince.*
- **prince** [prɪnts] a male of high esteem or regard in his profession or class. □ *Jerry is a prince of a boss.*
- **prints** [prɪnts] the plural of *print* 'a copy of a photograph or piece of artwork.' □ *The prints are ready to be picked up at the store.*
- **prints** [prɪnts] the plural of *print* 'a fingerprint.' □ *The police found Bill's prints on the doorknob.*
- **prints** [prɪnts] the present tense, third person singular of *print* 'to press inked type on paper or a similar surface; to publish in type.' □ *The newspaper only prints an early edition of the paper.* □ *His business prints facsimiles of government materials.*
- **prints** [prɪnts] the present tense, third person singular of *print* 'to write using the letters of Roman type rather than script.' □ *She never prints her name; she always writes in script.*

princes–princess

- **princes** ['prɪnsəz] the plural of *prince* 'a male member of a royal family, especially the son of a king or queen.' □ *The princes are vacationing with the queen at an exclusive resort.*
- **princes** ['prɪnsəz] the plural of *prince* 'a male who is held in high esteem by his peers.' □ *Both gentlemen were princes of kindness in the eyes of their friends.*
- **princess** ['prɪnsɛs] a female member of a royal family; the wife of a prince. □ *The princess was expected to marry nobly.* □ *The princess accompanies the prince on official state business.*
- **princess** ['prɪnsɛs] a woman known for her outstanding qualities. □ *Ann has always been a princess of graciousness.*
- **princess** ['prɪnsɛs] high-waisted. (A style of dress, gown, or blouse.) □ *The wedding gown featured a princess waistline.*

princess See the main entry beginning with *princes.*

principal—principle

- **principal** ['prɪnsəpl] most important or influential. ☐ *One of the principal characters in the story is a stray dog.*
- **principal** ['prɪnsəpl] the authoritative person in control, usually of a school. ☐ *Ms. Brown will be the new principal of the school.*
- **principal** ['prɪnsəpl] a sum of money that is loaned and upon which interest is paid and repayment is due; the main part of an estate. ☐ *The couple made monthly payments on the principal of their car loan.* ☐ *The elderly man lives on the interest of his estate and does not use the principal.*
- **principle** ['prɪnsəpl] a fundamental rule, law, or code of conduct. ☐ *Our system of justice is based on the principle of equality.*
- **principle** ['prɪnsəpl] the underlying facts of operation of nature. ☐ *This new invention is based on the principle of gravity.*

principle See the main entry beginning with *principal.*

prints See the main entry beginning with *prince.*

prize See the main entry beginning with *pries.*

profit—prophet

- **profit** ['prɑfət] a gain or return over and above an expenditure. ☐ *If you buy those stocks now, you stand to earn a nice profit in the future.*
- **profit** ['prɑfət] to benefit or gain from something. ☐ *We will all profit from our hard work.*
- **prophet** ['prɑfət] a person who tells of divinely inspired revelations or predicts the future. ☐ *Isaiah was a prophet in biblical times.*
- **prophet** ['prɑfət] a person gifted with uncommon moral and spiritual insights. ☐ *The minister was both a prophet and a great leader.*
- **prophet** ['prɑfət] a spokesperson for a cause or group. ☐ *In order for any progress to be made, a strong prophet for the cause needs to emerge.*

prophet See the main entry beginning with *profit.*

pros—prose

- **pros** [proz] the plural of *pro* 'professional.' ☐ *Two pros are available at the golf course to give you tips on your game.*
- **prose** [proz] the common, nonpoetic language of people,

either in the spoken or written form. □ *The author's prose was quite eloquent.*

- **prose** [proz] a literary style resembling that of common speech. □ *Our homework assignment included reading a selection of prose from our literature book.*

prose See the main entry beginning with *pros.*

purl See the main entry beginning with *pearl.*

Q

quarts—quartz

- **quarts** [kʍɔɚts] the plural of *quart* 'a measurement equalling one quarter of a gallon.' □ *Boil the pasta in two quarts of water.*
- **quarts** [kʍɔɚts] the plural of *quart* 'a container with the capacity of one quart.' □ *Please pick up a couple of quarts of milk at the grocery store when you come home.*
- **quartz** [kʍɔɚts] a mineral that occurs in transparent crystals and in natural crystalline masses. □ *The geology instructor brought in several samples of quartz for his class to examine.*

quartz See the main entry beginning with *quarts.*

quay See the main entry beginning with *key.*

queue See the main entry beginning with *cue.*

R

rabbet—rabbit

- **rabbet** [ˈræbɪt] a groove cut into a surface and designed to be fitted with a corresponding member to form a joint. □ *Carpenters will often use a rabbet to join two pieces of wood neatly.*
- **rabbet** [ˈræbɪt] to cut or fit a groove. □ *We need to rabbet this surface in order to get a good fit.*
- **rabbit** [ˈræbɪt] a small, long-eared mammal belonging to the hare family. □ *Sally plans to show her rabbit at the fair this summer.*
- **rabbit** [ˈræbɪt] the fur or pelt of a rabbit. □ *The jacket Mary bought is made of rabbit.*

rabbit See the main entry beginning with *rabbet.*

rack—wrack

- **rack** [ræk] a framework on or in which articles are placed, hung, or stored. □ *Lay that wet sweater on the rack rather than hanging it on the clothesline.*
- **rack** [ræk] an instrument of torture. □ *The guard used the rack to torture the prisoner.*
- **rack** [ræk] to cause acute pain, suffering, or anguish to someone or something. □ *The disease will continue to rack her weakening body.*
- **rack** [ræk] to stretch or strain something violently. □ *His violent coughs continued to rack his sore ribs.*
- **rack** [ræk] a horse's fast-moving, artificial pace. □ *The show horse must perform a series of gaits, including the rack.*
- **rack** [ræk] a cut of meat from the rib section of an animal. □ *The king served a rack of lamb at the feast.*
- **wrack** [ræk] to ruin something completely. □ *The hurricane*

will wrack the tiny island village.

- **wrack** [ræk] a shipwreck. □ *Scuba divers continued to search for the wrack on the reef.*
- **wrack** [ræk] a type of seaweed or other marine vegetation. □ *Much wrack washed up onto the shore after the storm.*
- **wrack** [ræk] the violent destruction of a vehicle, structure, or machine. □ *The wrack of the beautiful city by the typhoon was devastating.*

rail—rale

- **rail** [rel] a bar extending from one support to another that serves as a barrier or guard. □ *Use the rail along the stairs for extra support.*
- **rail** [rel] the fence that borders a racecourse. □ *The horse on the rail won the race.*
- **rail** [rel] a railroad or track. □ *Sue prefers to travel by rail rather than by air.*
- **rail** [rel] a small, marshland bird belonging to the crane family. □ *If we're lucky, we may spot a rail in the swamp.*
- **rail** [rel] to rant at or scold someone in harsh or abusive language. □ *Even after an apology, the angry man continued to rail at the sales clerk.*
- **rale** [rel] an abnormal breathing sound. □ *The doctor detected a rale in her patient's chest.*

rain—reign—rein

- **rain** [ren] falling precipitation in the form of droplets. □ *The cool, refreshing rain was a relief after the hot, windy day.*
- **rain** [ren] to fall or pour down on someone or something like rain. □ *Insult after insult continued to rain down on the unpopular speaker.*
- **rain** [ren] to deposit or bestow something abundantly. □ *Parents rain love and affection on their children.*
- **reign** [ren] to possess or exercise power or authority over someone or something. □ *Our bosses reign over everyone in the company.*
- **reign** [ren] to predominate or rule over someone or something. □ *Sometimes monarchs reign over their subjects for decades.*
- **reign** [ren] the period of influence of a monarch or sovereign. □ *The queen's reign was marred by much violence.*
- **rein** [ren] a check line on either side of a bridle or halter that is used to control an animal. □ *Pull back on the bridle rein to get control of the horse.*
- **rein** [ren] complete freedom. □ *Some parents give free rein*

to their children at an early age.

- **rein** [ren] a restraining influence. □ *A parent's control of the car keys will put a rein on any teenager's behavior.*

raise—rays—raze

- **raise** [rez] to lift or move someone or something upward. □ *Raise the hood of the car, please.*
- **raise** [rez] an increase in amount, usually in wages, salaries, bets, or bids. □ *After just six months on the job, Kurt received a raise.*
- **raise** [rez] to rouse or incite someone or something, usually to promote action. □ *If we raise a loud protest, perhaps they will listen to us.*
- **raise** [rez] to grow or cultivate someone or something. □ *Most parents raise their children carefully.* □ *The Joneses only raise cash crops.*
- **raise** [rez] to collect something. □ *Our goal is to raise $300 for a new park sign.*
- **raise** [rez] to bring something up for consideration. □ *Why does no one raise the obvious question?*
- **rays** [rez] the plural of *ray* 'a beam of light or some other radiant energy.' □ *Warm rays of sunlight shone through the forest canopy.*
- **rays** [rez] the plural of *ray* 'any line, such as a division or vein.' □ *The rays in those green leaves are dark purple.*
- **raze** [rez] to destroy or demolish something to ground level. □ *The work crew will raze the condemned building tomorrow.*
- **raze** [rez] to shave, cut, or scrape something off of something. □ *The young boy tried to raze the peach fuzz from his face.*

rale See the main entry beginning with *rail.*

rancor—ranker

- **rancor** ['ræŋkɚ, 'ræŋkɔɚ] hatred. □ *Evil thoughts and rancor seethed within the man.*
- **ranker** ['ræŋkɚ] an individual who serves or has served in the ranks, usually a commissioned officer who has been promoted. □ *As a ranker, she can identify with troops as well as officers.*

ranker See the main entry beginning with *rancor.*

rap—wrap

- **rap** [ræp] a sharp knock or blow. □ *I heard a rap on the door.*
- **rap** [ræp] a criticism; a rebuke. □ *The man offered a stinging rap to his opponent's comments.*
- **rap [on]** [ræp] to strike something suddenly or sharply. □

Rap that jar on the table to loosen the lid.

- **rap** [ræp] to arrest, retain, or charge with criminal action. (Police or underworld slang.) ☐ *The police plan to rap the suspect with the recent crimes.*
- **rap** [ræp] to perform in a rhythmic, musical style by the same name in which lyrics are spoken to a steady background beat rather than sung. ☐ *Many high school students learn to rap after school.*
- **wrap** [ræp] to enclose or bundle something or someone by enfolding or covering; to embrace someone or something. ☐ *Let's wrap ourselves in these warm blankets.* ☐ *The little boy likes to wrap his arms around his favorite stuffed bear when he goes to sleep.*
- **wrap [up]** [ræp] to completely immerse or involve someone in something. ☐ *Some people wrap themselves up completely in their work.*
- **wrap** [ræp] an outer garment, similar to a cloak, that wraps around the body. ☐ *Her wrap was a simple woolen shawl.*

rapped—rapt—wrapped

- **rapped [on]** [ræpt] the past tense and past participle of *rap [on]* 'to strike something suddenly or sharply.' ☐ *I rapped on the window until someone saw me.*
- **rapped** [ræpt] the past tense and past participle of *rap* 'to charge someone with a criminal action.' (Police or underworld slang.) ☐ *The cops rapped the vagabond with trespassing and vagrancy.*
- **rapped** [ræpt] the past tense and past participle of *rap* 'to perform in a rhythmic, musical style in which lyrics are spoken to a steady background beat.' ☐ *The musicians rapped until the wee hours of the night.*
- **rapt** [ræpt] wholly absorbed or engrossed in something or someone. ☐ *We listened to the speaker with rapt attention.*
- **wrapped** [ræpt] the past tense and past participle of *wrap* 'to enclose or bundle someone or something up by enfolding.' ☐ *I wrapped all of the gifts by myself.*
- **wrapped [around]** [ræpt] the past tense and past participle of *wrap [around]* 'to embrace or surround someone or something.' ☐ *The friends wrapped their arms around each other.*
- **wrapped [up]** [ræpt] the past tense and past participle of *wrap [up]* 'to completely immerse oneself in or involve oneself in someone or something.' ☐ *She got so wrapped up in the novel that she couldn't put it down.*

rapt See the main entry beginning with *rapped.*

rays See the main entry beginning with *raise.*

raze See the main entry beginning with *raise.*

read—red

(See also *read—reed.*)

- **read** [rɛd] the past tense and past participle of *read* 'to look at and comprehend written or printed matter.' □ *The child read at an early age.* □ *He read aloud from the morning newspaper.*
- **red** [rɛd] a color that resembles the color of blood. □ *Jackie wants to buy a red sports car.*
- **red** [rɛd] something resembling the color red. □ *His face turned red with embarrassment.*
- **red** [rɛd] a Communist. □ *The artist was once accused of being a red.*
- **red** [rɛd] a person advocating the overthrow of an existing political or social order. □ *The conservatives hoped to rid the government of every red who threatened the political system.*

read—reed

- **read** [rid] to understand or utter aloud written or printed matter. □ *Most children learn to read in first or second grade.* □ *Would you please read that part of the article again?*
- **read** [rid] to interpret the meaning of someone or something. □ *How do you read the sudden change in John's behavior?* □ *How do you read John on this matter?*
- **read** [rid] to predict or foretell something. □ *Astrologers claim to read the future by studying the stars.*
- **reed** [rid] a tall, slender grass, usually found growing in marshy areas. □ *The stem of a reed is hollow.*
- **reed** [rid] a thin, flexible slat of wood or cane fixed to the end of the mouthpiece of some musical instruments. □ *The saxophone and clarinet are two instruments that require a reed to produce sound.*
- **reed** [rid] a comblike device used to separate the yarns on a loom. □ *You must straighten the fibers using a reed before you begin weaving.*

real—reel

- **real** [ril] actual; true; authentic. □ *I saw a real giraffe at the zoo.*
- **real** [ril] something stationary, fixed, or permanent, usually land or buildings. □ *My sister deals in real estate management.*
- **real** [ril] measured by purchasing power. □ *His real income is fairly substantial.*

- **real** [ril] very. (Informal.) □ *The students were real happy when they finished their exams.*
- **reel** [ril] a device around which something is wound. □ *The reel on my fishing pole jammed when I dropped it.*
- **reel** [ril] a quantity of something wound on a reel. □ *I need a reel of cable to complete the job.*
- **reel** [ril] to wind something in or upon as if on a reel. □ *Reel the fish in close to the side of the boat so we can see it.*
- **reel** [ril] to fall or teeter backward as if from a blow. □ *The lack of oxygen made my head reel.*
- **reel** [ril] a Scottish Highland dance or the music to which it is performed. □ *The dancers kicked and stomped their feet during the lively reel.*

recede—reseed

- **recede** [rə'sid] to draw or pull back or away from something. □ *After two days at flood level, the river began to recede.*
- **recede** [rə'sid] to decrease. □ *His financial debt finally began to recede.*
- **recede** [ri'sid] to cede something back to someone. □ *The landowner decided not to recede his property to his previous tenants.*
- **reseed** ['ri'sid] to sow seed again. □ *After the heavy rain, we had to reseed the garden.* □ *Each year they reseed their winter wheat field.* □ *Some fields naturally reseed themselves.*

receipt—reseat

- **receipt** [rɪ'sit] the act of receiving. □ *You will be paid upon the receipt of the signed contract.*
- **receipt** [rɪ'sit] a written acknowledgement of items or goods received. □ *Bring your receipt if you must return an item to the store.*
- **receipt** [rɪ'sit] to mark something as paid. □ *I will receipt the invoice when I receive the payment.*
- **reseat** ['ri'sit] to seat someone again. □ *The ushers were asked to reseat the audience following the false fire alarm.*
- **reseat** ['ri'sit] to reinstall someone in an office or seat of dignity. □ *The council will reseat its chairperson following his long illness.*
- **reseat** ['ri'sit] to repair or replace the seat of something. □ *It will be necessary to reseat four of the antique chairs we purchased at the auction.*

red See the main entry beginning with *read.*

reed See the main entry beginning with *read.*

reel See the main entry beginning with *real.*

reign See the main entry beginning with *rain.*

rein See the main entry beginning with *rain.*

reseat See the main entry beginning with *receipt.*

reseed See the main entry beginning with *recede.*

residence—residents

- **residence** [ˈrɛzədənts] the place where a person resides or lives. ☐ *You must list your permanent residence on the application form.*
- **residence** [ˈrɛzədənts] a dwelling. ☐ *The police discovered the residence of the suspect was empty.*
- **residence** [ˈrɛzədənts] the period of time one dwells in a location for the fulfillment of duty or to receive a benefit. ☐ *Members of Congress must establish residence in their home districts.*
- **residence** [ˈrɛzədənts] a period for study, research, practice, or teaching of medicine. ☐ *The doctor will serve her residence at a local hospital.*
- **residents** [ˈrɛzədənts] the plural of *resident* 'someone who lives in a place.' ☐ *The residents of that house are rarely at home.*
- **residents** [ˈrɛzədənts] the plural of *resident* 'a doctor who is going through a period for study, research, practice, or teaching.' ☐ *The young residents correctly diagnosed the patient's illness.*

residents See the main entry beginning with *residence.*

rest—wrest

- **rest** [rɛst] to repose in sleep or relaxation. ☐ *I think I'll rest after that vigorous walk.*
- **rest** [rɛst] a place for resting or lodging. ☐ *My aunt's cat uses her mantle as a rest.*
- **rest** [rɛst] peace of mind or spirit. ☐ *He won't have any rest until he knows whether he passed his exams.*
- **rest** [rɛst] to bring something to an end. ☐ *Let's just let that unlikely idea rest.*
- **rest** [rɛst] remains; leftovers. ☐ *Put the rest of the food in the refrigerator.*
- **rest** [rɛst] a rhythmic silence in music. ☐ *The drummer ignored the rest and continued playing.*
- **wrest** [rɛst] to take something or someone forcibly; to gain something with difficulty. ☐ *The prince was unable to wrest*

power from the king. □ *The officers had to wrest the gun from the attacker.*

- **wrest** [rɛst] to change the significance or truth of something. □ *Joan tends to wrest the truth when making excuses for herself.*

retch—wretch

- **retch** [rɛtʃ] to vomit; to try to vomit. □ *The grisly sight made me retch.*
- **wretch** [rɛtʃ] a miserable, unfortunate person; an outcast or vile individual. □ *The poor wretch had no job or means of support.* □ *In the movie, the villian was a terrible wretch.*

review—revue

- **review** [rɪ'vju] to look over, inspect, or survey something. □ *Let's review the results of the questionnaire.*
- **review** [rɪ'vju] to examine something again. □ *Be sure to review all of the course material before taking the final exam.*
- **review** [rɪ'vju] a critical evaluation of a movie, book, or play. □ *The off-Broadway play did not receive a very favorable review.*
- **review** [rɪ'vju] a judicial examination. □ *The appeals court has agreed to a review of that particular case.*
- **review** [rɪ'vju] a magazine devoted chiefly to reviews. □ *The monthly business review has increased its readership recently.*
- **revue** [rɪ'vju] a theater production comprised of short songs, dances, and comic sketches. □ *Audiences were excited about the rollicking revue.*

revue See the main entry beginning with *review.*

rigger—rigor

- **rigger** ['rɪgɚ] a specialized, sable brush used in painting portraits or pictures. □ *As a portrait artist, Maggie must periodically replace her rigger with a new one.*
- **rigger** ['rɪgɚ] a ship with a specific rig setup. □ *The square-rigger sailed serenely in the calm seas.*
- **rigger** ['rɪgɚ] a person who fits, arranges, or sets up something. □ *The house alarm is so complicated that the company sends a rigger to install it for the customer.*
- **rigor** ['rɪgɚ] strictness; severity. □ *The father of that family rules with rigor.*
- **rigor** ['rɪgɚ] stiffness; rigidity. □ *The rigor of the old woman's muscles makes stairs difficult to climb.*
- **rigor** ['rɪgɚ] inflexibility of judgment, opinion, or temperament. □ *All of the rigor of his younger days disappeared as he mellowed with age.*

- **rigor** [ˈrɪgɚ] a situation or condition that makes life difficult. □ *The rigor of Marie's lifestyle finally took its toll on her health.*

right—rite—wright—write

- **right** [rɑɪt] correct; appropriate. □ *Please wear the right type of clothing on the camping trip.* □ *I finally had to admit that you were right.*
- **right** [rɑɪt] righteous. □ *He is a right and honorable man.*
- **right** [rɑɪt] genuine. □ *Make sure the antiques you purchase are right and are not reproductions.*
- **right** [rɑɪt] to justify or change something that is wrong. □ *It is too late to right the damage that has been done.*
- **right** [rɑɪt] a direction that is opposite of left. □ *Turn right at the next traffic light.*
- **rite** [rɑɪt] ceremony; a precise manner of carrying out a ceremonial tradition. □ *The priest will perform the rite of baptism at the church this morning.*
- **wright** [rɑɪt] someone who makes or repairs certain things. (Usually seen in compounds such as *wheelwright* and *shipwright*.) □ *Grandpa looked all over the county for a wheelwright who could fix up the old buggy.*
- **write** [rɑɪt] to draw up, author, or compose something in writing. □ *The author hopes to write a biography about that famous sculptor.* □ *Sue can write very poetic phrases.*

rigor See the main entry beginning with *rigger*.

ring—wring

- **ring** [rɪŋ] a circular band used to pull, hold, or hang something. □ *I keep my keys on a big ring so I don't lose any of them.*
- **ring** [rɪŋ] a piece of jewelry worn on the finger. □ *Tom gave Ann an engagement ring on Thanksgiving Day.*
- **ring** [rɪŋ] a circular form or shape. □ *The glass of iced tea left a water ring on the tabletop.*
- **ring** [rɪŋ] an arena where boxing matches take place. □ *The audience applauded as the two boxers entered the ring.*
- **ring** [rɪŋ] to form or place a ring around something. □ *We'll ring the base of the tree with flowers.*
- **ring** [rɪŋ] a clear, resonant sound. □ *The teenager ran quickly to the phone when she heard a ring.*
- **ring** [rɪŋ] to make a clear, resonant sound. □ *When I tried to ring the doorbell, I discovered it didn't work.*
- **ring** [rɪŋ] a telephone call. □ *I'll give you a ring as soon as I get home.*

- **wring** [rɪŋ] to twist or squeeze something in order to extract moisture or liquid. □ *Wring the water from your socks after you take them off.*
- **wring** [rɪŋ] to obtain or acquire something by coercion or violence. □ *The nasty cop tried to wring a confession from the innocent man.*
- **wring** [rɪŋ] to twist the hands together in an expression of grief or anguish. □ *Her mother used to wring her hands whenever she was upset.*
- **wring** [rɪŋ] to shake hands vigorously. □ *Why must he always wring everyone's hands so hard?*
- **wring** [rɪŋ] to contort something by twisting. □ *Did your mother ever tell you that she would wring your neck if you misbehaved?*

rite See the main entry beginning with *right.*

road—rode—rowed

- **road** [rod] an open pathway for vehicles, people, and animals. □ *The rural road is a very scenic drive.*
- **road** [rod] a somewhat protected anchorage place for ships and boats. □ *Lahaina road was a favorite port for early visitors to the island of Maui.*
- **rode** [rod] the past tense of *ride* 'to travel in or on something.' □ *Jane rode the bus to work for years.*
- **rode** [rod] the past tense of *ride* 'to be sustained by something; to continue something without interference.' □ *The candidate rode a wave of popularity during his campaign.* □ *The team rode all the way to the championship.*
- **rode** [rod] the past tense of *ride* 'to nag, tease, or harass someone.' □ *Jane continually rode her husband about his poor golf game.*
- **rowed** [rod] the past tense and past participle of *row* 'to propel a boat by using oars.' □ *We rowed across the lake against the wind.*
- **rowed** [rod] the past tense and past participle of *row* 'to form someone's hair into rows.' □ *The hair stylist rowed her client's hair.*

rode See the main entry beginning with *road.*

roe—row

- **roe** [ro] the eggs of fish. □ *The roe of sturgeon is known as caviar.*
- **roe** [ro] a speckled figure sometimes seen in sawn lumber. □ *The lumber buyer would not buy any wood containing a roe.*

- **row** [ro] to propel a boat by using oars. ☐ *If you don't want to row, we can use the outboard motor.*
- **row** [ro] to form something into rows. ☐ *Be careful how you row the vegetable plants in the garden.*
- **row** [ro] a number of objects in a sequence or series. ☐ *Each row of desks was neatly aligned in the classroom.*
- **row** [ro] a street occupied by a specific kind of enterprise. ☐ *They live in a row of homes in the new development area.*

roes—rose—rows

(See also *rouse—rows.*)

- **roes** [roz] the plural of *roe* 'the eggs of fish.' ☐ *Roes are usually either red, yellow, or black and are often eaten in Japanese restaurants.*
- **roes** [roz] the plural of *roe* 'a speckled figure sometimes seen in sawn lumber.' ☐ *Because of so many roes in that wood, the sawmill decided to discount its price.*
- **rose** [roz] the fragrant blossom of a shrub with thorny stems by the same name. ☐ *Be sure to cover the rose during the winter.* ☐ *On her birthday, Katie's husband gave her a single sweetheart rose.*
- **rose** [roz] a cut of gemstone that resembles a rose. ☐ *The ring contained a single rose garnet.*
- **rose** [roz] resembling a rose in shape, fragrance, or color. ☐ *Mother always wears rose perfume.* ☐ *She wore a rose dress to the party.*
- **rose** [roz] the past tense of *rise* 'to elevate oneself or itself; to ascend.' ☐ *He rose slowly from his comfortable chair.*
- **rows** [roz] the plural of *row* 'a number of objects in a straight line.' ☐ *The new cars stood in long rows on the factory lot.* ☐ *Rows of commercial buildings make up the business district.*
- **rows** [roz] the present tense, third person singular of *row* 'to propel a boat by using oars.' ☐ *The avid fisherman rows around the entire pond every afternoon.*

roil—royal

- **roil** [roɪl] to disturb or rile someone. ☐ *Don't roil your brother by nagging at him.*
- **roil** [roɪl] to stir up or move something about violently. ☐ *The floodwaters will no doubt roil the sediment at the mouth of the river.*
- **royal** [roɪl] of noble ancestry; relating to the crown. ☐ *Mark comes from a royal family.* ☐ *The royal couple will attend the parade.*
- **royal** [roɪl] of great magnitude, quality, or size. (Colloquial.)

☐ *"I have a royal headache," moaned Liz.*

- **royal** [roɪl] a male deer of at least eight years that has an antler configuration of at least twelve points. ☐ *We saw a magnificent royal on the mountainside.*
- **royal** [roɪl] a shade of bright purplish-blue. ☐ *His royal shirt was very handsome.*

role–roll

- **role** [rol] a part played by a singer or actor. ☐ *Her role in the play was a minor one.*
- **role** [rol] a function. ☐ *We'll never know for sure what role he played in the discovery.*
- **roll** [rol] a scroll. ☐ *The messenger handed the roll to the king.*
- **roll** [rol] a list of names. ☐ *Before we begin, let me call roll.*
- **roll** [rol] something formed into the shape of a roll. ☐ *Jessie had a roll of dollar bills in his pocket.*
- **roll** [rol] to cause someone or something to move forward by turning over and over. ☐ *It is easier to roll an object down a hill than to carry it.*
- **roll** [rol] to rob a person by pilfering his or her pockets. ☐ *Someone entered the dormitory room and tried to roll the occupants while they slept.*
- **roll** [rol] to travel along something. ☐ *I like the sound of trains as they roll along the tracks.*
- **roll** [rol] a sound of sustained, rapid drumbeats. ☐ *The drummer was required to perform a long roll during the march.*

roll See the main entry beginning with *role.*

rose See the main entry beginning with *roes.*

rote–wrote

- **rote** [rot] the use of memory with little understanding or intelligence. ☐ *Learning by rote is not the best way to learn.*
- **rote** [rot] an automatic or mechanical repetition or routine involving little thought. ☐ *Through shear rote Daniel was able to clean his apartment even though he had the flu.*
- **wrote** [rot] the past tense of *write* 'to spell out words, usually on paper.' ☐ *Mike wrote the alphabet on the blackboard.* ☐ *Dad wrote us a letter to tell us the time his plane would arrive.*

rough–ruff

- **rough** [rəf] coarse or irregular. ☐ *The dog has a rough coat.*
- **rough** [rəf] wild; turbulent. ☐ *We had a rough flight over the mountains.*

- **rough** [rəf] taxing; difficult. □ *The orphan had a rough childhood.*
- **rough** [rəf] crude; unrefined; something in a preliminary or unfinished state. □ *Jane's manners are a little rough.* □ *A rough copy of that report is due by noon.*
- **rough** [rəf] the brushy, uneven area bordering a golf fairway. □ *Bob hit the ball into the rough between the sand traps.*
- **rough** [rəf] to maul or manhandle someone or something. □ *The thug tried to rough up and frighten the old man.*
- **rough** [rəf] a freshwater perch found in Europe. □ *The restaurant serves a tasty rough every Wednesday night.*
- **ruff** [rəf] the hair or feathers around the neck of an animal. □ *The dark red dog has a ruff of thick golden hair.*
- **ruff** [rəf] a stiff, pleated collar worn by women and men in the 1500's and 1600's. □ *The Elizabethan actor looked uncomfortable in the starched ruff.*

rouse—rows

(See also *roes—rose—rows.*)

- **rouse** [rɑʊz] to wake someone or something from slumber or repose. □ *It is very difficult to rouse someone from a deep sleep.*
- **rouse** [rɑʊz] to stir up or excite someone or something. □ *The mob's leader tried to rouse his followers into action.*
- **rows** [rɑʊz] the plural of *row* 'a loud quarrel or argument.' □ *Police were called to the couple's residence because of the noisy rows.*

rout—route

- **rout** [rɑʊt] a disorderly retreat. □ *During the rout, the soldiers fled in all directions.*
- **rout** [rɑʊt] a state of wild confusion. □ *There was a rout as both baseball teams cleared the benches.*
- **rout** [rɑʊt] a disastrous defeat. □ *The game ended in a rout for the home team.*
- **rout** [rɑʊt] a disturbance; a riot. □ *Someone reported a rout in the apartment building late last night.*
- **rout** [rɑʊt] to defeat someone or something decisively. □ *The commander told his troops they would surely rout the enemy.*
- **rout** [rɑʊt] to cut an edge or groove in a surface. □ *Carpenters often rout decorative edges on furniture.*
- **rout** [rɑʊt] to dig up or discover something. □ *Let's see if you can rout the truth about what really happened.*
- **rout** [rɑʊt] to search something awkwardly; to rummage something. □ *If we rout the room, we may destroy valuable evidence.* □ *Rout around in the drawer for some scissors.*

- **route** [rɑʊt, rut] a course or territory to be covered; an established passage for travel. □ *The girl's paper route covers several neighborhoods.* □ *The route I take to work is always busy in the morning.*
- **route** [rɑʊt, rut] to cause something or someone to take a specific direction or path. □ *The detour will route traffic away from the road repair area.*

route See the main entry beginning with *rout.*

row See the main entry beginning with *roe.*

rowed See the main entry beginning with *road.*

rows See the main entry beginning with *roes* and the main entry beginning with *rouse.*

royal See the main entry beginning with *roil.*

rude—rued

- **rude** [rud] lacking refinement or tact; offensive in action or manner. □ *His supervisor is a rude person.* □ *The supervisor's rude comments offended many employees.*
- **rued** [rud] the past tense and past participle of *rue* 'to feel sorrow or regret about something.' (Almost always in the expression *rue the day.*) □ *As a lonely millionaire, John rued the day he wished for fame and fortune.*

rued See the main entry beginning with *rude.*

ruff See the main entry beginning with *rough.*

rung—wrung

- **rung** [rəŋ] a crosspiece of a ladder. □ *Don't use that ladder until the cracked rung is replaced.*
- **rung** [rəŋ] a stage or degree of ascent. □ *He eventually reached the top rung in the corporation.*
- **rung** [rəŋ] a spoke of a wheel. □ *A rung in the front wheel is bent.*
- **rung** [rəŋ] a connecting support in the legs of a chair. □ *Is it possible to replace a broken rung in a chair?*
- **rung** [rəŋ] the past participle of *ring* 'to make a clear, musical sound, by striking metal or glass.' □ *The alarm had rung loudly for many minutes before Bill turned it off.*
- **rung** [rəŋ] the past participle of *ring* 'to place a telephone call.' □ *The telephone operator has rung the number repeatedly.*
- **wrung [out]** [rəŋ] the past participle of *wring [out]* 'to twist or squeeze something to extract moisture.' □ *I had wrung the*

wet clothing out before hanging it on the clothesline.

- **wrung** [rəŋ] the past participle of *wring* 'to twist one's hands together in grief or anguish.' ☐ *When first confronted with the bad news, he had wrung his hands, but now he is calmer.*
- **wrung** [rəŋ] the past participle of *wring* 'to grasp and shake someone's hand vigorously.' ☐ *It seems the politician had wrung the hands of everyone in town.*
- **wrung** [rəŋ] the past participle of *wring* 'to twist.' ☐ *He had wrung the necks of the three chickens in preparation for the big chicken dinner.*

rye—wry

- **rye** [rɑɪ] a hardy grain used for cereal or grown for cover. ☐ *Most of the farmland is planted in barley and rye.*
- **wry** [rɑɪ] cleverly humorous, often with a grim or ironic twist. ☐ *Tom has a wry sense of humor.*
- **wry** [rɑɪ] made with facial contortions. ☐ *His wry smile made me suspicious.*
- **wry** [rɑɪ] marked by impropriety. ☐ *None of us appreciated her pointed, wry comments.*

S

sac—sack

- **sac** [sæk] a pouch containing fluid inside a plant or animal. □ *Among seahorses, the male carries the egg sac containing the young.*
- **sack** [sæk] a container made of paper or other material that is used to carry items. □ *I carried my groceries home in a sack.*
- **sack** [sæk] a loose-fitting style of coat or dress. □ *The sack was once a very popular dress style.*
- **sack** [sæk] dismissal. □ *After working for the company for ten years, his sack was totally unexpected.*
- **sack** [sæk] to plunder or loot something after capture. □ *The soldiers continued to sack the city for days.*
- **sack** [sæk] to put something into a sack. □ *Will you help me sack these groceries?*
- **sack** [sæk] to fire or let someone go. □ *Most employers don't like to sack faithful workers in bad times.*

sack See the main entry beginning with *sac.*

sacks—sax

- **sacks** [sæks] the plural of *sack* 'a container made of paper or other material.' □ *Put all of the empty sacks in the cupboard.*
- **sacks** [sæks] the plural of *sack* 'a loose-fitting style of coat or dress.' □ *The models wore sacks of various colors over their dresses.*
- **sacks** [sæks] the present tense, third person singular of *sack* 'to plunder or loot something after capture.' □ *The platoon sacks each city that it conquers.*
- **sacks** [sæks] the present tense, third person singular of *sack* 'to pack things into a sack.' □ *Bob sacks groceries after school*

and on weekends.

- **sacks** [sæks] the present tense, third person singular of *sack* 'to dismiss someone from employment.' ☐ *If your company sacks you, file a complaint immediately.*
- **sax** [sæks] a saxophone. ☐ *A sax is an essential part of a jazz band.*

sail—sale

- **sail** [sel] an expanse of fabric hoisted above sailing vessels to catch the wind and propel the ships through water. ☐ *Due to the heavy seas and high winds, the main sail tore.*
- **sail** [sel] to travel aboard a vessel propelled by the wind. ☐ *The couple wanted to sail from Florida to Bermuda.*
- **sail** [sel] to glide through something without much effort. ☐ *Henry hoped to sail through his interview and get the job without any problems.*
- **sale** [sel] the act of selling something or transferring ownership of something from one person to another. ☐ *The sale of our home was completed quickly.*
- **sale** [sel] the disposal of items at bargain prices. ☐ *The department store sale will last through the weekend.*
- **sale** [sel] the availability of something for purchase. ☐ *His tractor is not for sale.*
- **sale** [sel] gross receipts. ☐ *The total month's sale was above average.*

sale See the main entry beginning with *sail.*

sane—seine

- **sane** [sen] mentally sound or stable. ☐ *The accused man was declared sane and capable of standing trial.*
- **seine** [sen] a large, weighted net with floats on one side designed to drag through water and catch fish. ☐ *We tried to catch minnows in the stream by using a large seine.*
- **seine** [sen] to fish or catch something with a seine. ☐ *Terry wanted to seine the pond in hopes of catching the big bass.*

saver—savor

- **saver** ['sevɚ] a person who collects and keeps something. ☐ *Bernice is a compulsive saver of food coupons.*
- **saver** ['sevɚ] a person who rescues someone or something from harm. ☐ *Mr. Smith is known as a saver of lost or injured animals.*
- **savor** ['sevɚ] to relish or delight in something. ☐ *The smell of the first campfire of the season is an odor to savor.*
- **savor** ['sevɚ] to smell or taste something with great pleasure.

☐ *Mary likes to savor her first cup of coffee of the morning.*

- **savor** ['sevɚ] a distinctive smell or flavor. ☐ *Vintage wine has a unique savor all its own.*

savor See the main entry beginning with *saver.*

sax See the main entry beginning with *sacks.*

scene—seen

- **scene** [sin] the site of an action or occurrence. ☐ *The scene of the accident was secured by police.*
- **scene** [sin] a stage setting. ☐ *During the play, the scene was darkened to create a feeling of the unknown.*
- **scene** [sin] a division of a theatrical performance. ☐ *She does not appear in the play until the third scene.*
- **scene** [sin] a display of inappropriate behavior or anger. ☐ *The angry customer made quite a scene.*
- **seen** [sin] the past participle of *see* 'to visualize someone or something.' ☐ *In her mind she has seen the man of her dreams.*
- **seen** [sin] the past participle of *see* 'to understand something.' ☐ *We have seen the value of saving money.*
- **seen** [sin] the past participle of *see* 'to perceive someone or something with the eye.' ☐ *I have never seen him look so happy in his whole life.*
- **seen** [sin] the past participle of *see* 'to examine or watch someone or something.' ☐ *The investigators have seen all of the evidence.*
- **seen [to]** [sin] the past participle of *see [to]* 'to escort or accompany someone to a place.' ☐ *The volunteers have seen each of the patients safely to his room.*

scent See the main entry beginning with *cent.*

scents See the main entry beginning with *cents.*

scull—skull

- **scull** [skəl] a type of oar used at the stern or back of a boat to move it forward. ☐ *The scull accidentally fell into the water.*
- **scull** [skəl] a racing boat propelled by sculls. ☐ *A great deal of strength is needed to man a racing scull.*
- **scull** [skəl] to propel a boat using a scull or large oar. ☐ *The plan was to scull the vessel rather than use its motor.*
- **skull** [skəl] the skeleton of the head of a vertebrate that encloses and protects the brain. ☐ *Workmen uncovered the skull of a large mammal at the building site.*
- **skull** [skəl] a mind. ☐ *Try to get this message into your skull.*

sea—see

- **sea** [si] the body of saltwater covering most of the earth's surface; a large body of saltwater that is not quite landlocked. ☐ *Not all fish can live in the sea.* ☐ *The sea is surrounded on three sides by land.*
- **sea** [si] a motion or rough disturbance on the surface of a large body of water. ☐ *The brisk wind and fairly calm sea made for ideal sailing conditions.*
- **see** [si] to visualize something or someone. ☐ *I can see trouble brewing.*
- **see** [si] to understand something. ☐ *Susan did not see the point he was trying to make.*
- **see** [si] to perceive someone or something. ☐ *We could see storm clouds forming on the horizon.*
- **see** [si] to examine or watch someone or something. ☐ *Wait and see what develops.*
- **see** [si] to escort or accompany someone or something to some place. ☐ *The boys promised to see their dates home.*

sealing See the main entry beginning with *ceiling.*

seam—seem

- **seam** [sim] a joint where two pieces of fabric are sewn together. ☐ *A seam on my new blouse came apart.*
- **seam** [sim] to stitch two pieces of fabric together. ☐ *He will seam the torn tent flap.*
- **seam** [sim] a ridge, line, or groove formed by the joining of edges. ☐ *I felt every seam in the bumpy road.*
- **seam** [sim] a thin layer of mineral between two distinctive layers of earth. ☐ *A seam of silver runs through the bedrock.*
- **seem** [sim] to appear; to give evidence of the existence or presence of someone or something. ☐ *The new nurses seem to enjoy their hard work.* ☐ *There doesn't seem to be anyone here.*

seas—sees—seize

- **seas** [siz] the plural of *sea* 'a body of saltwater.' ☐ *The seas near the arctic are cold and rough.* ☐ *Three different seas surround the country of Greece.*
- **seas** [siz] the plural of *sea* 'the surface conditions of a large body of water.' ☐ *The ship's captain alerted the crew to the rough seas ahead.*
- **sees** [siz] the present tense, third person singular of *see* 'to visualize something.' ☐ *Jane sees her future goals as being attainable.*
- **sees** [siz] the present tense, third person singular of *see* 'to

understand something.' □ *Mother sees the value of teaching her children to be independent.*

- **sees** [siz] the present tense, third person singular of *see* 'to perceive someone or something with the eye.' □ *Larry awakens early and sees the sun rise each day.*
- **sees** [siz] the present tense, third person singular of *see* 'to make sure that something is done.' □ *The bus driver sees that the children get off the bus safely.*
- **sees [to]** [siz] the present tense, third person singular of *see [to]* 'to escort someone to some place.' □ *The butler sees all visitors to the door when they leave.*
- **seize** [siz] to grasp someone or something; to take something by force. □ *The military will someday try to seize control of the government.* □ *I wanted to seize her arm so we could talk.*
- **seize** [siz] to capture someone or something. □ *The troops tried without success to seize a truck convoy.*
- **seize** [siz] to take over one's mind completely. □ *Try not to let jealousy seize your mind.*

sects—sex

- **sects** [sɛkts] the plural of *sect* 'a religious denomination.' □ *Many different sects were represented at the religious conference.*
- **sects** [sɛkts] the plural of *sect* 'a party, cult, or faction.' □ *The leaders of those sects demand total obedience from their followers.*
- **sex** [sɛks] either of the two sexual divisions of organisms, male or female. □ *The expectant parents did not wish to know the sex of their unborn child.*
- **sex** [sɛks] pertaining to sexual phenomena or behavior. □ *The sex offender was sent to prison.*
- **sex** [sɛks] to determine the sex of some creature. □ *His job at the chicken hatchery is to sex newly hatched chicks.*

see See the main entry beginning with *sea.*

seed See the main entry beginning with *cede.*

seeder See the main entry beginning with *cedar.*

seem See the main entry beginning with *seam.*

seen See the main entry beginning with *scene.*

sees See the main entry beginning with *seas.*

seine See the main entry beginning with *sane.*

seize See the main entry beginning with *seas.*

sell See the main entry beginning with *cell.*

seller See the main entry beginning with *cellar.*

sense See the main entry beginning with *cents.*

senses See the main entry beginning with *census.*

sensor See the main entry beginning with *censer.*

sensual—sensuous
- **sensual** ['sɛnʃul] having to do with physical or sexual satisfaction. □ *The exotic dance was very sensual in nature.*
- **sensuous** ['sɛnʃuəs] having to do with the senses. □ *Walking through the field of wildflowers was a sensuous delight.*

sensuous See the main entry beginning with *sensual.*

sent See the main entry beginning with *cent.*

serf—surf
- **serf** [sɚf] a member of the peasant class bound to the land and subject to the will of the owner or overseer in a feudal society. □ *Each serf was allowed to keep a portion of the crops he grew.*
- **surf** [sɚf] the swell, foam, splash, or sound of breaking waves upon a shore. □ *The sound of the surf lulled me to sleep.*
- **surf** [sɚf] to ride the waves. □ *Curt learned to surf while visiting relatives in California.*

serial See the main entry beginning with *cereal.*

session See the main entry beginning with *cession.*

set—sit
- **set** [sɛt] to place something onto something. □ *Would you please set this vase on the mantel?*
- **sit** [sɪt] to rest on one's buttocks, as in a chair. □ *Please sit over there.*

sew—so—sow
- **sew** [so] to stitch or hold something together using needle and thread. □ *Sew that loose button on the shirt before it falls off.*
- **so** [so] as indicated or suggested. □ *Dad gave us an idea about how to handle the problem, and we agreed to do so.*
- **so** [so] therefore. □ *That is a silly plan, so let's forget about it.*
- **so** [so] conforming to actual facts. □ *Lisa said certain things that were not so.*

- **so** [so] very; to a great degree. □ *Jeff's job promotion made him so happy that he took his family out to dinner.*
- **sow** [so] to plant with seed. □ *Farmers sow winter wheat in the fall.*
- **sow** [so] to set something into motion. □ *Mike will try to sow the plans needed to get the project underway.*

sex See the main entry beginning with *sects.*

shall—will

- **shall** [ʃæl] in the future. (A form used with the first person, *I* or *we* in formal speech or writing.) □ *I shall consider your idea carefully.* □ *We shall try not to be late.*
- **will** [wɪl] in the future. (A form used with all three persons *I, we; you;* or *he, she, it, they* except in formal speech or writing.) □ *I will have your report finished by noon.* □ *You will be reimbursed for the lost article.* □ *They will no longer work here after June.*
- **will** [wɪl] determination; resolve. □ *Where there's a will there's a way.*
- **will** [wɪl] a legal document that specifies how one's property is disposed of after one's death. □ *My grandfather mentioned me in his will, but there was nothing left of the estate after the lawyers and the tax people took what was theirs.*

shear—sheer

- **shear** [ʃiɚ] to cut, shave, or clip something, usually hair or wool. □ *Many farmers must shear their own lambs and sheep.*
- **shear** [ʃiɚ] to cut something with something sharp. □ *A good knife can shear even the toughest pieces of meat.*
- **shear** [ʃiɚ] a scissors or cutting tool. □ *I need to have my sewing shear sharpened.*
- **sheer** [ʃiɚ] pure, complete, or utter. □ *People bungee jump for sheer excitement.* □ *It was sheer luck that they met after so many years.*
- **sheer** [ʃiɚ] transparent; filmy. □ *The costume was made from a sheer fabric.*
- **sheer** [ʃiɚ] to swerve suddenly or change course. □ *The sudden appearance of the mountaintop caused the pilot to sheer to his left.*

sheer See the main entry beginning with *shear.*

sheik See the main entry beginning with *chic.*

shoe—shoo

- **shoe** [ʃu] an article of footwear. □ *The toddler put his shoe* *on the wrong foot.*

- **shoe** [ʃu] something resembling a shoe. ☐ *The shoe on the sled runner is rusted.*
- **shoe** [ʃu] a device that controls, slows, or stops the motion of some object. ☐ *One brake shoe on the car has gone bad.*
- **shoe** [ʃu] to provide or fit someone or something with a shoe. ☐ *Those blacksmiths travel around to farms to shoe any horses needing new horseshoes.*
- **shoo** [ʃu] to brush, scare, or send someone or something away. ☐ *Shoo those flies away from the freshly baked pies.*

shone—shown

- **shone** [ʃon] the past tense and past participle of *shine* 'to give off rays of light.' ☐ *The sun shone after the rainstorm.*
- **shone** [ʃon] the past tense and past participle of *shine* 'to be bright and luminous.' ☐ *His eyes shone brightly as he stepped forward to receive his award.*
- **shone** [ʃon] the past tense and past participle of *shine* 'to be distinguished or eminent.' ☐ *Her career as an educator shone above all of her peers.*
- **shown** [ʃon] the past participle of *show* 'to exhibit something; to demonstrate something.' ☐ *That house has been shown by several different real estate agents.* ☐ *Nancy has shown her crafts at various local shows.*

shoo See the main entry beginning with *shoe.*

shoot See the main entry beginning with *chute.*

shown See the main entry beginning with *shone.*

side—sighed

- **side** [saɪd] the left or right edge of the body. ☐ *The left side of her body was affected by the stroke.* ☐ *I prefer to sleep on my side.*
- **side** [saɪd] a space or place in relation to the center of something. ☐ *Put the book on the left side of the shelf.*
- **side** [saɪd] an outer edge or boundary. ☐ *Players must remain at the side of the field when not in the game.*
- **side** [saɪd] an activity or attitude of one body or persons with regard to another. ☐ *My mother's side of the family has brown eyes.*
- **side** [saɪd] to support or agree with someone or something. ☐ *I refuse to side with either of the quarrelers.*
- **side** [saɪd] to furnish something with sides or siding. ☐ *Our neighbors want to side their house with a bright color.*

- **sighed** [saɪd] the past tense and past participle of *sigh* 'to emit a drawn-out, audible breath.' ☐ *The weary woman sighed after a long day's work.*
- **sighed** [saɪd] the past tense and past participle of *sigh* 'to say something with a drawn-out, audible breath.' ☐ *"How much farther do we have to go?" sighed the tired child.*

sighed See the main entry beginning with *side.*

sighs—size

- **sighs** [saɪz] the plural of *sigh* 'a drawn-out, audible breath.' ☐ *After the tense situation ended, people gave many sighs of relief.*
- **sighs** [saɪz] the present tense, third person singular of *sigh* 'to utter a drawn-out, audible breath.' ☐ *Her father always sighs when puzzled.*
- **size** [saɪz] a physical measurement or dimension. ☐ *Because of Tom's immense size, several pro teams were interested in recruiting him as a blocker.*
- **size** [saɪz] a series of graduated measures. ☐ *He wears a large size in clothing.*
- **size** [saɪz] actual state or condition. ☐ *We cannot alter the size of the circumstances.*
- **size** [saɪz] to make a judgment of something or someone. ☐ *"How do you size up this situation?" asked Jim.*
- **size** [saɪz] to arrange or classify something by size. ☐ *The grocer has to size all of the oranges before he can price them.*
- **size** [saɪz] to stiffen something, usually with starch. ☐ *The dry cleaners will size your shirts if you request it.*

sight See the main entry beginning with *cite.*

sign—sine

- **sign** [saɪn] a signal, motion, or gesture indicating some thought. ☐ *The referee gave the sign for the game to begin.*
- **sign** [saɪn] a placard or lettered board used to display advertising or information. ☐ *The highway sign was visible at night.*
- **sign** [saɪn] one of the twelve divisions of the zodiac. ☐ *Jerry was born under the sign of Leo.*
- **sign** [saɪn] to communicate manually with sign language. ☐ *The deaf woman never learned to sign.*
- **sign** [saɪn] to place one's signature on formal written matter. ☐ *Please sign on the bottom line.*
- **sine** [saɪn] a mathematical function in trigonometry dealing with angles. ☐ *The math student was unable to figure the sine of the diagram.*

sine See the main entry beginning with *sign.*

sit See the main entry beginning with *set.*

site See the main entry beginning with *cite.*

size See the main entry beginning with *sighs.*

skull See the main entry beginning with *scull.*

slay—sleigh

- **slay** [sle] to kill or murder someone or something violently. ☐ *It was wrong to slay the deer merely for its antlers.*
- **slay** [sle] to overwhelm; to impress. (A slang exaggeration.) ☐ *Gerry thought he could slay the girls with his good looks.*
- **sleigh** [sle] a sled with runners designed to carry goods or people over ice and snow. ☐ *That country inn offers rides in an antique sleigh to its guests during the wintertime.*

sleigh See the main entry beginning with *slay.*

sleight—slight

- **sleight** [slɑɪt] deception; craftiness. ☐ *The magician's skillful sleight fooled everyone.*
- **slight** [slɑɪt] trivial. ☐ *His error was so slight that no one even noticed.*
- **slight** [slɑɪt] scanty. ☐ *Jane's dress was very slight.*
- **slight** [slɑɪt] having a delicate, slim build. ☐ *The suspect was described as blond and slight.*
- **slight** [slɑɪt] small in amount, number, or kind. ☐ *Add just a slight amount of salt to the soup.*
- **slight** [slɑɪt] to treat someone or something as unimportant; to ignore or neglect someone. ☐ *I didn't mean to slight your question.* ☐ *If you slight the guest of honor, you'll be considered rude.*
- **slight** [slɑɪt] an insult; rude behavior. ☐ *Mary's obvious slight of her mother-in-law was noted by many people.*

slight See the main entry beginning with *sleight.*

so See the main entry beginning with *sew.*

soar—sore

- **soar** [soɚ] to sail or fly high and unencumbered. ☐ *I wonder what it is like to soar in a glider plane.*
- **soar** [soɚ] to move upward in status or position. ☐ *The actor's popularity began to soar with the release of his first movie.*
- **sore** [soɚ] an open, often infected wound. ☐ *You should put some salve on that sore.*

- **sore** [soə-] a source of irritation or pain. ☐ *Any discussion of his past was a sore for him.*
- **sore** [soə-] to be painfully sensitive. ☐ *My back is sore today for some reason.*
- **sore** [soə-] vexed or angered. ☐ *Don't be a sore loser.*

soared—sword

- **soared** [soə-d] the past tense and past participle of *soar* 'to sail or fly high and unencumbered.' ☐ *The gull soared gracefully with the wind.*
- **soared** [soə-d] the past tense and past participle of *soar* 'to move upward in status or position.' ☐ *The singer's hit record soared to the top of the record charts.*
- **sword** [soə-d] a long, sharp blade used for stabbing, cutting, or thrusting. ☐ *The marine's sash and sword are part of his dress uniform.*

sold—soled—souled

- **sold** [sold] the past tense and past participle of *sell* 'to offer something for sale; to exchange something for money.' ☐ *The store sold only sporting goods.* ☐ *Jack sold his old lawn mower to his neighbor.*
- **soled** [sold] the past tense and past participle of *sole* 'to equip footwear with a sole.' ☐ *The cobbler soled Mary's hiking boots twice in one season.*
- **souled** [sold] the past participle of *soul* 'to equip someone with a kind spirit.' (This occurs only as a past participle.) ☐ *My aunt was always a kind-souled lady.*

sole—soul

- **sole** [sol] the bottom part of a foot or shoe. ☐ *I have a cut on the sole of my foot.*
- **sole** [sol] the lower part or base of something on which something else rests. ☐ *The sole of her golf club has been damaged.*
- **sole** [sol] to furnish something with the lower part or base of something. ☐ *The cobbler will sole a pair of shoes for only eight dollars.*
- **sole** [sol] a tasty, white-fleshed fish. ☐ *He couldn't decide whether to order the shrimp or the sole on the menu.*
- **sole** [sol] only; lone. ☐ *A baby girl was the sole survivor of the auto accident.* ☐ *The sole judge in the case found the defendant not guilty.*
- **soul** [sol] the spiritual part of a human being. ☐ *Fred felt that his soul would live on after his death.*

- **soul** [sol] a person's total self. ☐ *Sara poured her heart and soul into the difficult project.*
- **soul** [sol] an essential or active part. ☐ *Mike was the soul behind the business's success.*

soled See the main entry beginning with *sold.*

some—sum

- **some** [səm] an unspecified number, amount, part, person, or thing. ☐ *Tomorrow the company will be forced to lay off some of its workers.*
- **some** [səm] noteworthy; important. ☐ *That was some movie!*
- **some** [səm] somewhat. ☐ *I was irritated some at her lack of manners.*
- **sum** [səm] the total or whole amount; the end result of adding numbers or amounts. ☐ *The sum of money in the cash register is small.* ☐ *None of the math students came up with the correct sum.*
- **sum** [səm] the utmost degree; the highest point. ☐ *The sum of all her happiness was realized on her wedding day.*
- **sum [up]** [səm] to summarize something. ☐ *Would you please sum up his comments in a few words?*

son—sun

- **son** [sən] a male offspring of human beings. ☐ *In Scotland it is considered lucky to be the seventh son of a seventh son.*
- **son** [sən] a person closely associated with a formative body, usually a town, school, or country. ☐ *The newly elected president is a favorite son of the state of Iowa.*
- **sun** [sən] a warmth-providing celestial body around which the Earth and other planets revolve. ☐ *I remember seeing a total eclipse of the sun once as a child.*
- **sun** [sən] the light or heat given off from the sun. ☐ *The bright sun seemed to lighten our spirits.*
- **sun** [sən] something resembling the sun's brilliance. ☐ *The lawyer had her moment in the sun when she won the famous court case.*

sore See the main entry beginning with *soar.*

soul See the main entry beginning with *sole.*

souled See the main entry beginning with *sold.*

sow See the main entry beginning with *sew.*

spade—spayed

- **spade** [sped] a digging tool usually pushed into the ground with either the hand or foot. □ *Using a spade in soft, sandy soil is not difficult.*

- **spade** [sped] a tool resembling a spade in shape or function. □ *A tree spade was used to plant the large evergreen tree.*
- **spade** [sped] a playing card having the symbol of a spade on it. □ *Tony threw a high spade on my four to win the hand.*
- **spayed** [sped] the past tense and past participle of *spay* 'to remove the ovaries of a female animal.' □ *After breeding her once, we decided to have our collie spayed.*

spayed See the main entry beginning with *spade.*

staid—stayed

- **staid** [sted] serious. □ *The professor's somber expression and staid manner made him seem unapproachable.*
- **stayed** [sted] the past tense and past participle of *stay* 'to remain in a certain status, position, or place.' □ *The children stayed friends during their entire lives.* □ *The driver stayed in the passing lane for miles.*
- **stayed** [sted] the past tense and past participle of *stay* 'to take up temporary residence somewhere.' □ *We stayed with my sister and her family while our parents were on vacation.*
- **stayed** [sted] the past tense and past participle of *stay* '[for a judge] to issue an order preventing something from happening.' □ *The judge stayed the execution of the man on death row.*

stair—stare

- **stair** [stɛɚ] a flight of steps leading from one level to another. □ *I took the stair rather than the elevator.*
- **stair** [stɛɚ] a single step in a staircase. □ *He left his shoes on the stair beside the door.*
- **stare** [stɛɚ] to look fixedly, conspicuously, or searchingly at something or someone. □ *The man taught his children not to stare at other people.* □ *The young man could not help but stare at his beloved whenever she spoke.*

stake—steak

- **stake** [stek] a sharp, pointed piece of wood or metal driven into the ground as a marker or support. □ *The tent stake was bent.*
- **stake** [stek] the prize in a contest. □ *A stake of fifty dollars goes to the winner of the race.*
- **stake** [stek] something to be lost or gained. □ *If this rumor spreads, the senator's reputation is at stake.*
- **stake** [stek] an interest in a commercial venture. □ *He has very little stake in the new building project.*

- **stake** [stek] to place stakes or mark with stakes. □ *Let's stake out the dimensions for the new playhouse.*
- **stake** [stek] to back someone or something financially. □ *I'll stake you in that business venture if you like.*
- **stake** [stek] to bet something. □ *The cowboys decided to stake their favorite saddles on the horse race.*
- **steak** [stek] a cut of meat, usually beef. □ *John likes steak and eggs for breakfast on Sunday mornings.*

stare See the main entry beginning with *stair.*

stationary—stationery

- **stationary** ['steʃənɛɚi] not moving; unchanging in place or condition. □ *The weatherman said a stationary storm front had settled over the region.*
- **stationery** ['steʃənɛɚi] letter-writing materials such as ink, pen, paper, and envelopes. □ *Dad went into the store to buy some stationery items.* □ *I have several pretty styles of stationery.*

stationery See the main entry beginning with *stationary.*

stayed See the main entry beginning with *staid.*

steak See the main entry beginning with *stake.*

steal—steel

- **steal** [stil] to take something illegally. □ *The boys tried to steal a car from the parking lot.*
- **steal** [stil] to move about in a quiet, secret manner. □ *A cat burglar knows how to steal about in a home without being seen or heard.*
- **steal** [stil] to gain or win something by daring, skill, or trickery. □ *The actor's dashing manner and rugged good looks were enough to steal away the girl's heart.*
- **steal** [stil] an act of stealing. □ *The baseball player's steal at home plate won the ball game.*
- **steal** [stil] a bargain. □ *I really got a steal when I bought that table at the garage sale.*
- **steel** [stil] commercial iron that comes from ore and is used in manufacturing. □ *Large amounts of steel were once used to make cars.*
- **steel** [stil] something made from steel or resembling steel. □ *Those stainless steel knives are guaranteed not to rust.*
- **steel** [stil] to fill someone with resolve or determination. □ *Police officers are taught to steel themselves against the less pleasant aspects of their jobs.*

steel See the main entry beginning with *steal.*

step—steppe

- **step** [stɛp] a stair. □ *She twisted her ankle on the slippery step.*
- **step** [stɛp] a ladder rung. □ *"Go up one more step," called Janet from the bottom of the ladder.*
- **step** [stɛp] a stride. □ *Mark always walks with a jaunty step.*
- **step** [stɛp] the amount of space passed over in one step. □ *The runner lost the race by a single step.*
- **step** [stɛp] a rank, grade, or degree in scale or quality. □ *The houses in this neighborhood are a step above the others we looked at.*
- **step** [stɛp] an action taken. □ *It is necessary to take this step in order to avoid further trouble.*
- **step** [stɛp] to move by raising and lowering the foot over some distance. □ *Please step over here.*
- **step** [stɛp] to press something down with the foot. □ *Step on the brake slowly and carefully.*
- **step** [stɛp] to move in a spritely manner. □ *The show dogs step around the ring with style.*
- **steppe** [stɛp] a vast expanse of flat, treeless plain. □ *Only coarse grasses grow on a steppe.*

steppe See the main entry beginning with *step.*

stile—style

- **stile** [stɑɪl] a set of steps leading up to and crossing over a wall or fence. □ *Grandpa built a stile over the pasture fence.*
- **stile** [stɑɪl] a vertical piece of a frame or panel into which other pieces are fitted. □ *The stile of the door frame is cracked.*
- **style** [stɑɪl] a way to express thought in language, art, or music. □ *His writing style is one of wry humor.*
- **style** [stɑɪl] a mode of mannerism, behavior, or conduct. □ *The nurse's style when dealing with her patients is friendly.*
- **style** [stɑɪl] a writing instrument. □ *The poet picked up his style to write a few lines of verse.*
- **style** [stɑɪl] to design or copy something from an existing mode. □ *The young acting student has tried to style her work after the famous actor.*

straight—strait

- **straight** [stret] unwavering or direct. □ *The easiest way to the city is straight up the main road.*
- **straight** [stret] free from curves, angles, or bends. □ *The*

shortest distance between two points is a straight line.

- **straight** [stret] upright; virtuous. ☐ *Gene is a straight, upstanding citizen.*
- **straight** [stret] frank; candid. ☐ *The mother demanded a straight answer.*
- **straight** [stret] marked by no deviations, usually with reference to a political party. ☐ *Her dad always votes a straight Republican ticket.*
- **straight** [stret] a homestretch. ☐ *The stock cars were three abreast coming into the straight.*
- **straight** [stret] an unbroken sequence in a game resulting in a perfect score. ☐ *The pool player ran the table for a straight in the pool match.*
- **straight** [stret] in poker, a combination of five sequential cards. ☐ *Dad's straight beat my pair of kings.*
- **strait** [stret] a narrow passage where two large bodies of water meet. ☐ *The ships sailed through the strait during the night.*
- **strait** [stret] a perplexing or difficult situation. ☐ *Helen was in a strait and didn't know what to do.*
- **strait** [stret] tightly or closely. ☐ *Her gown was very strait fitting.*

strait See the main entry beginning with *straight.*

style See the main entry beginning with *stile.*

succor—sucker

- **succor** ['səkɚ, 'səkɔr] relief or help. ☐ *The relief workers provided succor to the homeless people just before winter.*
- **succor** ['səkɚ, 'səkɔr] to go to the aid of someone. ☐ *It is difficult for parents not to succor their children in times of trouble.*
- **sucker** ['səkɚ] a device used to produce suction. ☐ *A type of sucker was used to remove the water from the ditch.*
- **sucker** ['səkɚ] a lollipop. ☐ *The corner drugstore sells every flavor of sucker imaginable.*
- **sucker** ['səkɚ] a type of freshwater fish related to the carp family. ☐ *The boys caught a sucker yesterday afternoon.*
- **sucker** ['səkɚ] a person that is easily fooled or cheated. ☐ *The con artist was constantly on the lookout for a sucker.*
- **sucker** ['səkɚ] to deceive someone intentionally. ☐ *The older boy tried to sucker the younger boy out of his lunch money.*

sucker See the main entry beginning with *succor.*

suede—swayed

- **suede** [swed] leather with a napped surface. □ *Suede is used to make shoes, purses, and clothing.*
- **suede** [swed] made of leather with a napped surface. □ *You'll have to take your suede coat to the cleaners to have the stains removed.*
- **swayed** [swed] the past tense and past participle of *sway* 'to move rhythmically and slowly, usually from side to side.' □ *The dancers swayed to the sounds of the music.*
- **swayed [from]** [swed] the past tense and past participle of *sway [from]* 'to divert or influence someone or something from something.' □ *The woman swayed her little girl's attention from the candy counter.*
- **swayed** [swed] the past tense and past participle of *sway* 'to persuade someone to change an opinion.' □ *The testimony could not have swayed the jury's position.*

suite—sweet

- **suite** [swit] a group of rooms occupied as a single unit. □ *The only vacancy in the hotel was a large suite.*
- **suite** [swit] the collection of personnel accompanying a dignitary or ruler on official business. □ *The king's entire suite traveled with him wherever he went.*
- **suite** [swit] a musical composition with a number of movements, usually in the same key. □ *The audience applauded after the orchestra played the suite of ballet music.*
- **sweet** [swit] pleasing to the taste, mind, or feelings. □ *The child's sweet temperament was the opposite of her twin sister's.*
- **sweet** [swit] dearest; much beloved. □ *"Marry me, my sweet," implored the suitor to his lady friend.*
- **sweet** [swit] great; terrific. □ *Winning the tournament was such a sweet experience.*
- **sweet** [swit] having a high sugar content. □ *This fudge is so sweet!*

sum See the main entry beginning with *some.*

sun See the main entry beginning with *son.*

surf See the main entry beginning with *serf.*

swayed See the main entry beginning with *suede.*

sweet See the main entry beginning with *suite.*

sword See the main entry beginning with *soared.*

symbol See the main entry beginning with *cymbal.*

T

tacked–tact

- **tacked [down]** [tækt] the past tense and past participle of *tack [down]* 'to attach or fasten something down with tacks.' □ *The workers tacked the carpet down rather than just laying it on the floor.*
- **tacked [together]** [tækt] the past tense and past participle of *tack [together]* 'to make or build something rapidly and carelessly.' □ *The old man tacked the shack together in one afternoon.*
- **tacked [onto]** [tækt] the past tense and past participle of *tack [onto]* 'to add something onto something in haste.' □ *Emily tacked a postscript onto the end of her letter.*
- **tacked** [tækt] the past tense and past participle of *tack* 'to change the direction of a sailing vessel.' □ *The racing schooner tacked several times during the course of the race.*
- **tacked** [tækt] the past tense and past participle of *tack* 'to follow after something in a zigzagging course.' □ *The guided missile tacked its target through the sky.*
- **tact** [tækt] a sense of what to do or say under given circumstances in order to avoid offending others. □ *Joan always handles the delicate subject of money with tact.*

tacks–tax

- **tacks** [tæks] the plural of *tack* 'a sharp-pointed, flat-headed pin.' □ *I spilled the box of tacks all over the desktop.*
- **tacks** [tæks] the plural of *tack* 'the direction of a sailing ship in relation to the set of its sails.' □ *The sailors continually changed the tacks of the ship.*

- **tacks [up]** [tæks] the present tense, third person singular of *tack [up]* 'to fasten onto a surface with tacks.' ☐ *Henry tacks up notes all over his apartment to remind himself to do things.*
- **tacks [together]** [tæks] the present tense, third person singular of *tack [together]* 'to put something together hastily and insecurely.' ☐ *It seems that contractor tacks together houses wherever he finds an empty lot.*
- **tacks [on]** [tæks] the present tense, third person singular of *tack [on]* 'to add something onto something.' ☐ *Mary always tacks on the question "Don't you think?" to her statements.*
- **tacks** [tæks] the present tense, third person singular of *tack* 'to change direction of a sailing vessel in relation to the wind.' ☐ *The captain tacks each time the wind changes.*
- **tax** [tæks] a charge placed by a government body on persons or property. ☐ *Most people think the amount of property tax they pay is too high.*
- **tax** [tæks] to levy an assessment on something. ☐ *The government will tax some items more heavily in the future.*
- **tax** [tæks] to place someone or something under heavy demands or conditions. ☐ *Such vigorous exercise might tax her heart beyond its limits.*

tact See the main entry beginning with *tacked.*

tail—tale

- **tail** [tel] an extension of the spine at the rear end of an animal, usually covered with hair. ☐ *My dog has a short, stubby tail.*
- **tail** [tel] something resembling a tail. ☐ *The tail of the kite is made from old rags.*
- **tail** [tel] the end or final process of something. ☐ *We were all glad to see the tail end of the project in sight.*
- **tail** [tel] to follow behind or trail something or someone. ☐ *Streams of exhaust tail the jets through the sky.*
- **tail** [tel] to follow someone in order to conduct surveillance. ☐ *The detective decided to tail the suspect all night long.*
- **tale** [tel] an untrue report or piece of gossip. ☐ *We could not believe her tale.*
- **tale** [tel] a report of facts or events. ☐ *Each listener was spellbound by his tale of adventure.*
- **tale** [tel] a story. ☐ *She read the tale with much expression.*
- **tale** [tel] a lie. ☐ *She fooled no one with her tale of what happened.*

tale See the main entry beginning with *tail.*

taper—tapir

- **taper** ['tepɚ] a candle that is narrower at the top than at the bottom. □ *A single taper burned on the altar during the wedding ceremony.*
- **taper** ['tepɚ] a faint light. □ *A thin taper of light shone through the crack in the door.*
- **taper** ['tepɚ] to make something gradually narrower at one end. □ *The seamstress wants to taper the trousers at the ankles.*
- **taper [off]** ['tepɚ] to diminish gradually. □ *The holiday shopping season usually starts to taper off after the first of the year.*
- **tapir** ['tepɚ] a large, shy mammal related to the rhinoceros and horse that inhabits the equatorial regions of the Far East and the Americas. □ *The tapir is a gentle but unattractive beast.*

tapir See the main entry beginning with *taper.*

tare—tear

(See also *tear—tier.*)

- **tare** [tɛɚ] a weedy plant often used as ground cover. □ *Many gardeners use a tare to keep the soil from eroding.*
- **tare** [tɛɚ] the calculation of the weight of a substance and its container minus the weight of the container. □ *Your cost will be figured by the tare of the liquid.*
- **tear** [tɛɚ] a hole or flaw caused by tearing. □ *Did you know this shirt has a tear in it?*
- **tear** [tɛɚ] to separate or pull something into parts. □ *We need to tear this paper into long strips.*
- **tear** [tɛɚ] to remove or wrench something from someone or something forcibly. □ *He could not tear himself away from the interesting novel.*
- **tear** [tɛɚ] to move or act hastily or violently. □ *The speeding car continued to tear down the street in a dangerous manner.*

tarry—terry

- **tarry** ['tæɚi, 'tɛɚi] to linger or lag behind; to stay in one place or location. □ *Sally liked to tarry after school to talk with her teachers.*
- **terry** ['tɛɚi] an absorbent fabric made up of uncut loops of cotton. □ *Towels made of terry feel nice against the skin.*

taught—taut

- **taught** [tɔt] the past tense and past participle of *teach* 'to educate or train someone or something in a particular subject;

to perform schooling in general.' □ *She taught school for many years.* □ *The owner of that store taught each of his children the basics of sound business management.*

- **taut** [tɔt] pulled tightly; stretched. □ *The taut rope suddenly snapped.* □ *Her face was lean and taut.*

taut See the main entry beginning with *taught.*

tax See the main entry beginning with *tacks.*

tea—tee

- **tea** [ti] a beverage made from steeping the leaves of various plants, usually the tea plant, in hot water. □ *Diane likes her tea very strong.*
- **tea** [ti] a plant that is known for its aromatic leaves and is used to make a beverage by the same name. □ *The fortune-teller claims that she can read tea leaves.*
- **tea** [ti] a light, late afternoon refreshment usually of cookies, cakes, or crackers served with tea. □ *Our bed and breakfast serves tea every day between three and four o'clock.*
- **tea** [ti] a reception at which light refreshments are served. □ *The ladies attended a tea after the art show.*
- **tee** [ti] the areas of a golf course in which the ball is put into play at each hole. □ *Because the golf course was crowded, golfers were lined up at each tee to continue play.*
- **tee** [ti] a small peg with a flat top on which a golf ball is set to begin play. □ *I lost my tee in the deep grass.*
- **tee [off]** [ti] to begin play by hitting a golf ball off a tee. □ *It's your turn to tee off at this hole.*

team—teem

- **team** [tim] a group of individuals associated in a work or sport activity. □ *The wrestling team traveled by bus to each meet.*
- **team** [tim] a pair of harnessed draft animals. □ *His team of Belgians won a blue ribbon at the fair.*
- **team [up]** [tim] to join together as a team. □ *Let's team up for the wheelbarrow race.*
- **team** [tim] performed as a team. □ *With some team effort, this task can be quickly accomplished.*
- **teem** [tim] to overflow with something. □ *Their personalities seem to teem with energy.*
- **teem** [tim] to be present in large quantity. □ *Our favorite stream begins to teem with spunky rainbow trout each spring.*

tear—tier

(See also *tare—tear.*)

- **tear** [tɪɚ] a clear, salty liquid secreted by a gland in the eye. ☐ *A single tear rolled down her cheek.*
- **tear** [tɪɚ] a transparent drop of liquid that resembles a tear. ☐ *There was a tear of some unknown substance on the surface of the material.*
- **tear** [tɪɚ] to produce tears; to weep. ☐ *The odor of the hot onions caused his eyes to tear.*
- **tier** [tɪɚ] a layer or row of things arranged one above the other. ☐ *Each tier of the wedding cake was larger than the one above it.*
- **tier** [tɪɚ] to arrange something in layers or rows one above the other. ☐ *Let's tier this stack of boxes so they don't fall over.*

teas—tease

- **teas** [tiz] the plural of *tea* 'a beverage made from steeping the leaves of various plants, usually the tea plant, in hot water.' ☐ *The restaurant serves several different teas.*
- **teas** [tiz] the plural of *tea* 'a plant that is known for its aromatic leaves or buds and is used to make a beverage by the same name.' ☐ *The plantation grows a number of exotic teas.*
- **teas** [tiz] the plural of *tea* 'a light, late afternoon refreshment of cookies, cakes, or crackers served with tea.' ☐ *The women tried to outdo each other at their afternoon teas.*
- **teas** [tiz] the plural of *tea* 'a reception at which light refreshments are served.' ☐ *The final campaign week was filled with countless informal teas and meetings.*
- **tease** [tiz] to poke fun at, annoy, or harass someone. ☐ *It is not nice to tease people who are different from you.*
- **tease** [tiz] to tantalize someone. ☐ *Those yummy desserts are enough to tease anyone's appetite.*
- **tease** [tiz] to untangle by laying flat and carding or combing. ☐ *You must tease the raw wool before spinning it.*
- **tease** [tiz] a person who pokes fun at, harasses, or annoys someone. ☐ *Linda is such a tease!*

tease See the main entry beginning with *teas.*

tee See the main entry beginning with *tea.*

teem See the main entry beginning with *team.*

tense—tents

- **tense** [tɛnts] nervous; anxious. ☐ *Tom is always tense before an airplane flight.*

- **tense** [tɛnts] taut; rigid. □ *My neck muscles feel tense when I am under stress.*
- **tense** [tɛnts] to become taut, rigid, or nervous. □ *My muscles tense when I am getting an injection.*
- **tense** [tɛnts] a distinction of verbs indicating time variances. □ *The words* shall *and* will *indicate the future tense.*
- **tents** [tɛnts] the plural of *tent* 'a collapsible structure made of canvas, nylon, or other material, supported by a framework and used for shelter.' □ *The older campers will sleep in tents instead of in the log cabins.*
- **tents** [tɛnts] the present tense, third person singular of *tent* 'to camp out or stay in a tent.' □ *Mike tents in the mountains for a week each summer.*

tents See the main entry beginning with *tense.*

tern—turn
- **tern** [tɚn] a small, compact bird belonging to the sea gull family. □ *As each wave rolled onto the beach, the tern curiously inspected the shoreline.*
- **turn** [tɚn] a change of direction or course. □ *His condition took a turn for the worse.*
- **turn** [tɚn] a chance to do something. □ *"When will it be my turn?" asked the small boy.*
- **turn** [tɚn] to rotate something or someone; to change the direction or course of something or someone. □ *Turn the chicken on the grill every ten minutes.* □ *The plane will turn at the end of the runway.*
- **turn** [tɚn] to sour; [for food] to go bad. □ *This cider is beginning to turn.*

terry See the main entry beginning with *tarry.*

their—there—they're
- **their** [ðɛɚ] the third person plural pronoun indicating possession or relationship by a group of people or things. □ *Their new house is very beautiful.* □ *The trees shed their leaves each fall.*
- **there** [ðɛɚ] a place that has been pointed out; a place some distance from the speaker. □ *Please put the blueprints there on the drafting table.* □ *Put it there, not here.*
- **there** [ðɛɚ] a word used to introduce a sentence or clause, usually when the verb has no definite subject. □ *There have been few changes since you left.*
- **there** [ðɛɚ] an interjection indicating a variety of emotions. □ *"There, I am finally finished with that job," the man sighed*

triumphantly. □ *"There, everything will be all right," the boy's mother said comfortingly.*

- **they're** [ðɛɚ] the contraction of *they* and *are.* □ *I think they're going to meet us at the stadium.*

there See the main entry beginning with *their.*

they're See the main entry beginning with *their.*

threw—through

- **threw** [θru] the past tense of *throw* 'to cast something or someone through the air.' □ *The outfielder threw the ball all the way to home plate.* □ *The unruly horse threw its jockey into the dirt.*
- **threw** [θru] the past tense of *throw* 'to form something on a potter's wheel.' □ *The potter threw some interesting clay vases on his wheel.*
- **threw** [θru] the past tense of *throw* 'to project something.' □ *The moon threw an eery light through the trees.*
- **threw** [θru] the past tense of *throw* 'to make or break a connection with a power source using a lever or switch.' □ *The electrician threw a switch to cut off the source of power.*
- **through** [θru] by means of something. □ *Through sheer willpower, Julie finally reached her goals.*
- **through** [θru] in one way and out another. □ *We will have to travel through the tunnel in the mountain to reach the other side.*
- **through** [θru] over or across something. □ *We sailed through some rough seas.*
- **through** [θru] from one point up to and including another point. □ *That specialty shop is open Monday through Friday.*

throe—throw

- **throe** [θro] a painful spasm. □ *With each throe of giving birth, the dog whined pitifully.*
- **throe** [θro] a difficult or painful struggle. □ *In his throe to achieve stardom, the actor lost sight of his roots.*
- **throw** [θro] to catapult something through the air. □ *How far can you throw a javelin?*
- **throw** [θro] to cause something to fall. □ *Throw down the bat and run to first base.*
- **throw** [θro] to form something on a potter's wheel. □ *Despite my best efforts, I was unable to throw a single piece of pottery on the wheel.*
- **throw** [θro] to project something. □ *Throw a little more light into that dark corner.*

- **throw** [θro] to produce something. □ *Carrie wants to breed her mare to a horse that will throw a lot of color.*
- **throw** [θro] to make or break a connection with a power source using a lever or switch. □ *A switchman will throw the switch to divert the engine from one track to another.*

throne—thrown

- **throne** [θron] a seat or place of royalty, deity, or authority. □ *Queen Elizabeth II now sits on the throne of England.*
- **throne** [θron] the person who occupies a seat of authority. □ *The final say in the matter rests with the throne.*
- **thrown** [θron] the past participle of *throw* 'to cast or hurl someone or something.' □ *He has thrown the frisbee onto the roof of the house.* □ *The child had thrown herself on the floor in a fit of temper.*
- **thrown** [θron] the past participle of *throw* 'to form something on a potter's wheel.' □ *The artist has thrown many interesting pieces on her wheel.*
- **thrown** [θron] the past participle of *throw* 'to project something.' □ *The setting sun has thrown long shadows across the lawn.*
- **thrown** [θron] the past participle of *throw* 'to produce offspring.' □ *That stud dog has never thrown an unusual color pattern in any of its offspring.*
- **thrown** [θron] the past participle of *throw* 'to turn an electrical switch; to make or break a connection with a power source using a lever or switch.' □ *He has accidentally thrown a switch and cut off the power to the building.*

through See the main entry beginning with *threw.*

throw See the main entry beginning with *throe.*

thrown See the main entry beginning with *throne.*

thyme—time

- **thyme** [taɪm] an aromatic garden herb that belongs to the mint family and is used in cooking. □ *The recipe calls for one-half teaspoon of thyme.*
- **time** [taɪm] the period during which something occurs. □ *I never seem to have enough time to do my chores.*
- **time** [taɪm] an appointed moment or hour when something should happen. □ *At what time do you expect to be home?*
- **time** [taɪm] a tempo, rhythm, or beat. □ *The drummer kept time with the other musicians.*
- **time** [taɪm] a geological or historical age. □ *There was a time*

when dinosaurs roamed the earth.

- **time** [taɪm] an experience. ☐ *We had a wonderful time on our vacation.*
- **time** [taɪm] an hourly wage rate. ☐ *The workers will get time-and-a-half if they work on the weekend.*
- **time** [taɪm] to keep the time of something or someone. ☐ *Jody was asked to time the swimmers at the swim meet.*

tic—tick

- **tic** [tɪk] a frequent, localized twitch, usually involving facial muscles. ☐ *His awful experiences during the war left the soldier with a nervous tic.*
- **tick** [tɪk] a bloodsucking insect that is dependent upon a warm-blooded host for survival and often spreads disease. ☐ *The common deer tick is responsible for spreading Lyme disease.*
- **tick** [tɪk] a soft, rhythmic beat often associated with timepieces. ☐ *The loud tick of the clock kept Joe awake at night.*
- **tick** [tɪk] a light mark used as an indicator. ☐ *Put a tick next to each item on the invoice.*
- **tick** [tɪk] a straw, feather, or fabric-filled case used as a mattress. ☐ *This sleeping tick is not very comfortable.*
- **tick** [tɪk] to make a ticking sound. ☐ *Those clocks all tick in different tones.*

tick See the main entry beginning with *tic.*

tide—tied

- **tide** [taɪd] a rising and falling of the surface of an ocean, sea, or gulf, influenced by the gravitational pull of the sun and moon. ☐ *Do not go swimming at high tide.*
- **tide** [taɪd] something that fluctuates like the tide. ☐ *The tide of her mood swings is unpredictable.*
- **tied** [taɪd] the past tense and past participle of *tie* 'to make a knot or bow.' ☐ *The child tied his shoelaces all by himself.*
- **tied [together]** [taɪd] the past tense and past participle of *tie [together]* 'to unite two or more people or things.' ☐ *The two corporations tied together to form one company.*
- **tied** [taɪd] the past tense and past participle of *tie* '[for two teams] to have the same score in a competition.' ☐ *At the end of nine innings, the score was tied twelve to twelve.*

tied See the main entry beginning with *tide.*

tier See the main entry beginning with *tear.*

'til—till

- **'til** [tɪl] until. ☐ *We won't see you again 'til much later.*

- **till** [tɪl] to plow, cultivate, or sow crops. □ *It is much easier to till soft, moist ground than hard, dry earth.*
- **till** [tɪl] a cash register or money drawer including its receipts. □ *If you're working alone in the store, do not leave the till unattended.*
- **till** [tɪl] a mixture of rocks, sand, clay, and gravel left behind by receding glaciers. □ *The geologists studied the till of the river basins.*

till See the main entry beginning with *'til.*

timber—timbre

- **timber** ['tɪmbɚ] standing trees. □ *The forest fire destroyed many acres of timber.*
- **timber** ['tɪmbɚ] the wood of living trees. □ *The timber on that mountainside is very valuable.*
- **timber** ['tɪmbɚ] wood material used for construction, either in raw or finished form. □ *It will take a lot of timber to build that cedar log lodge.*
- **timber** ['tɪmbɚ] the rib of a ship. □ *A timber on that ship cracked during the violent storm.*
- **timbre** ['tɪmbɚ, 'tæmbr] the tone or quality of a vocal or musical sound as heard by the ear. □ *The timbre of the alto's voice stood out among the other choir members' voices.*

timbre See the main entry beginning with *timber.*

time See the main entry beginning with *thyme.*

to—too—two

- **to** [tu] a preposition indicating movement toward something, purpose or result of, relation in time, extent, or degree, comparison or proportion. □ *After the soccer match we went to the ice-cream parlor for cold drinks.*
- **too** [tu] also. □ *Besides the house, we plan to sell the car and boat, too.*
- **too** [tu] an extensive degree. □ *I am too tired to stay awake any longer.*
- **two** [tu] the cardinal number between one and three. □ *Those two houses have exactly the same floor plan.* □ *The last card she played was the two of hearts.*
- **two** [tu] a pair. □ *The schoolchildren lined up two by two.*

toad—toed—towed

- **toad** [tod] an amphibian related to the frog but darker in color with dry, warty skin. □ *There is a huge toad in the flower garden.*

- **toad** [tod] a person or object worthy of contempt. ☐ *I don't understand what Alice sees in that toad, Dave.*
- **toed** [tod] the past participle of *toe* 'to equip something with toes; to be equipped with toes.' (This occurs only as a past participle.) ☐ *The three-toed sloth is a homely creature.* ☐ *The workers are required to wear steel-toed shoes on the job.*
- **toed** [tod] the past tense and past participle of *toe* 'to touch or move something about with one's toe.' ☐ *I toed the drowsy snake until it slithered away.*
- **towed** [tod] the past tense and past participle of *tow* 'to pull something behind something or someone.' ☐ *Heavy machinery towed the fallen trees out of the roadway.* ☐ *After the accident, the cars were towed away by the police.*

toe—tow

- **toe** [to] one of the digits of the foot. ☐ *I dropped the heavy sack on my big toe.*
- **toe** [to] the tip of a shoe. ☐ *The toe of his shoe has a hole in it.*
- **toe** [to] to equip something with toes. ☐ *The cobbler can toe these old work boots for me.*
- **toe** [to] to operate, move, or reach something or someone with a toe. ☐ *If you toe my foot again, I'll kick you.*
- **toe** [to] to drive nails in at a slant. ☐ *Toe that board to the one beneath it.*
- **tow** [to] to haul or pull something or someone behind something or someone. ☐ *We'll have to tow the truck to the repair garage.* ☐ *The baby-sitter towed the screaming child to the car.*

toed See the main entry beginning with *toad.*

told—tolled

- **told** [told] the past tense and past participle of *tell* 'to say something; to utter something; to reveal something.' ☐ *Linda always told the truth.* ☐ *She never told me the well-kept secret.* ☐ *The empty candy wrappers told the mother why her son had no appetite for dinner.* ☐ *I told my boss that I would be late for work.* ☐ *The clock on the bank told us the time.*
- **told [on]** [told] to betray someone; to tattle on someone. ☐ *My older brother always told on me for sneaking cookies.*
- **tolled** [told] the past tense and past participle of *toll* 'to sound a bell.' ☐ *The bell in the steeple tolled midnight.*
- **tolled** [told] the past tense and past participle of *toll* 'to signal or announce something.' ☐ *The town crier tolled the royal betrothal.*
- **tolled** [told] the past tense and past participle of *toll* 'to

charge or collect a toll.' □ *The toll collector tolled each of the travelers a dollar to cross the bridge.*

tole—toll

- **tole** [tol] a decorative, painted metal surface of various colors often found on ornamental wall hangings, curios, and boxes. □ *She made many attractive gifts with her new-found ability to tole paint.*
- **toll** [tol] a tax, fee, or levy paid for the privilege of using some public facility, usually a bridge or turnpike. □ *Drivers must pay a toll when entering the turnpike.*
- **toll** [tol] the cost in loss or detriment at which something is gained. □ *His difficult life took a toll on his health.*
- **toll** [tol] to sound a bell. □ *The church bells toll the hour of the day.*
- **toll** [tol] to signal or announce. □ *Trumpets and waving flags toll the end of the fighting.*
- **toll** [tol] to place or take a toll. □ *The state will toll the use of the new stretch of highway.*

toll See the main entry beginning with *tole.*

tolled See the main entry beginning with *told.*

too See the main entry beginning with *to.*

tort—torte

- **tort** [tɔɚt] a wrongful act against which civil action may be brought. □ *Trespass is an example of a civil tort.*
- **torte** [tɔɚt] a rich, layered dessert topped with frosting. □ *Mom always serves her famous four-layer torte at Thanksgiving dinner.*

torte See the main entry beginning with *tort.*

tough—tuff

- **tough** [təf] strong; firm. □ *These old shoes are tough enough to last many more years.*
- **tough** [təf] stubborn. □ *Janice has a tough manner about her.*
- **tough** [təf] capable of enduring stress, difficulty, or hardship. □ *The journey will require tough adventurers.*
- **tough** [təf] difficult to deal with. □ *Bill is a tough person to work for.*
- **tough** [təf] a rough, rowdy individual. □ *The boss always sends his tough to do his dirty work for him.*
- **tuff** [təf] rock or rock deposits made of disintegrating material, usually volcanic in nature. □ *The heavy spring rains*

washed much tuff out of the mountains and into the river and streambeds.

tow See the main entry beginning with *toe.*

towed See the main entry beginning with *toad.*

tracked—tract

- **tracked** [trækt] the past tense and past participle of *track* 'to follow or trail someone or something.' □ *Rescuers tracked the lost hiker through the snow.*
- **tracked** [trækt] the past tense and past participle of *track* 'to observe the path of something, using specialized equipment.' □ *Scientists tracked the path of the new comet.*
- **tracked** [trækt] the past tense and past participle of *track* 'to carry soil or other material on one's feet and deposit it on the floor.' □ *The children tracked mud all through the house.*
- **tract** [trækt] a pamphlet containing religious or political information. □ *I picked up a tract to read in the waiting room.*
- **tract** [trækt] an area of land; a parcel of land. □ *The couple purchased a small tract of land as an investment.* □ *That vast tract of land in the foothills is ideal for grazing cattle.*
- **tract** [trækt] a system of the body whose parts collectively perform some function. □ *This week the class is studying the digestive tract.*

tract See the main entry beginning with *tracked.*

tray—trey

- **tray** [tre] a flat-surfaced, open receptacle, often without sides or with shallow sides, used for carrying or displaying articles. □ *Grandmother's silver tea service sits on a tray in the china cabinet.*
- **trey** [tre] a card, die, or domino displaying three symbols or dots. □ *His poker hand revealed two pairs and a trey.*

trey See the main entry beginning with *tray.*

troop—troupe

- **troop** [trup] a group of soldiers. □ *The small troop entered the city after dark.*
- **troop** [trup] a collection of objects or people. □ *An interested troop of listeners heard the speaker talk.*
- **troop** [trup] a flock of birds; an assembly of mammals. □ *A baboon troop is a highly organized and complex unit.*
- **troop** [trup] a unit of Girl or Boy Scouts under the direction of a leader. □ *When my brothers were young, my father served*

as leader of their troop.

- **troop** [trup] to move as a group or crowd. □ *Let's all troop over to the park to play ball after our cookout.*
- **troupe** [trup] a group of stage or traveling performers. □ *That theatrical troupe has been on the road performing for a long time.*

troupe See the main entry beginning with *troop.*

trussed–trust

- **trussed** [trəst] the past tense and past participle of *truss* 'to bind or secure someone or something tightly.' □ *The police found the victim trussed but otherwise unharmed.* □ *After the turkey was stuffed and trussed, I put it into the oven.*
- **trussed [up]** [trəst] the past tense and past participle of *truss [up]* 'to strengthen or support something with trusses.' □ *We first put up the sidewalls and then trussed them up temporarily.*
- **trust** [trəst] to have confidence in someone or something. □ *Something about the way she smiled told me not to trust her.*
- **trust** [trəst] an obligation or charge imposed in faith. □ *She put trust in his ability to invest her money wisely.*
- **trust** [trəst] a property interest held by one party for the benefit of another. □ *Funds were put in a trust to help the family whose house burned.*
- **trust** [trəst] to believe in or rely on someone or something. □ *I trust that you will see to all of the details of the contract.*

trust See the main entry beginning with *trussed.*

tuff See the main entry beginning with *tough.*

turn See the main entry beginning with *tern.*

two See the main entry beginning with *to.*

U

undo—undue

- **undo** [ən'du] to open or unfasten something by releasing. ☐ *I was unable to undo the padlock on the gate.*
- **undo** [ən'du] to nullify something. ☐ *He could not undo the damage done to his garden by the heavy rain.*
- **undo** [ən'du] to ruin or reverse the fortunes of someone or something. ☐ *The athlete tried to undo his competitor's chances of winning.*
- **undue** [ən'dju, ən'du] unnecessary or inappropriate. ☐ *The political candidate thought undue attention was being given to his private life.*
- **undue** [ən'dju, ən'du] not due. ☐ *The bill is undue until the end of the month.*

undue See the main entry beginning with *undo.*

uninterested See the main entry beginning with *disinterested.*

urn See the main entry beginning with *earn.*

use See the main entry beginning with *ewes.*

V

vail—vale—veil

- **vail** [vel] to remove one's hat to show respect. (Archaic English.) □ *The peasant was told to vail his hat in the presence of the noble family.*
- **vale** [vel] a valley; a dale. □ *From the mountaintop the little hamlet nestled in the vale looked like a miniature village.*
- **veil** [vel] a covering of cloth worn to conceal the face. □ *Women in some countries are required to wear a veil when in public.* □ *The bride's veil was made of white netting.*
- **veil** [vel] a covering used to conceal or hide something. □ *A veil was used to cover the sculpture until the dedication ceremony.*
- **veil** [vel] to conceal something. □ *The man tried to veil his uneasiness by laughing.*

vain—vane—vein

- **vain** [ven] conceited; self-centered. □ *The movie star is a very vain person.*
- **vain** [ven] unsuccessful. □ *Her many vain attempts to pass the driver's test left her unhappy.*
- **vane** [ven] a device used to determine the direction of the wind. □ *The vane on the roof of the barn is pointing north.*
- **vane** [ven] the wide, flat part of a feather. □ *The vane on the bird's wing is bright red.*
- **vane** [ven] a group of feathers or a piece of plastic attached to the rear of an arrow to help guide its flight. □ *One vane was torn as the arrow bounced off a tree.*
- **vane** [ven] a blade of a windmill. □ *Only a single vane remained on the rusted windmill.*
- **vein** [ven] a layer of minerals in the earth. □ *The prospector*

discovered a vein of silver in the earth.

- **vein** [ven] a blood vessel that carries blood to the heart. □ *The nurse will draw blood from a vein in your arm.*
- **vein** [ven] the part of a leaf that gives it the appearance of containing lines. □ *The vein of that yellow leaf is dark purple.*
- **vein** [ven] a line of thought. □ *The speaker continued his discussion in a serious vein.* □ *The business will continue to operate along the same vein.*

vale See the main entry beginning with *vail.*

vane See the main entry beginning with *vain.*

vary—very

- **vary** ['væɚi, 'vɛɚi] to change something; to cause something to deviate. □ *Each year the firm tries to vary its marketing campaign.*
- **very** ['vɛɚi] to a high degree. □ *Janice has been very successful in her new job.*
- **very** ['vɛɚi] precise. □ *His comments struck my very conscience.* □ *My aunt bought the very dress I liked.*
- **very** ['vɛɚi] mere. □ *The very idea of eating insects sickened him.*

veil See the main entry beginning with *vail.*

vein See the main entry beginning with *vain.*

very See the main entry beginning with *vary.*

vial—vile

- **vial** [vaɪl] a small, usually cylindrical container. □ *The lab technician carefully marked and dated each vial of pills.*
- **vile** [vaɪl] wicked. □ *That man is a vile individual.*
- **vile** [vaɪl] foul. □ *Decaying debris has a vile odor.*

vice—vise

- **vice** [vaɪs] corruption; crime. □ *The gangster was involved in all sorts of vice.*
- **vice** [vaɪs] a moral or physical shortcoming, imperfection, or taint. □ *Her only vice is a weakness for chocolate.*
- **vice** [vaɪs] secondary; serving in the place of someone. (Part of a title.) □ *His father was the vice-president of the poetry society.*
- **vise** [vaɪs] a device used to hold some object in place by means of a clamp. □ *A vise has many uses in carpentry.*

vile See the main entry beginning with *vial.*

vise See the main entry beginning with *vice.*

W

wade—weighed

- **wade** [wed] to enter or walk about in shallow water. ☐ *The children wanted to wade in the stream.*
- **wade** [wed] to proceed or move about with labor or difficulty. ☐ *It will take me all day to wade through this paperwork.*
- **wade** [wed] to approach a project with vigor and enthusiasm. ☐ *Sam likes to wade right into any challenging task.*
- **weighed** [wed] the past tense and past participle of *weigh* 'to determine the weight or heaviness of someone or something.' ☐ *As children, we were weighed at each visit to the doctor's office.*
- **weighed** [wed] the past tense and past participle of *weigh* 'to consider something carefully.' ☐ *The judge carefully weighed all of the evidence in the case.*
- **weighed** [wed] the past tense and past participle of *weigh* 'to pull up an anchor in readiness for departure.' ☐ *After a night in port, the ship weighed anchor at dawn.*
- **weighed** [wed] the past tense and past participle of *weigh* 'to be a burden on someone or something.' (Figurative.) ☐ *Their constant financial worries weighed heavily on their minds.*

wail—wale—whale

- **wail** [wel] a mournful cry. ☐ *The forlorn wail of the coyote was heard throughout the valley.*
- **wail** [wel] a prolonged expression of grief, sadness, or pain. ☐ *The wail of the mourners was terrible to hear.*
- **wail** [wel] to utter a cry of grief or pain. ☐ *We heard the woman wail from a distance.*
- **wale** [wel] a raised rib in a piece of fabric. ☐ *That corduroy*

fabric comes in both a wide and narrow wale.

- **wale** [wel] a welt, usually on the surface of the skin. ☐ *The scratch by the tree branch left a long wale on his arm.*
- **wale** [wel] the long, thick, wooden plates on the side of a ship. ☐ *Each wale of the boat was handmade.*
- **wale** [wel] to raise or mark the skin with welts. ☐ *"If you don't behave, I'll wale your behind!" threatened the upset mother.*
- **whale** [ʍel] a large, ocean mammal that bears and suckles live young. ☐ *The blue whale is the earth's largest living creature.*
- **whale** [ʍel] a person, event, or object massive or impressive in size or qualities. ☐ *"Boy, that was a whale of a concert!" commented Todd.*
- **whale** [ʍel] to fish or hunt whales. ☐ *Coastal people in many countries whale for a living.*
- **whale** [ʍel] to thrash someone. ☐ *The attackers continued to whale the helpless man.*

waist—waste

- **waist** [west] the mid-section of a human torso between the ribs and the hips. ☐ *Scarlett O'Hara boasted the tiniest waist in three counties.*
- **waist** [west] a short garment or part of a garment covering the body from the neck to the waist; a bodice. ☐ *The waist of her gown was richly detailed.*
- **waste** [west] debris; garbage. ☐ *All of this waste must be hauled to the dump.*
- **waste** [west] scrap. ☐ *Collect all of the waste metal to be recycled.*
- **waste** [west] a broad, barren tract of land; a vast body of open water. ☐ *We could see nothing but the horizon across the waste of land.*
- **waste** [west] loss of body weight, tissue, or vigor. ☐ *To see his waste over a long period of time was very sad.*
- **waste** [west] sewage or excrement. ☐ *The city's waste is treated at a nearby sewage treatment plant.*
- **waste** [west] to ravage; to devastate. ☐ *The war continues to waste the impoverished nation.*
- **waste** [west] to cause something to diminish in size, strength, or vitality. ☐ *We watched her enthusiasm slowly waste away.*
- **waste** [west] to consume something carelessly; to allow something to be lost or discarded unused. ☐ *We must be careful not to waste our precious natural resources.*

wait—weight

- **wait** [wet] to remain in place in expectancy. ☐ *Let's wait and see what happens next.*
- **wait [for]** [wet] to delay or postpone. ☐ *He decided to wait for the rain to stop before dashing to the parking lot.*
- **wait** [wet] to serve as a waitress or waiter. ☐ *Greg has decided to wait tables at the local pub for a summer job.*
- **weight** [wet] a heavy object. ☐ *A weight is needed to keep this drapery hanging straight.*
- **weight** [wet] a burden or pressure. ☐ *The weight of the difficult decision was almost unbearable.*
- **weight** [wet] a unit of mass or measure. ☐ *Alex put some weight in the back of his car to give added traction.*
- **weight** [wet] the relative value or importance given to something. ☐ *The weight of this issue is very apparent to everyone involved.*
- **weight** [wet] to place heaviness or weight upon someone or something. ☐ *Weight down those papers so they don't blow away.*
- **weight** [wet] to impose a burden upon someone. ☐ *I didn't mean to weight you down with all of my troubles.*

waive—wave

- **waive** [wev] to voluntarily relinquish something or give up a right to something. ☐ *The accused decided to waive his right to a jury trial.*
- **waive** [wev] to temporarily put something aside. ☐ *Will you waive some of your course electives until next year?*
- **waive** [wev] to refrain from prosecuting or enforcing something. ☐ *The policy will no longer waive those restrictions.*
- **wave** [wev] a hand motion used as a greeting, farewell, or signal. ☐ *He gave a quick wave before boarding the ship.*
- **wave** [wev] a swell on the surface of a body of water. ☐ *A huge wave washed over the bow of the boat.*
- **wave** [wev] something resembling a wave. ☐ *A sudden wave of nausea made her dizzy.*
- **wave** [wev] an energy transmission through some medium from one point to another. ☐ *The pictures are being transmitted via a complex radio wave.*
- **wave** [wev] a distinct condition of weather or temperature. ☐ *An unexpected heat wave settled over the region.*
- **wave** [wev] to float or move about in an air current. ☐ *I love to see palm leaves wave about in the tropical breeze.*

wale See the main entry beginning with *wail.*

war—wore

- **war** [wɔɚ] a state of declared, armed hostilities. ☐ *The war lasted only a few short months.*
- **war** [wɔɚ] a state or period of conflict or struggle. ☐ *Those two giant beverage companies have been at war for years.*
- **war** [wɔɚ] to engage in war, conflict, or hostility. ☐ *The once-feuding nations have agreed not to war any longer.*
- **wore** [wɔɚ] the past tense of *wear* 'to dress in or adorn oneself with an article of clothing.' ☐ *The groom wore a dark grey tuxedo.*
- **wore** [wɔɚ] the past tense of *wear* 'to display some type of appearance.' ☐ *Her father always wore a look of dismay on his face.*
- **wore** [wɔɚ] the past tense of *wear [down]* 'to diminish something through persistence.' ☐ *The persistent child eventually wore down his mother's defense.*

ware—wear—where

- **ware** [wɛɚ] a manufactured commodity or article; merchandise. ☐ *The only ware that the company produces is transistor radios.* ☐ *The peddler's best-selling ware was a variety of pots and pans.*
- **ware** [wɛɚ] pottery of fired clay. ☐ *After painting the ceramic ware, the artist must fire it again.*
- **wear** [wɛɚ] to dress in or adorn oneself with articles of clothing. ☐ *Many tennis players now choose to wear bright colored clothing.*
- **wear** [wɛɚ] to display or have an appearance of something. ☐ *Wear a look of confidence at your job interview.*
- **wear** [wɛɚ] to diminish or deteriorate through use. ☐ *The carpeting by the front door is beginning to wear.*
- **where** [ʍɛɚ] in, at, or to what place, position, or situation. ☐ *"Where did you find such a deal?" quizzed Ray.*
- **where** [ʍɛɚ] wherever. ☐ *The cats tend to wander where they like.*
- **where** [ʍɛɚ] locale or place. ☐ *No one is sure of the where and why of the crime.*

warn—worn

- **warn** [wɔɚn] to alert, notify, or counsel someone. ☐ *Doctors must warn their patients of the side effects of medication.*
- **warn** [wɔɚn] to tell someone to go or leave. ☐ *The referees had to warn the disruptive players off the playing field.*
- **worn** [wɔɚn] the past participle of *wear* 'to dress in or adorn

oneself with an article of clothing.' ☐ *Have you worn that hat before?*

- **worn** [wɔɚn] the past participle of *wear* 'to display or have an appearance of something.' ☐ *It seems he hasn't worn a smile in weeks.*
- **worn [away]** [wɔɚn] the past participle of *wear [away]* 'to cause something to diminish or deteriorate.' ☐ *Her illness has worn away her energy.*

waste See the main entry beginning with *waist.*

wave See the main entry beginning with *waive.*

wax—whacks

- **wax** [wæks] a substance secreted by bees that is used to make their honeycombs. ☐ *Those candles are made from the wax of bees.*
- **wax** [wæks] any of numerous plant or animal secretions resembling a waxy substance. ☐ *A doctor removed the excess wax from his patient's ears.*
- **wax** [wæks] paraffin. ☐ *Use a good wax to coat the bottom of your skis.*
- **wax** [wæks] to rub or treat something with wax. ☐ *If you wax the underside of your toboggan, it will travel faster down the hill.*
- **wax** [wæks] to grow or increase. ☐ *The profits of the company tend to wax with buyer demand.*
- **wax** [wæks] the period of the lunar cycle between a new moon and a full moon. ☐ *At what time this month will the moon wax?*
- **whacks** [ʍæks] the plural of *whack* 'a resounding blow.' ☐ *The baby-sitter gave the naughty child three whacks with a paddle.*
- **whacks** [ʍæks] the plural of *whack* 'an attempt or opportunity to do something.' (Slang.) ☐ *The coach offered the second-string pitcher a couple of whacks at starting games.*
- **whacks** [ʍæks] the present tense, third person singular of *whack* 'to strike or bat at something or someone.' ☐ *That volleyball player really whacks the ball around the court.*

way—weigh—whey

- **way** [we] a course of passage or travel. ☐ *The homing pigeon found its way back to its coop.*
- **way** [we] a condition. ☐ *The way I felt led me to take a nap.*
- **way** [we] a manner or style of doing something. ☐ *"That is*

no way to eat!" scolded the man.

- **way** [we] a distance. ☐ *It's a long way from Florida to California.*
- **way** [we] connected with a stage or point along a route. ☐ *Fresh horses are available at each way station along the trail.*
- **weigh** [we] to determine the weight or heaviness of something; to measure something on a scale. ☐ *We must weigh the cargo of the truck before it goes on the road.*
- **weigh** [we] to consider something carefully. ☐ *Weigh the consequences of your actions before you act.*
- **weigh** [we] to make something heavy. ☐ *Citizens are asked to weigh down anything that might blow away during the hurricane.*
- **weigh** [we] to pull up an anchor in readiness for departure. ☐ *The ship will weigh anchor at dawn.*
- **weigh** [we] to have a disheartening effect on someone. ☐ *I hope this sad news will not weigh heavily on you.*
- **whey** [ʍe] the watery part of whole milk as separate from the part containing the butterfat. ☐ *Whey is a by-product in the cheese-making process.*

we—wee

- **we** [wi] the first person, plural pronoun. ☐ *"Let's see if we can win the relay race," Mitch urged his teammates.*
- **wee** [wi] very tiny. ☐ *When born, a bear cub is just a wee thing.*
- **wee** [wi] miniscule. ☐ *Add only a wee bit of seasoning to the soup.*
- **wee** [wi] very early. ☐ *Doctors are quite used to getting up in the wee hours of the morning to handle emergencies.*

weak—week

- **weak** [wik] lacking strength, vigor, or stamina. ☐ *He felt very weak following his long illness.*
- **weak** [wik] deficient in mental or physical capabilities. ☐ *As she aged, my aunt's eyesight grew weak.*
- **weak** [wik] not based soundly on fact or logic. ☐ *The evidence supporting that theory is weak.*
- **weak** [wik] lacking required or usual ingredients. ☐ *This coffee tastes weak and watery.*
- **weak** [wik] lame or ineffective. ☐ *The boy offered a weak excuse for his tardiness.*
- **weak** [wik] barely sounded. ☐ *The kitten uttered a weak meow.*
- **week** [wik] a seven-day cycle or period. ☐ *They will be vacationing out East for a week in July.*

wear See the main entry beginning with *ware.*

weather—wether—whether

- **weather** ['wɛðɚ] climatic or atmospheric conditions. ☐ *The weather in Michigan is very unpredictable.*
- **weather** ['wɛðɚ] the wind. ☐ *The captain turned his vessel into the weather.*
- **weather** ['wɛðɚ] to expose something to the open air and the elements. ☐ *The man wanted to weather the lumber before he used it.*
- **weather** ['wɛðɚ] to endure and come safely through some trying experience. ☐ *Susan seems able to weather almost any misfortune that comes her way.*
- **wether** ['wɛðɚ] a male sheep castrated before reaching sexual maturity. ☐ *The sheep farmer kept the ewes but sold off each wether.*
- **whether** ['ʍɛðɚ] a word indicating options or alternatives. ☐ *Whether he'll take the job in Colorado or the one in Idaho is unknown.*

weave—we've

- **weave** [wiv] to interlace strands of materials. ☐ *She likes to weave old rags into useful rugs.*
- **weave** [wiv] to make cloth on a loom. ☐ *His mother taught him to weave at a young age.*
- **weave** [wiv] to spin something. ☐ *We must first weave the raw material into yarn.*
- **weave** [wiv] to create something by elaborately combining elements. ☐ *That author is able to weave the most compelling stories.*
- **weave** [wiv] to move in an unsteady, zigzag fashion. ☐ *We noticed a car weave across the divided highway.*
- **weave** [wiv] a pattern or method for interlacing thread into woven fabric. ☐ *Do you know how to weave that pattern?*
- **we've** [wiv] the contraction of *we have.* ☐ *We've always enjoyed living in a state with so many outdoor opportunities.*

we'd—weed

- **we'd** [wid] the contraction of *we had, we would,* or *we should.* ☐ *We'd better leave before dark, or we'll never find our way.*
- **weed** [wid] a useless plant that tends to choke out areas of desirable plant growth. ☐ *The weed had roots that extended deep into the ground.*
- **weed** [wid] any undesirable or obnoxious person or thing. ☐ *My uncle used to say that his brother was a weed in a family*

of roses.

- **weed** [wid] to clean an area of soil by pulling out undesirable plants. □ *The best time to weed the flower bed is right after a rain.*
- **weed [out]** [wid] to remove someone or something not wanted. □ *The foreman wants to weed out all of the unproductive workers.*
- **weed** [wid] marijuana. (Slang.) □ *The student bought a special pipe for smoking weed.*

wee See the main entry beginning with *we.*

weed See the main entry beginning with *we'd.*

week See the main entry beginning with *weak.*

weigh See the main entry beginning with *way.*

weighed See the main entry beginning with *wade.*

weight See the main entry beginning with *wait.*

weir—we're

- **weir** [wiɚ] a fencelike enclosure built in a waterway and used to trap and collect fish. □ *Salmon are trapped and stripped of their eggs at the weir.*
- **weir** [wiɚ] a dam or diversion in a waterway used to stop or redirect its flow or raise the water level. □ *A weir was used to funnel the excess water away from the main arm of the river.*
- **we're** [wiɚ] the contraction of *we are.* □ *"Do you know where we're at?" asked Dave.*

weld—welled

- **weld** [wɛld] to fasten or join metal parts together using a heating process in which the parts melt and run together. □ *Jerry will weld the broken pieces of axle.*
- **weld** [wɛld] to join intimately or closely. □ *A formal announcement will weld the two business ventures together.*
- **weld** [wɛld] a welded joint. □ *He did not get a good weld on his first attempt.*
- **welled [up]** [wɛld] the past tense and past participle of *well [up]* 'to flow up and overflow.' □ *Water welled up in the sink during the flood.* □ *Tears of joy welled up in the bride's father's eyes as he walked his daughter down the aisle.* □ *Oil welled up from the rigs in record amounts.*

we'll—wheal—wheel

- **we'll** [wil] the contraction of *we will* or *we shall.* □ *I can't* *promise that we'll be there, but we'll try.*

- **wheal** [ʍil] a suddenly raised formation on the skin; a flat itching or burning area on the skin. ☐ *The bee sting left a wheal on her face.*
- **wheel** [ʍil] a circular device made of steel, rubber, or wood mounted on an axle and capable of turning. ☐ *The wheel on the wagon is wobbly.*
- **wheel** [ʍil] something resembling a wheel. ☐ *The steering wheel of that automobile contains an airbag.*
- **wheel** [ʍil] to change direction in a pivotal movement suddenly. ☐ *If you suddenly stop and wheel about, you may accidently bump into someone.*
- **wheel** [ʍil] to convey on or as if on wheels. ☐ *Wheel those building supplies over here.*

welled See the main entry beginning with *weld.*

we're See the main entry beginning with *weir.*

were—whir

- **were** [wɚ] the past subjunctive tense of *be.* ☐ *The kittens in the pet shop window were adorable.*
- **whir** [ʍɚ] to revolve, fly, or move very rapidly, creating a whirring sound. ☐ *The automated turnstile doors at the store's entrance whir constantly.*

wet—whet

- **wet** [wɛt] moist, damp. ☐ *His shirt was wet with sweat.*
- **wet** [wɛt] containing liquid. ☐ *This towel is soaking wet.*
- **wet** [wɛt] processed using water or some other liquid. ☐ *Wet drilling cement requires fewer drill bits than does dry drilling.*
- **wet** [wɛt] rainy. ☐ *Yesterday was a wet day.*
- **wet** [wɛt] permitting the manufacture and sale of alcoholic beverages. ☐ *Hubbard County is one of the few wet counties in the state.*
- **wet** [wɛt] all wrong. (Slang.) ☐ *Harry was all wet in his recollection of the accident.*
- **wet** [wɛt] to make something wet. ☐ *Wet down the driveway to keep the dust from blowing around.*
- **wet** [wɛt] to urinate on or in something. ☐ *The child got so excited that she wet her trousers.*
- **whet** [ʍɛt] to sharpen something by rubbing on or with an object. ☐ *You may whet that knife on this special stone.*
- **whet** [ʍɛt] to make something sharp or more acute. ☐ *A glass of wine before dinner will only whet your appetite.*

wether See the main entry beginning with *weather.*

we've See the main entry beginning with *weave.*

whacks See the main entry beginning with *wax.*

whale See the main entry beginning with *wail.*

wheal See the main entry beginning with *we'll.*

wheel See the main entry beginning with *we'll.*

where See the main entry beginning with *ware.*

whet See the main entry beginning with *wet.*

whether See the main entry beginning with *weather.*

whey See the main entry beginning with *way.*

which—witch

- **which** [ʍɪtʃ] what one or ones out of a group. ☐ *Which picture do you prefer?*
- **which** [ʍɪtʃ] a pronoun that introduces a clause. ☐ *The stolen items, which were thought to be lost forever, were finally located.*
- **which** [ʍɪtʃ] whichever. ☐ *You may choose which you like best.*
- **witch** [wɪtʃ] a woman who practices witchcraft. ☐ *The woman who lived alone down by the creek was thought to be a witch.*
- **witch** [wɪtʃ] to bewitch someone or something. ☐ *Don't try to witch me with your black magic.*

while—wile

- **while** [ʍɑɪl] during the time of something. ☐ *Annette was stationed in Germany while she was in the army.*
- **while** [ʍɑɪl] at the same time as something. ☐ *I sat on a park bench while he jogged.*
- **while** [ʍɑɪl] to pass time in a boring or leisurely manner. ☐ *The retiree likes to while away his days fishing.*
- **wile** [wɑɪl] a trick or deception. ☐ *Her clever wile fooled no one.*
- **wile** [wɑɪl] to entice or lure someone as if by a magic spell. ☐ *The man tried to wile the woman into believing him.*

whine—wine

- **whine** [ʍɑɪn] a plaintive, prolonged cry. ☐ *The constant whine of the puppy upset the entire household.*
- **whine** [ʍɑɪn] to cry in a forlorn or distressed way. ☐ *The baby continued to whine after getting an injection.*
- **whine** [ʍɑɪn] to complain in a manner resembling a whine.

☐ *My sister is not one to whine when things don't go her way.*

- **wine** [waɪn] a fermented, alcoholic beverage made from fruit or plants; something that intoxicates or makes heady. ☐ *The wine has a full, fruity flavor.* ☐ *Sudden success is like wine to the spirit.*
- **wine** [waɪn] a purplish-red color. ☐ *The new house is decorated in colors of forest green and wine.*
- **wine** [waɪn] to drink wine. ☐ *The company likes to wine and dine its new executives.*

whir See the main entry beginning with *were.*

whither—wither

- **whither** [ˈʍɪðɚ] where. ☐ *"Whither thou goest . . . " is the beginning of a verse from the book of Ruth in the Bible.*
- **wither** [ˈwɪðɚ] to droop, dry up, or shrivel, usually from lack of moisture. ☐ *Without rain, the crops began to wither.*
- **wither** [ˈwɪðɚ] to lose vigor, stamina, or spirit. ☐ *The runner began to wither near the end of the race.*
- **wither** [ˈwɪðɚ] to stun someone or something. ☐ *She threw me a look that would wither anyone.*

whoa—woe

- **whoa** [wo] a command given to a horse or draft animal to stop or stand still. ☐ *Pulling back on the reins, Nathan called "whoa" to his horse.*
- **woe** [wo] misfortune, suffering, or grief. (Also in the fixed form *woe is me.*) ☐ *How could so much woe befall one person?* ☐ *"Oh, woe is me," lamented Candy over her misfortune.*

whole See the main entry beginning with *hole.*

wholly See the main entry beginning with *holy.*

whoop See the main entry beginning with *hoop.*

who's—whose

- **who's** [huz] the contraction of *who is.* ☐ *He is one of the boys who's going to the summer music festival.*
- **whose** [huz] a pronoun indicating that which belongs to whom. ☐ *Whose watch is this?*

whose See the main entry beginning with *who's.*

wild—wiled

- **wild** [waɪld] untamed; uncivilized. ☐ *The wild West appealed to many people living in the 1800's.*
- **wild** [waɪld] growing of its own accord without help or care

from humans. □ *Wild strawberries grow in the field behind our home.*

- **wild** [waɪld] uncontrolled. □ *As they grew tired, the children became wild.*
- **wild** [waɪld] having to do with the wilderness or wildlife. □ *The men enjoy camping in the wild.*
- **wild** [waɪld] deviating from the expected. (Slang or colloquial.) □ *The movie had a wild ending.*
- **wiled [out of]** [waɪld] the past tense and past participle of *wile [out of]* 'to trick or deceive someone into giving something up.' □ *The con artists wiled the old man out of his life savings.*
- **wiled [into]** [waɪl] the past tense and past participle of *wile [into]* 'to entice or lure someone into doing something.' □ *She wiled her husband into buying her a mink stole.*

wile See the main entry beginning with *while.*

wiled See the main entry beginning with *wild.*

will See the main entry beginning with *shall.*

wine See the main entry beginning with *whine.*

witch See the main entry beginning with *which.*

wither See the main entry beginning with *whither.*

woe See the main entry beginning with *whoa.*

won See the main entry beginning with *one.*

wood—would

- **wood** [wʊd] the hard, fibrous interior of a tree or shrub lying beneath the bark. □ *The wood of the cherry tree is reddish in color.*
- **wood** [wʊd] timber. □ *How much wood does it take to build a log home?*
- **wood** [wʊd] a stand of trees. □ *The deer disappeared into the wood.*
- **wood** [wʊd] something made out of wood. □ *The wood box was carved and painted by a skilled carpenter.*
- **would** [wʊd] a word indicating desire, preference, or intent. □ *The druggist said he would be happy to deliver your prescription.*
- **would** [wʊd] could or should. □ *A leather pouch would actually hold liquids quite well.*

wore See the main entry beginning with *war.*

worn See the main entry beginning with *warn.*

would See the main entry beginning with *wood.*

wrack See the main entry beginning with *rack.*

wrap See the main entry beginning with *rap.*

wrapped See the main entry beginning with *rapped.*

wrest See the main entry beginning with *rest.*

wretch See the main entry beginning with *retch.*

wright See the main entry beginning with *right.*

wring See the main entry beginning with *ring.*

write See the main entry beginning with *right.*

wrote See the main entry beginning with *rote.*

wrung See the main entry beginning with *rung.*

wry See the main entry beginning with *rye.*

Y

yew See the main entry beginning with *ewe.*

yews See the main entry beginning with *ewes.*

yoke—yolk

- **yoke** [jok] a wooden frame worn over the necks of work animals. □ *The team of oxen were joined by a yoke.*
- **yoke** [jok] a pair of yoked draft animals. □ *The yoke of mules was greatly admired by the farmers.*
- **yoke** [jok] some oppressive or restrictive bond, duty, or agency. □ *His impending court appearance was a yoke he did not look forward to.*
- **yoke** [jok] a shaped and fitted piece of fabric that is part of the shoulders of a garment; the top portion of a skirt. □ *The dress had a smocked yoke.*
- **yoke** [jok] to harness something with a yoke. □ *When you yoke the horses, be sure not to tangle the reins.*
- **yolk** [jok] the mass of yellow inside an egg. □ *I cracked open an egg that had a double yolk.*

yolk See the main entry beginning with *yoke.*

yore—your—you're

- **yore** [jɔɚ] days past or distant times. □ *In days of yore, knights in shining armor rescued princesses from castle towers.*
- **your** [juɚ, jɔɚ] the possessive pronoun showing a relationship to you, yourself, or yourselves. □ *Your helpfulness has been greatly appreciated.*
- **your** [juɚ, jɔɚ] relating to oneself. □ *The party store is on your left as you enter the plaza.*

- **you're** [juɚ, jɔɚ] the contraction of *you are.* □ *If you're hungry, there are some snacks in the refrigerator.*

you See the main entry beginning with *ewe.*

you'll—yule

- **you'll** [jul, juəl] the contraction of *you will* or *you shall.* □ *Hurry up or you'll be late for your appointment.*
- **yule** [jul] Christmastime. □ *The yule season is a time for joy, celebration, and happiness.*

your See the main entry beginning with *yore.*

you're See the main entry beginning with *yore.*

yule See the main entry beginning with *you'll.*